Guide to Web Development with Java

Tim Downey

Guide to Web Development with Java

Understanding Website Creation

 Springer

Tim Downey
Computing and Information Sciences
Florida Inernational University
11200 SW 8th Street
Miami, FL
USA

ISBN 978-1-4471-2442-9   e-ISBN 978-1-4471-2443-6
DOI 10.1007/978-1-4471-2443-6
Springer London Dordrecht Heidelberg New York

British Library Cataloguing in Publication Data
A catalogue record for this book is available from the British Library

Library of Congress Control Number: 2011945783

Printed on acid-free paper

Springer is part of Springer Science+Business Media (www.springer.com)

To Bobbi, my sweetheart, with all my love.

Preface

I have been teaching web development for 14 years. I started with Perl. I can still remember the behemoth programs that contained all the logic and HTML. I remember using a text editor to write the program. Debugging consisted of a lot of print statements. It was a fun time, full of exploration, but I do not miss them.

Nine years ago, I made the move to Java and Java servlets. Life became much simpler with the use of NetBeans. It has been a critical component in developing web applications using Java. Debugging a web application in NetBeans is just as easy as debugging any Java application.

This book is meant for students who have a solid background in programming, but who do not have any database training. Until six years ago, my students used a glorified HashMap to save data. Then, a former student gave me the word: Hibernate. For anyone with a programming background in Java, using Hibernate to save data to a relational database is a simple task.

I have always been a proponent of automating the common tasks that web applications perform. There are many packages that can simplify the job of a web developer: Log4j, BeanUtils and Hibernate. I have created additional classes that can automate additional tasks.

The book uses HTML, HTML Forms, Cascading Style Sheets (CSS) and XML as tools. Each topic will receive an introduction, but the full scope of the area will not be explored. The focus of the book is on Java servlets that use Java Server Pages and connect to a MySQL database using Hibernate. No SQL will be covered in the book, because SQL is not needed. A short section in the Appendix explains some basic SQL concepts for those who want to see what Hibernate is doing.

Web services are useful tools for developers. Complex features can be added to a web application by using web services. The development environments for Java now have tools and wizards that simplify accessing a service, but there is still plenty of work left for the programmer.

The book has eight chapters. In a typical one-semester course, the first five chapters can be covered in detail. Chapter 7 only requires the sections on HTML tables and CSS style sheets from Chap. 6. One of the web service applications from Chap. 8 uses the shopping cart application from Chap. 7. While it might not be feasible to cover all eight chapters in a single semester, it is possible to pick and choose topics from Chaps. 6, 7 and 8.

Chapter 1 introduces the browser-server communication process, HTML, Tomcat and dynamic pages using Java Server Pages. The chapter does not go into depth in any of these topics, but introduces enough material to be able to write simple pages that send data to the web.

Chapter 2 introduces the concept of a controller. The controller is in charge of directing data to the next page. The controller makes it easier to add new pages to the application. It is better to write the controller as a Java program, known as a servlet, rather than as a Java Server Page. The details of developing a servlet are covered, including modifying the configuration file of the web application to allow access to the servlet.

Chapter 3 introduces Java beans and member variables. Java beans provide support for encapsulating the data. In later chapters, the data in the bean can be stored in a database. Member variables are troublesome in servlets; they can cause errors that are hard to debug. A helper class is introduced to allow the application to use member variables. Some member variables use the same class for all servlets; other member variables use a different class for each servlet. Inheritance is used to separate the first group into a base class that can be reused by all servlets. The member variables in the second group must be placed in a class that changes for each servlet.

The first three chapters introduce the basic structure of web applications. Chapter 4 adds features to the web application and provides code for simplifying some of the common tasks of a controller. The Log4j package is added to the web application and a logger is added to the controller. Students learn how easy it is to add external resources to an application. Some of the features of the application can be streamlined: eliminating the need for hidden fields by using the session, automating the controller logic, filling the bean from the request parameters.

Chapter 5 completes the picture of a web application. Required validation and data persistence are introduced. Both are implemented using the Hibernate package. By the end of the chapter, the student will understand how most websites work. The student will be able to gather data, validate it, save it to a database and retrieve it.

Chapter 6 contains additional HTML tags and introduces cascading style sheets. Most of Chap. 6 can be covered at any time in the course, for those who want to allow the students to create more interesting-looking websites early in the course.

Chapter 7 covers HTML cookies and completes the coverage of Hibernate by removing records from the database and validating a few fields at a time. Half of the chapter is devoted to developing a shopping cart. Generics are used to create a shopping cart that can be used with any bean.

The first seven chapters are for creating web applications from the ground up; Chap. 8 is about accessing resources that someone else created. Three applications are developed that access web services. One application is developed that creates Java classes from database tables that already exist. Once the Java classes exist, all the techniques from the book can be used to access the database.

My goal is for students to understand how it all fits together. Sometimes I want them to know the details and sometimes I want them to just use the tools. In the beginning, I want them to learn how things work. Chapters 1, 2 and 3 introduce how websites work. Later, I want them to simplify as much as possible. Chapter 4 shows them how to use Java to automate some of the common tasks. Chapters 5 and 8 teach them to use tools to validate data, access a database and implement web services. Chapters 6 and 7 show them the details of advanced HTML elements and shopping carts.

The book develops a framework for implementing websites. There are many frameworks on the market. I want students to understand how a framework might be implemented at the code level and to understand the problems that frameworks must solve. In the future, when they are introduced to other frameworks, they will understand them better.

I am grateful to the community of web developers who have provided all the excellent tools for creating web applications: Apache, Tomcat, Hibernate, Java Servlets, Java Server Pages, NetBeans, Eclipse, Log4j, Apache Commons, Google web services, FedEx web services, PayPal web services, JBoss Community.

I am thankful to Bobbi, my sweetheart, for all of her love and support. Without Bobbi, this book would not have been finished. I also want to thank Kip Irvine for encouraging me to write. Without Kip, this book would not have been started.

Miami   Tim Downey

Contents

Browser-Server Communication

1

This chapter explains how information is sent from a browser to a server. It begins with a description of the request from a browser and a response from a server. Each of these has a format that is determined by the *Hypertext Transfer Protocol* (HTTP).

The chapter continues with the explanation of markup languages, with a detailed description of the *Hypertext Markup Language* (HTML), which is used to send formatted content from the server to the browser. One of the most important features of HTML is its ability to easily request additional information from the server through the use of hypertext links.

HTML forms are also covered. These are used to send data from the browser back to the server. Information from the form must be formatted so that it can be sent over the web. The browser and server handle encoding and decoding the data.

Simple web pages cannot process form data that is sent to them. One way to process form data is to use a web application and a *Java Server Page* (JSP). In a JSP, the *Expression Language* (EL) simplifies access to the form data and can be used to initialise the form elements with the form data that is sent to the page.

JSPs are processed by a program known as a servlet engine. The servlet engine receives the request and response data from the web server and processes the request from the browser. The servlet engine translates all JSPs into programs known as servlets.

Servlets and JSPs must be run from a servlet engine. Tomcat is a popular servlet engine. NetBeans and Eclipse are *Integrated Development Environments* (IDE) for Java programs. NetBeans is tailored for web development and is packaged with Tomcat. Eclipse must be configured for web development and requires a separate download and configuration for Tomcat.

1.1   Hypertext Transfer Protocol

Whenever someone accesses a web page on the Internet, there is communication between two computers. On one computer there is a software program known as a browser, and on the other is a software program known as a web server. The browser

T. Downey, *Guide to Web Development with Java: Understanding Website Creation*,
DOI 10.1007/978-1-4471-2443-6_1, © Springer-Verlag London Limited 2012

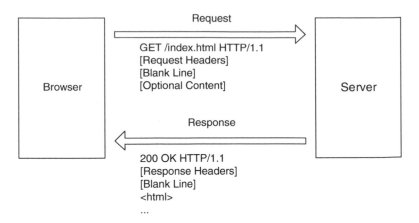

Fig. 1.1 The request and response have specific formats, as specified by the HTTP protocol

sends a request to the server and the server sends a response to the browser. The request contains the name of the page that is being requested and information about the browser that is making the request. The response contains the page that was requested (if it is available), information about the page and information about the server sending the page (see Fig. 1.1).

When the browser makes the request, it mentions the protocol that it is using: HTTP/1.1. When the server sends the response, it also identifies the protocol it is using: HTTP/1.1. A protocol is not a language; it is a set of rules that must be followed. For instance, one rule in HTTP is that the first line of a request will contain the type of request, the address of the page on the server and the version of the protocol that the browser is using. Another rule is that the first line of the response will contain a numeric code indicating the success of the request, a sentence describing the code and the version of the protocol that the server is using.

Protocols are used in many places, not just with computers. When the leaders of two countries meet, they must decide on a common protocol in order to communicate. Do they bow or shake hands when they meet? Do they eat with chopsticks or silverware? It is the same situation for computers; in order for the browser and server to communicate, they must decide on a common protocol.

1.1.1   Request Format

The request from the browser has the following format in HTTP:
1. The first line contains the type of request, the name of the requested page and the protocol that is being used.
2. Subsequent lines are the request headers. They contain information about the browser and the request.
3. A blank line in the request indicates the end of the request headers.
4. In a POST request, there can be additional information sent after the blank line.

Table 1.1 Common request headers

User-agent	Identifies the type of browser that made the request
Accept	Specifies the MIME types that the browser prefers
Accept-language	Indicates the user's preferred language, if multiple versions of the document exist
Accept-charset	Indicates the user's preferred character set. Different character sets can display characters from different languages

Table 1.2 Common response headers

Server	Identifies the type of server that made the response
Content-type	Identifies the MIME type of the response
Content-length	Contains the number of characters that are in the response

Typical information that is contained in the request headers is the brand of the browser that is making the request, the types of content that the browser prefers, the languages and character set that the browser prefers and the type of connection that is being used. The names of these request headers are User-agent, Accept, Accept-language and Accept-charset, respectively (Table 1.1).

1.1.2 Response Format

The response from the server has the following format in HTTP:
1. The first line contains the status code, a brief description of the status code and the protocol being used.
2. Subsequent lines are the response headers. They contain information about the server and the response.
3. A blank line in the response indicates the end of the response headers.
4. In a successful response, the content of the page will be sent after the blank line.
   Typical information that is contained in the response headers is the brand of the server that is making the response, the type of the file that is being returned and the number of characters that are in the file. The names of these response headers are Server, Content-Type and Content-length, respectively (Table 1.2).

1.1.3 Content Type

The server must also identify the type of information that is being sent. This is known as the *Content Type*. There are content types for text, graphics, spreadsheets, word processors and more.

These content types are expressed as *Multipurpose Internet Mail Extensions* (MIME) types. MIME types are used by web servers to declare the type of content that is being sent. MIME types are used by the browser to decode the type of content that is being received. If there is additional data being included in the request, the browser uses special MIME types and headers to inform the server. The server and browser will each contain a file that has a table of MIME types with the associated file extension for that type.

The basic structure of a MIME type is a general type, a slash and a specific type. For example, there is a general type for text that has several specific types for plain text, HTML text and style sheet text. These types are represented as text/plain, text/html and text/css, respectively. When the server sends a file to the browser, it will also include the MIME type for the file in the header that is sent to the browser.

MIME types are universal. All systems have agreed to use MIME types to identify the content of a file transmitted over the web. File extensions are too limiting for this purpose. Many different word processor programs might use the extension *.doc* to identify a file. For instance, *.doc* might refer to an MS Word document or to an MS WordPad document. It is impossible to tell from the extension which program actually created the program. In addition, other programs could use the *.doc* extension to identify a program: for instance, Word Perfect could also use the *.doc* extension. Using the extension to identify the content of the file would be too confusing.

The most common content type on the web is HTML text, represented as the MIME type text/html.

1.2   Markup Language

I am confident that most students have seen a markup language. I remember my days in English composition classes: my returned papers would always have cryptic squiggles written all over them (Fig. 1.2).

Some of these would mean that a word was omitted (^), that two letters were transposed (a sideways 'S', enclosing the transposed letters), or that a new paragraph was needed (a backward, double-stemmed 'P'). These marks were invaluable to the teacher who had to correct the paper because they conveyed a lot of meaning in just a few pen strokes. Imagine if there were a program that would accept such a paper that is covered with markup, read the markup and generate a new version with all the corrections made.

There are other forms of markup languages. The script of a play has a markup language that describes the action that is proceeding while the dialog takes place. For instance, the following is a hypothetical script for the Three Stooges:

```
Moe: Oh, a wise guy, huh? <Pulls Larry's hair>
Larry: It wasn't me. <Hits Curly in the stomach>
Moe: What are you doing? <Tries to poke Curly in the eye>
Curly: Nyuk, nyuk, nyuk. <Places hand in front of eyes>
Moe: Ignoramus. <Bonks Curly on top of the head>
```

Word processors have an internal markup language that is used to indicate the format of the text: bold, italic, font, colour, etc. These codes are hidden from the

The old man went <u>to</u> sea, he needed
a big catch, so that he would receive
a lot of money. ¶The fish was waiting
in the dark sea.

Fig. 1.2   Editors use markup to annotate text

Fig. 1.3   Word processors use markup to format text

user. *WordPerfect* has an additional view of the document that displays all of these hidden codes (Fig. 1.3).

There are two parts to any markup language:

1. The plain text
2. The markup, which contains additional information about the plain text

1.2.1   Hypertext Markup Language

HTML is the markup language for the web. It is what allows the browser to display colours, fonts, links and graphics. All markup is enclosed within the angle brackets < and >. Directly adjacent to the opening bracket is the name of the tag. There can be additional attributes after the name of the tag and the closing bracket.

HTML tags are intermixed with plain text. The plain text is what the viewer of a web page will see. The HTML tags are commands to the browser for displaying the text. In this example, the plain text 'This text is strong' is enclosed within the HTML tags for making text look strong:

```
<strong>This text is strong</strong>
```

The viewer of the web page would not see the tags, but would see the text rendered strongly. For most browsers, strong text is bold and the sentence would appear as

This text is strong

Table 1.3 Examples of singletons

Tag	Explanation
` `	Insert a line break into the document
`<input>`	Insert a form element into the document. This is a tag that has additional attributes, which will be explained below

Table 1.4 Examples of paired tags

Tag	Explanation
`<strong>strong</strong>`	Typically, the enclosed text is rendered in a thicker font
`<ins>inserted</ins>`	Typically, the enclosed text is rendered with an underline
`<em>emphasised</em>`	Typically, the enclosed text is rendered in an italic font
`<p>paragraph</p>`	The enclosed text will have at least one empty line preceding it

There are two types of HTML tags: singletons and paired tags.

Singletons have a limited amount of text associated with them or they have no text at all. Singletons only have one tag. Table 1.3 gives two examples of singleton tags.

Paired tags are designed to contain many words and other tags. These tags have an opening and a closing tag. The text that they control is placed between the opening and closing tags. The closing tag is the same as the opening tag, except the tag name is preceded by a forward slash /. Table 1.4 gives four examples of paired tags.

1.2.2   Basic Tags for a Web Page

We are very sophisticated listeners. We can understand many different accents. We can understand when words are slurred together. However, if we were to write out the phonetic transcription of our statements, they would be unreadable. There is a correct way to write our language, but a sophisticated listener can detect and correct many errors in pronunciation.

For instance, most English speakers would understand me if I asked the question

Jeet yet?

In print, it is incomprehensible. A proper response might be

No, joo?

Or,

Yeah, I already ate.

As we become more proficient in a language, we are able to understand it, even when people do not enunciate clearly.

In the same way, all markup languages have a format that must be followed in order to be correct. Some language interpreters are more sophisticated than others and can detect and correct mistakes in the written format. For example, a paragraph tag in HTML is a paired tag and most browsers will render paragraphs correctly, even if the closing paragraph tag is missing. The reason is that paragraph tags cannot be nested one inside the other, so when a browser encounters a new <p> tag before seeing the closing </p> for the current paragraph, the browser inserts a closing </p> and then begins the new paragraph. However, if an XML interpreter were used to read the same HTML file with the missing </p> tag, the interpreter would report an error instead of continuing to parse the file. It is better to code all the tags that are defined for a well-formed HTML document, than to rely on browsers to fill in the missing details.

Standard Tags

The HTML specification defines a group of standard tags that control the structure of the HTML document. These tags will contain plain text and other tags.

```
<html> html code</html>
```

The *html* tags enclose all the other tags and text in the document.

```
<head> browser command tags </head>
```

The *head* tags enclose tags that inform the browser about how to display the entire page. These control how the page appears in the browser, but do not contain any content for the page. This paired tag belongs within the paired <html> tags.

```
<body> body tags </body>
```

The *body* tags contain all the plain text and HTML tags that are to be displayed in the browser window. This paired tag belongs within the paired <html> tags.

The <head> section does not contain normal markup tags, like strong and em, but instead contains tags that indicate how the browser should display the page.

```
<title> title text </title>
```

The *title* tags enclose the text that will display in the title bar of the browser window.

```
<meta charset="utf-8">
```

The *meta* tag is a singleton that indicates extra information for the browser. This tag can be repeated to include different information for the browser. In a standard page, there should be a meta tag with *charset* of *utf-8*. This indicates the character set for the language that is being used to display the page.

HTML Validation

The *WWW Consortium* (W3C) publishes the HTML standard and provides tools for HTML validation that will test that a page has the correct HTML structure. In order to comply with the HTML specification, all web pages should have the following structure:

```
<!DOCTYPE HTML>
<html>
  <head>
    <meta charset="utf-8">
    <title>Simple Page</title>
  </head>
  <body>
    <p>
      This is a <em>simple</em> web page.
  </body>
</html>
```

1. The DOCTYPE defines the type of markup that is being used. It precedes the `<html>` tag because it defines which version of HTML is being used.
2. All the tags and plaintext for the page are contained within the paired `<html>` tags.
   (a) Place a `<head>` section within the paired `<html>` tags.
       Place a paired `<title>` tag within the `<head>` section.
       Place a singleton `<meta>` tag for the character set within the `<head>` section.
   (b) Place a `<body>` section within the paired `<html>` tags.
3. The DOCTYPE and meta tags are required if the page is to be validated by W3C for correct HTML syntax. Go to http://www.w3.org to access the HTML validator.

There is no excuse for a web page to contain errors. With the use of the validation tool at http://www.w3.org, all HTML pages should be validated to ensure that they contain all the basic tags.

Layout Versus Style

There are two different types of information that are contained in each HTML page: layout and style. The basic layout is covered in this chapter; advanced layout and style are covered in Chap. 6. Style information contains things like the colours and font for the page. The recommended way to handle style and layout is to place all the layout tags in the HTML page and to place all the style information in a separate file, called a style sheet. For the interested student, the HTML and style information from Chap. 6 can be read at any time.

Hypertext Markup Language Five (HTML5) is the latest version of the HTML standard. In the previous versions, tags could be used to specify the style of a page. In the new version, those tags have been deprecated. In order to validate that a page conforms to version 5, the tags that specify specific style cannot be used.

In previous versions of the HTML standard, there were different DOCTYPE statements that could be used for HTML pages: strict and transitional. The strict one was the recommended one, since it enforced the rule that all style information be contained in a separate file. In version five, there are no choices for the DOCTYPE: all pages must use strict HTML. All pages for this book will use the new DOCTYPE for HTML5.

```
<!DOCTYPE HTML>
```

Word Wrap and White Space

Most of us are used to typing text in a word processor and letting the program determine where the line breaks belong. This is known as *word wrap*. The only time that we are required to hit the enter key is when we want to start a new paragraph.

Browsers will use word wrap to display text, even if the enter key is pressed. Browsers will treat a new line character, a tab character and multiple spaces as a single space. In order to insert a new line, tab or multiple spaces in an HTML page, markup must be used: if it is not plain text, then it must be placed in markup.

Browsers take word wrap one step further. Browsers will compress all consecutive white space characters into a single space character. The common white space characters are the space, the tab and the new line character. If there are five spaces at the start of a line, they will be compressed into one space.

The following listing contains a web page that has a poem.

```
<!DOCTYPE HTML>
<html>
   <head>
     <meta charset="utf-8">
     <title>A Poem</title>
   </head>
   <body>
     Roses are red
     Violets are blue
     This could be a poem
     But not a haiku

     A haiku has a fixed structure. The first line has five
     syllables, the second line has seven syllables and the
     third line has five syllables. Therefore, the previous
     poem cannot be a haiku.
   </body>
</html>
```

Even though the poem has four lines, the poem will appear as one line in the browser. This is because there is no markup to indicate that one line has ended and another line should begin. The browser will start a new line if the poem would extend beyond the right margin of the browser.

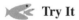 **Try It**

http://bytesizebook.com/book/ch1/poem.html

Open the link in a browser and view the poem (Fig. 1.4). Resize the window and note how the browser will break the text in different places. If the window is large enough, the entire page would be displayed on one line.

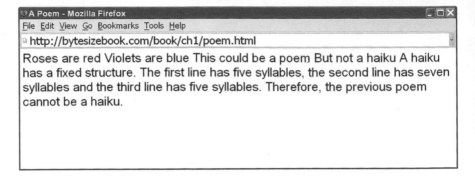

Fig. 1.4 How the poem will appear in the browser

Line Breaks

Two of the tags that can be used to start a new line are <br> and <p>. The <br> tag is short for *break* and starts a new line directly under the current line. It is a singleton tag, so it does not have a closing tag. The <p> tag is short for *paragraph* and skips at least one line and then starts a new line. It is a paired tag, so it is closed with the </p> tag.

As was mentioned above, browsers have the ability to interpret HTML even if some tags are missing. The closing paragraph tag is such a tag. It is not possible to nest one paragraph inside another, so if the browser encounters two paragraph tags without closing tags, as in <p> One <p> Two, then it will interpret this as <p> One</p> <p> Two</p>. Even the validators at *w3.org* will accept HTML that does not have closing paragraph tags.

Listing 1.1 contains the HTML page for the poem using markup for line breaks and paragraph tags.

```
<!DOCTYPE HTML>
<html>
  <head>
    <meta charset="utf-8">
    <title>A Poem</title>
  </head>
  <body>
    <p>
        Roses are red<br>
        Violets are blue<br>
        This could be a poem<br>
        But not a haiku<br>
    <p>
    A haiku has a fixed structure. The first line has five
    syllables, the second line has seven syllables and the
    third line has five syllables. Therefore, the previous
    poem cannot be a haiku.
  </body>
</html>
```

Listing 1.1 A four-line poem displayed using HTML

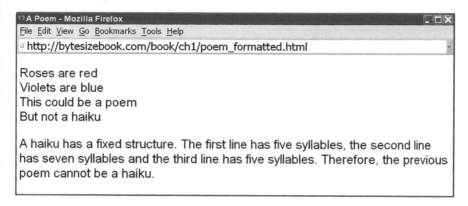

Fig. 1.5 How the formatted poem will appear in the browser

When displayed in a browser, each line of the poem will appear on a separate line. The paragraph that follows the poem will still be displayed using word wrap since no line breaks were inserted into it.

 Try It

http://bytesizebook.com/book/ch1/poem_formatted.html

Open the page in a browser to see how it looks (Fig. 1.5). Resize the window and note that the poem displays on four lines unless the window is very small.

Most browsers have an option for viewing the actual HTML that was sent from the server. If you view the source, you will see the same HTML code that was displayed in Listing 1.1.

1.2.3   What Is the HT in HTML?

The **HT** in **HTML** stands for *Hypertext*. Hypertext is the ability to click on a link in one page and have another page open. If you have ever clicked on a link in a web page to open another page, then you have used a hypertext link.

There are two parts to a hypertext link: the location of the new page and the link text that appears in the browser. The location of the pages is specified as a *Uniform Resource Locator* (URL), which contains four parts: protocol, server, path and name. The protocol could be http, ftp, telnet or others. The protocol is followed by a colon and two slashes (://). After the protocol is the server. The server is followed by a slash and the path of the directory that contains the resource. The name of the resource follows the path. `protocol://server/path/name`

The URL of the hypertext link is not displayed in the browser, but it is associated with the underlined text on the web page. Another way to say this is that the URL has to be included in the markup, since it does not appear as plain text.

Anchor Tag

The tag for a hypertext link is the paired tag <a>, which is short for *anchor*.

```
<a href="hidden_URL_of_a_file">
  Visible text in browser
</a>
```

Note that the text that is visible in the browser is not inside a tag, but that the URL of the file is. This is an example of a tag that has additional information stored in it. The additional information is called an *attribute*. The URL of the page is stored in an attribute named *href*. Attributes in HTML tags provide extra information that is not visible in the browser.

This agrees with the basic definition of HTML as having plain text and tags. The tags contain extra information about how to display the plain text. In this case, when the user clicks on the plain text, the browser will read the URL from the *href* attribute and request that page from the server.

It may not seem apparent why this tag is called an anchor tag. An anchor tag in HTML is like the anchor of a ship. The anchor for a ship connects two parts: the ship, which is visible from the surface of the water, and the bottom of the ocean. When the anchor is in use, it is not in the ship, it is in the bottom of the ocean. The anchor HTML tag connects the visible text in the browser to the physical location of a file.

Absolute and Relative References

The *href* attribute of the anchor tag contains the URL of the destination page. When using the anchor tag to reference other pages on the web, you must know the complete URL of the resource in order to create a link to it. However, depending on where the resource is located, you may be able to speed up the loading of your page by using a *relative reference*.

1. If the resource is the entire URL, starting with http://. This is known as an *absolute reference*.

   ```
   <a href="http://server.com/path/page.html">
     Some Page Somewhere on the web
   </a>
   ```

2. If the resource is on the same server, but is not descended from the current directory, then include the full path from the document root, starting with a /.

   ```
   <a href="/path/from/root/page.html">
     Some Page on the Current Server
   </a>
   ```

3. If the resource is in the same directory as the HTML page that references it, then only include the file name, not the server or the directory.

```
<a href="page.html">
   Some Page
</a>
```

4. If the resource is in a subdirectory of the directory where the HTML page that references it is located, then include the name of the subdirectory and the file name.

```
<a href="subdir/of/current/dir/page.html">
   Some Page in Some Subdir
</a>
```

There are three types of references.
1. Absolute
2. Relative from document root
3. Relative from current directory

There are just a few rules to determine the kind of reference.
1. If the URL begins with a protocol (like http://, ftp:// or telnet://), then it is an
   absolute reference to that location.
2. If the URL begins with a /, then it is a relative reference from the document root
   of the current server.
3. In all other cases, the URL is a relative reference from the current directory.

Calculating Relative References

To calculate a relative reference, start with the absolute reference of the current page
and the absolute reference to the new page. For instance, suppose that the current
page and the next page are referenced as

```
http://www.bytesizebook.com/book/ch1/poem.html
http://www.bytesizebook.com/book/ch1/poem_formatted.html
```

To find the relative reference, start from the protocol in each reference and
remove all common parts. The protocol and server are the same, so remove them.
The entire path is the same, so remove it. For these two references, the common
parts are http://www.bytesizebook.com/book/ch1/, so the relative
reference is poem_formatted.html.

Consider these two references:

```
http://www.bytesizebook.com/book/ch1/poem.html
http://www.bytesizebook.com/book/ch1/OnePage/First.jsp
```

To calculate the reference, remove the protocol and server, since they are the
same. Remove the path, since the path of the first is contained in the path to
the second. The relative reference is OnePage/First.jsp.

Consider the same references, but in a different order:

```
http://www.bytesizebook.com/book/ch1/OnePage/First.jsp
http://www.bytesizebook.com/book/ch1/poem.html
```

The protocol and server can be removed, but not the path. The path of the first reference is not contained completely within the path to the second. There are two alternatives.
1. Include the path in the relative reference: `/book/ch1/poem.html`.
2. Use the special symbol .. to indicate to go up one folder in the path: `../poem.html`.

To improve portability, it is better to avoid adding the web app folder to references. In this case, it is better to use the second technique.

At some point you will need to decide which is more important, portability or legibility. Consider these references:

```
http://www.bytesizebook.com/book/ch1/OnePage/First.jsp
http://www.bytesizebook.com/book/ch2/jspController.jsp
```

The two possible relative references are
1. `/book/ch2/jspController.jsp`
2. `../../ch2/jspController.jsp`

When the relative references become more complicated, it becomes a personal preference for deciding which reference to use.

1.3   HTML Forms

If you have ever logged into a website, then you have used an HTML form to supply your username and password. A form will have places where a user can enter data. These are known as *form elements* and can be for one line of text, several lines of text, drop-down lists and buttons. The form in Fig. 1.6, which is from Florida International University, uses several form elements for lines of text and a button for submitting the data to the server.

Fig. 1.6 An entry form
from FIU

Table 1.5 Two essential form element types

Type	Example
text	`<input type="text" name="hobby" value="">` The *value* attribute is the text that appears within the element when the page is loaded
submit	`<input type="submit" name="nextButton" value="Next">` The *value* attribute is the text that appears on the button in the browser

1.3.1   Form Elements

The form and the form elements are defined using HTML tags. The opening form tag is `<form>` and the closing tag is `</form>`. Plain text, other HTML tags and form element tags can be placed between the opening and closing form tags. There are many form elements, but only two of them will be introduced now. Table 1.5 defines the two essential form elements: *text* and *submit*. Additional form elements are covered in Chap. 6.

Each of these has the same tag name (*input*) and attributes *(type, name, value)*.
1. The HTML tag name is *input*.
2. There are many different form elements that use the *input* tag. The *type* attribute identifies which form element to display.
3. There could be several form elements in a form. The *name* attribute should be a unique identifier for the element.
4. The *value* attribute stores the data that is in the element. The value that is hard coded in the element is the value that is displayed in the browser when the HTML page is loaded.
5. The *name* and *value* attributes are used to send data to the server. When the form is submitted, the data for this element will be sent as *name = value*. The value that will be sent will be the current data that is displayed in the element.

Listing 1.2 is an example of a simple web page that has a form in it.

```
<!DOCTYPE HTML>
<html>
  <head>
    <meta charset="utf-8">
    <title>First Form</title>
  </head>
  <body>
    <form>
      <p>
        This is a simple HTML page that has a form in it.
      <p>
        Hobby: <input type="text" name="hobby"
                                  value="">
        <input type="submit" name="confirmButton"
                                  value="Confirm">
    </form>
  </body>
</html>
```

Listing 1.2 A web page with a form

First Form - Mozilla Firefox

File Edit View Go Bookmarks Tools Help

http://bytesizebook.com/book/ch1/OnePage/SimpleForm.html

This is a simple HTML page that has a form in it.

Hobby: [   ] [Confirm]

Fig. 1.7 A form with a text box and a submit button

Table 1.6 A table of colour preferences

Foreground	Black
Background	White
Border	Red
Link	Blue

The form has an input element of type *text* with a name of *hobby* and an input element of type *submit* with a name of *confirmButton*. The name that appears on the button is *Confirm*. Note that there are HTML tags, plain text and form elements between the opening and closing form tags.

 Try It

http://bytesizebook.com/book/ch1/OnePage/SimpleForm.html

The page will display a text box and a submit button (Fig. 1.7). Open the page in a browser, enter some data in the text box and submit the form.

1.3.2   Representing Data

In a two-dimensional world, it is very easy to create lists of data. For example, Table 1.6 displays a list of colour preferences in a table.

How would these be written in a one-dimensional world? In other words, how would all of this data be combined into one string of text?

In addition to the data that is in the table, the structure of the table would also need to be stored in the string. This table has four rows and two columns. There would need to be a way to indicate the end of one row and the start of the next. There would need to be a way to indicate the end of one column and the start of the next.

One technique for data formatting is to choose special characters to represent the end of a row and the end of a column. It doesn't matter which characters are used, as long as they are different. It is also helpful if the characters that are chosen are not common characters. For example, the ampersand and equal sign could be used.
1. & is used to separate rows.
2. = is used to separate the two columns in a row.

Using this technique, the above list could be represented as a string. The structure of the table is embedded in the string with the addition of special characters.

```
foreground=black&background=white&border=red&link=blue
```

1.3.3   Transmitting Data over the Web

When the user activates a submit button on a form, the data in the form elements is sent to the server. The default destination on the server is the URL of the current page. All the data in the form elements are placed into one string that is sent to the server. This string is known as the *query string*. The data from the format is placed into the query string as *name = value* pairs.

1. Each input element of type *text* or *submit* with a *name* attribute will have its data added to the query string as a *name = value* pair.
2. If there are many *name = value* pairs, then they are separated by an ampersand, &.
3. If a form element does not have a *name* attribute, then it is not sent to the server.
4. In the default case, the query string is sent to the server by appending it to the end of the URL. A question mark is used to separate the end of the URL from the start of the query string.

If the user entered *skiing* in the *hobby* element and clicked the *Confirm* button of the form, then the query string that is sent from the browser would look like the following string.

```
hobby=skiing&confirmButton=Confirm
```

A question mark and the query string are appended to the URL. The request sent to the browser would contain the following URL.

```
http://store.com/buy.htm?hobby=skiing&confirmButton=Confirm
```

If the user had entered the hobby as *water skiing*, then the query string would appear as the following string.

```
hobby=water+skiing&confirmButton=Confirm
```

Note that the space between *water* and *skiing* has been replaced by a plus sign. A space would break the URL in two. This is the first example of a character that cannot be represented normally in a URL; there will be other characters that must be translated before they can be entered in a query string. Please be aware that the browser does this translation automatically and that the server will do the reverse translation automatically. This is known as URL encoding and URL decoding.

Fig. 1.8 After entering data and clicking the button, the query string will appear in the URL

Try It

http://bytesizebook.com/book/ch1/OnePage/SimpleForm.html

Open the form, enter a hobby and click the *Confirm* button. The same page will redisplay, but the query string will be appended to the URL (Fig. 1.8).

Many first-time observers will think that nothing is happening when the submit button on the form is clicked, except that the value that was entered into the text box has disappeared. In reality, a new request for the same page was made to the server with the query string, containing the data from the form appended to the URL of the request. A complete request was made by the browser; a complete response was sent by the server.

1.4   Processing Form Data

If the data from a form is sent to a simple HTML page, then there is no way for the HTML page to retrieve the data that was sent from the browser. In order to process the data, the page should be a *JSP* or a *Servlet* in a *web application*.

1.4.1 Web Application

A web application consists of a directory structure and some required files. The directory structure is the same for all web applications. One of the required files is the *web.xml* file, which is used to initialise the web application.

Directory Structure
The root directory can have any name, like *FistApp*, but the subdirectories must have the names *WEB-INF*, *lib* and *classes* as shown in Fig. 1.9.

The root directory (i.e. *FirstApp*) of the web application is the standard location for HTML files. The WEB-INF directory contains the *web.xml* file. The *lib* directory is where *jar* files will be placed to add nonstandard features to the web application. The *classes* directory is where the programs and supporting files for your web application will be placed.

Fig. 1.9 A web application has a specific directory structure

Only the root directory is visible from the Internet. That is why HTML files are placed in the root of the web application. Any file that is to be accessed from the web must be visible from the root of the web application.

The WEB-INF directory and its contents cannot be accessed directly from the web. A method will be covered in the next chapter for making selected files, which are descended from WEB-INF, visible from the web.

web.xml

The configuration file for the web application is named *web.xml* and belongs in the WEB-INF directory. It contains XML that defines any special features for the web application, such as initialisation parameters and security access roles. XML is similar to HTML, but there are no predefined tags. Each application defines its own tags.

The web application structure is defined in the Java Servlet specification. The current version is 3.0. In the current version, many of the tags that were normally in the *web.xml* file can be replaced with annotations. When practicable, the applications in the book will use the new annotations to simplify the *web.xml* file. There are a few times when the *web.xml* will need to be modified to implement features. The details of these modifications will be covered when the concept is introduced.

In this book, it will be assumed that the web application supports the Java Servlets 3.0 specification. As such, the *web.xml* file for a web application should contain the XML in the following listing, at the least. The web-app tag specifies that version 3.0 is being used.

```
<?xml version="1.0" encoding="UTF-8"?>

<web-app xmlns="http://java.sun.com/xml/ns/javaee"
         xmlns:xsi="http://www.w3.org/2001/XMLSchema-instance"
         xsi:schemaLocation="http://java.sun.com/xml/ns/javaee
             http://java.sun.com/xml/ns/javaee/web-app_3_0.xsd"
         version="3.0">
    <session-config>
       <session-timeout>
          30
       </session-timeout>
    </session-config>
</web-app>
```

The latest versions of the NetBeans and Eclipse IDEs do not include the *web.xml* file by default. It is assumed that all necessary configuration information can be implemented using annotations. There are still times when it is better to use the *web.xml* file, even when an annotation is available. When creating a web application, please follow the instructions in the Appendix for including a *web.xml* file in a web application for these IDEs.

Web Application Location

Web applications are run by servlet engines. Each servlet engine will have a special location for web applications. For the Tomcat servlet engine, all web applications should be located in the *webapps* directory.

NetBeans and Eclipse are Java development environments that can run web applications. All web applications in each IDE will automatically be added to the servlet engine. See the Appendix for instructions on running web applications in each IDE.

For other servlet engines, check the documentation to determine where web applications should be placed.

1.4.2   JSP

A *Java Server Page* (JSP) contains HTML tags and plain text, just like a regular web page. In addition, a JSP can contain Java code that is executed when the page is displayed. As long as it is contained in a web application, a JSP will be able to process the form data that is sent to it.

JSP Location

For now, the location of JSPs will be in the root directory of the web application, not in the WEB-INF directory. The WEB-INF directory is not accessible directly through a web browser. Later, you will see how it is possible to place a JSP inside the WEB-INF directory so that access to the JSP can be restricted.

Accessing Form Data

Starting with the servlet specification 2.0, a language was added to JSPs that simplifies access to objects that are available to a JSP. This language is known as the *Expression Language* (EL). EL statements start with a dollar sign and are surrounded by curly braces.

```
${EL-statement}
```

The EL statement for accessing data in the query string uses the word *param* and the name of the form element that contained the data.

```
${param.name_of_element}
```

Consider the query string of hobby=water+skiing. To retrieve the value of the hobby parameter from the query string, insert ${param.hobby} anywhere inside the JSP.

First JSP - Mozilla Firefox

File Edit View Go Bookmarks Tools Help

book.com/book/ch1/OnePage/First.jsp?hobby=water+skiing&confirmButton=Confirm

This is a simple HTML page that has a form in it.

The hobby was received as: **water skiing**

Hobby: [   ] [Confirm]

Fig. 1.10 The value from the query string is displayed in the page

```html
<!DOCTYPE HTML>
<html>
  <head>
    <meta charset="utf-8">
    <title>First JSP</title>
  </head>
  <body>
    <form>
      <p>
        This is a simple HTML page that has a form in it.
      <p>
        The hobby was received as: <strong>${param.hobby}</strong>
      <p>
        Hobby: <input type="text" name="hobby"
                              value="">
        <input type="submit" name="confirmButton"
                              value="Confirm">
    </form>
  </body>
</html>
```

The source code for this page looks just like the HTML page that contained the simple form in Listing 1.2, except that it includes one instance of an EL statement, ${param.hobby}, and has the extension *jsp* instead of *html*. These changes allow the value that is present in the query string to be displayed in the browser. This is an example of a dynamic page. It changes appearance based upon the data that is entered by the user.

 Try It

http://bytesizebook.com/book/ch1/OnePage/First.jsp

Type in a hobby and click the *Confirm* button. The form data will be sent back to the current page in the query string. Figure 1.10 shows the value that is in the query string being displayed in the body of the JSP.

1.4.3   Initialising Form Elements

Using the ${param.hobby} syntax, it is possible to initialise a form element with the value that was sent to the page. The trick is to set the *value* attribute of the form element with the parameter value: value="${param.hobby}". The *value* attribute holds the data that will appear in the form element when the page is loaded.

```html
<!DOCTYPE HTML>
<html>
  <head>
    <meta charset="utf-8">
    <title>Initialized JSP</title>
  </head>
  <body>
    <form>
      <p>
        This is a simple HTML page that has a form in it.
      <p>
        The hobby was received as: <strong>${param.hobby}</strong>
      <p>
        Hobby: <input type="text" name="hobby"
                                  value="${param.hobby}">
        <input type="submit" name="confirmButton"
                             value="Confirm">
    </form>
  </body>
</html>
```

Try It

http://bytesizebook.com/book/ch1/OnePage/FormInitialized.jsp

Before entering a hobby in the form element, examine the source of the page in the browser. Note that the value for the hobby element is the empty string.

```html
...
<form>
  <p>

    This is a simple HTML page that has a form in it.
  <p>
    The hobby was received as: <strong></strong>
  <p>
    Hobby: <input type="text" name="hobby"
                             value="">
    <input type="submit" name="confirmButton"
                         value="Confirm">
</form>
...
```

Now enter a hobby and click the *Confirm* button (Fig. 1.11).

Open the source of the page in the browser. You will see that the value that was sent from the browser to the server is now hard coded in the form element. Try a hobby that has multiple words, too.

Fig. 1.11   The input element is initialised with the value from the query string

```
...
<form>
  <p>
    This is a simple HTML page that has a form in it.
  <p>
    The hobby was received as: <strong>water skiing</strong>
  <p>
    Hobby: <input type="text" name="hobby"
                             value="water skiing">
    <input type="submit" name="confirmButton"
                         value="Confirm">
</form>
...
```

Remember to use the quotes around the values. If the quotes are omitted and the value has multiple words in it, then only the first will be placed in the element. Never write the value as value = ${param.hobby}; always include the quotes.

Try It

http://bytesizebook.com/book/ch1/OnePage/FormInitializedBad.jsp

In this example, the quotes have been omitted for the value. To see the problem, enter more than one word in the hobby element.

In Fig. 1.12, you will see that the correct value is displayed in the plain text, but that the value in the form element is incorrect. For example, if the hobby is entered as water skiing, then the form element will only display *water*.

The reason becomes clear when the HTML code for the form element is viewed in the browser.

```
<input type="text" name="hobby" value=water skiing>
```

Without the quotes around the *value* attribute, the browser sees the following attributes: *type*, *name*, *value* and *skiing*. The browser doesn't know what the *skiing* attribute is, so the browser ignores it. Compare this to the correct format for the input element.

```
<input type="text" name="hobby" value="water skiing">
```

Now the browser sees the correct attributes: *type*, *name* and *value*.

Fig. 1.12 The input element is not initialised properly for values that have multiple words

1.5   The Truth About JSPs

JSPs look like HTML pages, but they can generate dynamic content. Whenever there is dynamic content, there is a program working in the background. HTML pages are plain text. If a JSP is not in a web application, then there would be no dynamic content, and they would be treated as plain text.

JSPs are abstractions: they are translated into Java programs known as *servlets*. The program that translates them into servlets is known as the servlet engine. It is the task of the servlet engine to translate the JSPs into servlets and to execute them.

Servlets only contain Java code. All the plain text from the JSP has been translated into `write` statements. The EL statements have been translated into complicated Java expressions.

1.5.1   Servlet for a JSP

The following listing contains the servlet that was created by the servlet engine for the last page. The contents of the page can be seen in the `out.write` statements.

```
package ch1;

import javax.servlet.*;
import javax.servlet.http.*;
import javax.servlet.jsp.*;

public final class FormInitialized_jsp
    extends org.apache.jasper.runtime.HttpJspBase
    implements org.apache.jasper.runtime.JspSourceDependent {

  private static final JspFactory _jspxFactory =
        JspFactory.getDefaultFactory();

  private static java.util.List<String> _jspx_dependants;

  public java.util.List<String> getDependants() {
    return _jspx_dependants;
  }
```

```
public void _jspService(final HttpServletRequest request,
                    final HttpServletResponse response)
   throws java.io.IOException, ServletException {

final PageContext pageContext;
HttpSession session = null;
final ServletContext application;
final ServletConfig config;
JspWriter out = null;
final Object page = this;
JspWriter _jspx_out = null;
PageContext _jspx_page_context = null;

try {
  response.setContentType("text/html");
  pageContext = _jspxFactory.getPageContext(
      this, request, response,
          null, true, 8192, true);
  _jspx_page_context = pageContext;
  application = pageContext.getServletContext();
  config = pageContext.getServletConfig();
  session = pageContext.getSession();
  out = pageContext.getOut();
  _jspx_out = out;

  out.write("<!DOCTYPE HTML>\ n");
  out.write("<html>\ n");
  out.write("  <head>\ n");
  out.write("    <meta charset='utf-8'>\ n");
  out.write("    <title>Initialized JSP</title>\ n");
  out.write("  </head>\ n");
  out.write("  <body>\ n");
  out.write("    <form>\ n");
  out.write("      <p>\ n");
  out.write("        This is a simple HTML page that "
        + "has a form in it.\ n");
  out.write("      <p>\ n");
  out.write("        The hobby was received as: <strong>");
  out.write((String) org.apache.jasper.runtime.
      PageContextImpl.proprietaryEvaluate(
        "${param.hobby}", String.class,
        (PageContext)_jspx_page_context, null, false));
  out.write("</strong>\ n");
  out.write("      <p>\ n");
  out.write("        Hobby: <input type='text' name='hobby' \ n");
  out.write("                                  value='");
  out.write((String) org.apache.jasper.runtime.
      PageContextImpl.proprietaryEvaluate(
        "${param.hobby}", String.class,
        (PageContext)_jspx_page_context, null, false));
  out.write("'>\ n");
  out.write("        <input type='submit' name='confirmButton' \ n");
  out.write("                                value='Confirm'>\ n");
  out.write("    </form>\ n");
  out.write("  </body>\ n");
```

```
      out.write("</html>");
  }catch (Throwable t) {
    if (!(t instanceof SkipPageException)){
      out = _jspx_out;
      if (out != null && out.getBufferSize() != 0)
        try { out.clearBuffer(); }
        catch (java.io.IOException e) {}
      if (_jspx_page_context != null)
          _jspx_page_context.handlePageException(t);
    }
  }finally {
    _jspxFactory.releasePageContext(_jspx_page_context);
  }
  }
}
```

It is actually a complicated matter to generate dynamic content. The EL statement in the JSP is responsible for the dynamic content. In the above servlet, the actual Java code for the EL statement of ${param.hobby} is

```
out.write((String) org.apache.jasper.runtime.
    PageContextImpl.proprietaryEvaluate(
      "${param.hobby}", String.class,
      (PageContext)_jspx_page_context, null, false));
```

The beauty of a JSP is that the servlet engine implements most of the details automatically. The developer can simply write HTML statements and EL statements to generate programs that can process dynamic data.

1.5.2   Handling a JSP

Web servers know how to deliver static content, but need separate programs to handle dynamic content. Common web servers are Apache and Microsoft Internet Information Server. Apache is the most popular web server software on the market. If there is a request made to the web server for a JSP, then the web server must send the request to another program to complete the request. In particular, if a web page has a form for entering data and sends the data to a JSP, then a special program known as a *servlet engine* will handle the request.

A servlet engine is a program running on the server that knows how to execute JSPs and servlets. There are several different servlet engines: Tomcat and JRun are two popular choices.

JSP Request Process
When the user fills in data in a form and clicks a button, there is a request made from the browser to the web server (Fig. 1.13).

Fig. 1.13 The browser makes
a request to the server for a
dynamic page

Fig. 1.14 The web server
sends the request for a JSP to
the servlet engine

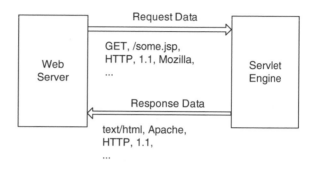

Fig. 1.15 The servlet engine
sends a response back to the
browser

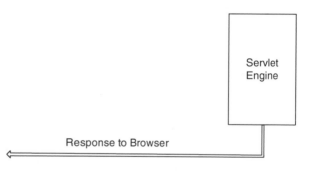

The web server recognises that the extension of the request is *.jsp*, so it calls a servlet engine to process the JSP. The web server administrator must configure the web server so that it sends all *.jsp* files to the servlet engine. There is nothing magical about the *.jsp* extension; it could be set to any extension at all (Fig. 1.14).

The web server sends the request information that it received from the browser to the servlet engine. If this were a request for a static page, the server would send a response to the browser; instead, the server sends the response information to the servlet engine. The servlet engine takes this request and response information and sends a response back to the browser (Fig. 1.15).

Putting all the steps together gives the complete picture of how a request for a JSP is handled: the request is made; the server calls another program to handle the request; the other program, which is known as a servlet engine, sends the response to the browser (Fig. 1.16).

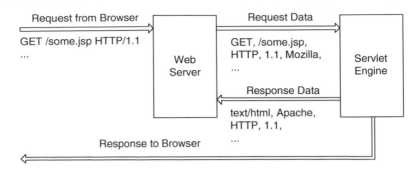

Fig. 1.16 The complete request and response cycle

Servlet Engine Response

Inside the servlet engine, there are steps that are followed to take the request information and generate a response. The servlet engine must translate the JSP into a servlet, load the servlet into memory, encapsulate the data from the browser and generate the response.

Translating the JSP: The servlet engine must translate all JSPs into servlets. The servlet engine will keep a copy of the translated servlet so that the engine does not need to retranslate the JSP on every request. The servlet engine will only create the servlet when the servlet does not exist or when the source JSP has been modified.

Loading the Servlet: A servlet is loaded into memory upon the first request made to it after the servlet engine has been started or restarted. The servlet .class file is stored on disk. Upon the first request to the servlet, the .class file is loaded into memory. Once a servlet has been loaded into memory, it will remain there – waiting for calls to its methods. It is not removed from memory after each request; this enables the servlet engine to process requests faster.

Request and Response Information: The web server sends the request information that it received from the browser to the servlet engine. The server also sends the response information to the servlet engine. The servlet engine takes this information and creates two objects: one that encapsulates the request information and one that encapsulates the response information. These two objects are all that are needed to communicate with the browser; all of the information that the browser sent is in the request object; all the information that is needed to send data to the browser is in the response object.

Servlet Method to Handle Request: Generating the response is done in the _jspService method of the generated servlet. The method has two parameters: the request and the response. These parameters are the objects that the servlet engine generated from the request data that was sent from the browser and from the response

Fig. 1.17 The servlet engine handling a request for a JSP

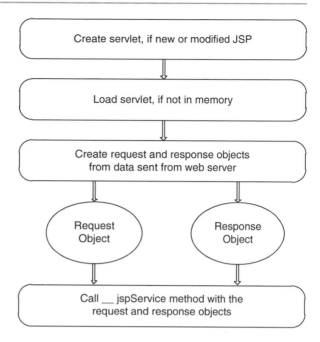

data that was forwarded by the web server. These objects are of the types javax. servlet.http.HttpServletRequest and javax.servlet.http. HttpServletResponse.

```
public void _jspService(HttpServletRequest request,
                        HttpServletResponse response)
        throws java.io.IOException, ServletException
```

Whenever a request is made for a JSP, the servlet engine might have to create the servlet and might have to load it into memory. If the servlet is recreated, then it will have to reload the servlet into memory. However, even if the servlet is not recreated, the servlet might need to be loaded into memory. Whenever the servlet engine is restarted, then all servlets are removed from memory; when the next request is made to the servlet, it will need to be reloaded into memory.

Figure 1.17 summarises the steps that are followed by the servlet engine when it receives a request for a JSP.

1.6   Tomcat and IDEs

In order to run servlets and JSPs, it is necessary to install a servlet engine. A popular servlet engine is Tomcat, which is an Apache project.

Table 1.7 Visible contents in a web application

Visible pages	This is the main folder for content that is visible from the web application. Place the JSPs from this chapter in this folder. NetBeans calls it *Web Pages*. Eclipse calls it *Web Content*
index.jsp	This is the default web page when this web application is loaded from Tomcat. Place hypertext links in this page to your JSPs and servlets. When the web application is run, this is the page that will appear in the web browser
WEB-INF	This sub-directory contains resources that cannot be viewed from the web, like the *web.xml* file

While it is possible to create Java programs with a text editor and to download and run Tomcat to run web applications, it is easier to use an IDE that interfaces with Tomcat. Two popular IDEs are NetBeans and Eclipse. The appendix contains information about these IDEs, including installing and configuring them.

Each IDE has similar features: code completion, syntax highlighting, fixing imports, refactoring. For first-time developers, I recommend NetBeans. For developers that must create Java files from an existing database, I recommend Eclipse.

1.6.1 Web Project

A web project in NetBeans and Eclipse is a set of directories and files that allow for servlets and JSPs to be executed and debugged. By placing the HTML, JSP and servlet files in the correct folders, a web project can be executed from within each IDE.

The web project does not have the structure of a web application; however, each IDE has the ability to create a *Web Archive* (WAR). The WAR file contains the corresponding web application structure. The files from the project folders will be copied into the folders of the web application. NetBeans creates the WAR file every time the project is cleaned and built. In Eclipse, the WAR file must be created from the File - > Export - > Web - > War File menu.

There are three main folders that are used for a web project: visible pages, class files and libraries. The visible pages folder will be discussed in this chapter. The other two folders will be covered in detail in Chaps. 2 and 4. In NetBeans, the folder is named *Web Pages*; in Eclipse, it is named *Web Content*.

Visible Pages

The visible pages folder is for HTML pages, images, CSS style sheets and some JSPs. Table 1.7 explains the directories and files that will be found in this folder when a new project is created.

 Try It

http://netbeans.org

Try It

http://www.eclipse.org

Download and install the latest NetBeans from http://netbeans.org or Eclipse from http://www.eclipse.org. In order to use the EL statements, Java 1.5 or higher must be installed on the system.

Create a web application and copy the JSPs into the visible pages folder. Subfolders can also be created. For now, do not place any JSPs under the WEB-INF directory. The Appendix has information about installing each IDE and running a web application.

Edit the *index.jsp* file by adding hypertext links to the JSPs.

Run the web application, follow the links to the JSPs and enjoy running a dynamic application.

1.7 Summary

The communication between the browser and server is controlled by the HTTP protocol. The two major parts of the protocol cover the request and response: the request from the browser and the response from the server must have specific formats. The server also indicates the type of the content that is being sent to the browser, so that the browser will know how to display it.

Markup languages are useful for annotating plain text. HTML is the markup language that is used on the Internet. The most common content sent on the web is HTML. Each HTML tag has a similar structure. To be well formed, an HTML page should have a set of basic tags. The most important tag in HTML is the anchor tag. The anchor tag can use relative and absolute references to other files.

HTML forms are the way that browsers accept information from a user and send it to the server. The basic input tags were covered: text and submit. When the browser sends the data to the server, the data must be formatted so that it can be passed in a URL. It is placed in the query string.

In order to process data from a user, the data must be received by a dynamic page in a web application. The most important file in a web application is the *web.xml* file, which is used to configure the web application. A web application must have a specific directory structure. JSPs are one of the ways that dynamic content can be displayed in a web application. The EL is used to display dynamic content from within a JSP. EL can be used to initialise form elements with data that is sent to the page.

JSPs are an abstraction: they are translated into Java programs, known as servlets, by the servlet engine. The servlet engine is an application that is called by the web server to handle JSPs and servlets. The servlet engine encapsulates the request and response information from the server into objects and passes them to the servlets.

NetBeans and Eclipse are excellent development environments for web applications. After creating a project, a web application can be executed with the click of a button.

1.8   Chapter Review

Terms
1. Browser
2. Server
3. Request
4. Response
5. Protocol
6. URL
7. MIME Type
8. Markup Language
9. HTML
    (a) Singleton Tag
    (b) Paired Tag
10. Word Wrap
11. White Space
12. Hypertext Link
    (a) Relative
    (b) Absolute
13. HTML Form
14. Query String
15. Web Application
16. Java Server Page
17. web.xml
18. Expression Language

New Java
1. _jspService

Tags
1. html
2. head
3. body
4. doctype
5. meta
6. title
7. br
8. p
9. input
    (a) text (name and value attributes)
    (b) submit (name and value attributes)
10. ${param.element_name}

Questions

1. What are the three things that belong in the first line of a request from the browser?
2. What are the three things that belong in the first line of a response from the server?
3. What types of information are contained in the request header?
4. What types of information are contained in the response header?
5. Besides the ?, = and &, list five additional characters that are encoded by the browser.
6. What is the purpose of MIME types?
7. What are the two parts of every markup language?
8. What two tags are needed in order to use the W3C validator?
9. How is white space treated in HTML pages?
10. What happens to a line of text that is longer than the width of the browser window that is displaying the HTML page?
11. Assume that a form has two text boxes named `firstName` and `lastName`.
    (a) Write the query string if the user enters *Fred* for the `firstName` and *Flintstone* for the `lastName`.
    (b) Write the query string if the user enters *John Quincy* for the `firstName` and *Adams III* for the `lastName`.
    (c) Write the query string if the user enters *Laverne & Shirley* for the `firstName` and leaves the `lastName` blank.
    (d) Write the EL statements that will display the values for the first name and last name.
12. What information is contained in the request object that is sent to the `_jspService` method?
13. What information is contained in the response object that is sent to the `_jspService` method?
14. How often is the servlet for a JSP generated?
15. When is the servlet for a JSP loaded into memory?

Tasks

1. Write a complete HTML page, including DOCTYPE and META tags. The content of the page should be a five-line poem; each line of the poem should display on a separate line in the browser. Validate the page for correct HTML syntax, at http://www.w3.org/. Introduce some errors into your page and validate again to see the error messages that the validator generates.
2. Write hypertext links to the following locations. Use a relative reference whenever possible.
    (a) To the site `http://www.microsoft.com`
    (b) To the file `page2.html` that is in the same directory as the current page
    (c) To the file `page3.html` that is in a subdirectory named `special` of the current directory
    (d) To the file `page4.html` that is in a subdirectory named `common` of the document root of the web server

3. Write a complete HTML page that has an HTML form with a text input field and a submit button. Validate the page for correct HTML syntax, at http://www. w3.org/
   (a) Rewrite the page so that it echoes the value for the input field as plain text, if it is in the Query String.
   (b) Rewrite the page so that it initialises the input element with the value for it in the Query String.
4. Write the Query String that would be created from an HTML form that has two input elements named first and last. Assume that the user has entered a value of *Fred* for first and *Flintstone* for last.
5. Create a web application with a complete *web.xml* file.
   (a) Place the HTML page from question 1 into the web application.
   (b) Place the JSP from question 3 into the web application.
   (c) In the HTML page, add a hypertext link to the JSP.
   (d) Access the HTML page from the web.
   (e) Access the JSP from the web.

Controllers

2

Web applications are more similar than different. If you describe a website where you buy things, you will probably say that there is a page where you enter personal information, then there is a page where you confirm that your information is correct and then the site processes your order. These pages could be named the *edit page*, the *confirm page* and the *process page*. For the next few chapters, this will be the basic structure of all the examples of web applications.

Web applications need to be able to send data from one page to the next. The form tag allows one page to send data to any other page. All the data that are in named form elements can be sent to any page when a button in a form is clicked.

Pages that have visible form elements for entering data can easily send data to another page; however, not all pages have visible form elements for entering data. Typically, the confirm page will display the user's data as plain text, not in visible form elements. There is a non-visible form element that can be added to a form that will hold the user's data, so that it can be sent to the next page when a button is clicked.

Some pages in a web application need to be able to send data to more than one page. The confirm page in a typical website is a common example. If there is an error in the data, the user will send the data back to the edit page. If the data is correct, the user will send the data to the process page. In order to handle this task efficiently, a separate page or program, known as a controller, will be used.

A task of the controller is to determine the next page to display. Based on the button that the user clicks, the controller will forward the request to the correct JSP. A controller can be written as a JSP, but it is better to write the controller as a Java program known as a servlet.

A servlet is a Java program that is compiled to a `.class` file. The `.class` file must be in the *classes* directory of a web application in order to be executed. By default, `.class` files cannot be accessed from the web, but they can be made visible by adding tags to the *web.xml* file of the web application.

T. Downey, *Guide to Web Development with Java: Understanding Website Creation*,
DOI 10.1007/978-1-4471-2443-6_2, © Springer-Verlag London Limited 2012

2.1   Sending Data to Another Form

When the user clicks a submit button in a form, by default, the data is sent back to
the current URL. At the server, the file at current URL then processes the data and
resends its content to the browser. It is possible to override this default behaviour so
that the data entered in one page can be sent to another page (Fig. 2.1).

Each form has an optional *action* attribute that specifies the URL of the page
that should receive the data.

2.1.1   Action Attribute

The *action* attribute should specify the URL of a JSP or servlet that will process the
data and return a new HTML page for the browser to display.

```
. . .
<form action="Confirm.jsp">
. . .
```

The *action* attribute of the form tag controls where the data is sent and the page
that will be displayed. For example, Listing 2.1 shows how the edit page, Edit.
jsp, could send its data to Confirm.jsp.

```
<!DOCTYPE HTML>
<html>
  <head>
    <meta charset="utf-8">
    <title>Simple Edit Page</title>
  </head>
  <body>
    <p>This is a simple HTML page that has a form in it.
    <form action="Confirm.jsp">
      <p>
        If there is a value for the hobby in the query
        string, then it is used to initialize the hobby
        element.
      <p>
        Hobby: <input type="text" name="hobby"
                                   value="${param.hobby}">
        <input type="submit" name="confirmButton"
                             value="Confirm">
    </form>
  </body>
</html>
```

Listing 2.1 A JSP that sends data to a different page

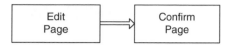

Fig. 2.1 The data from the edit page can be forwarded to the confirm page

Relative and Absolute References

Just like the *href* attribute in an anchor tag, the *action* attribute can be a relative reference to a JSP or Servlet, or can be an absolute reference to a JSP or Servlet on another server.

1. If the resource is not on the same server, then you must specify the entire URL, starting with `http://`.
   ```
   <form action="http://server.com/path/Confirm.jsp">
   ```
2. If the JSP or Servlet is on the same server, but is not descended from the current directory, then include the full path from the document root, starting with a /.
   ```
   <form action="/path/Confirm.jsp">
   ```
3. If the JSP or Servlet is in the same directory as the HTML page that references it, then only include the file name, not the server, nor the directory.
   ```
   <form action="Confirm.jsp">
   ```
4. If the JSP or Servlet is in a subdirectory of the directory where the HTML page that references it is located, then include the name of the subdirectory and the file name.
   ```
   <form action="subPath/Confirm.jsp">
   ```

Retrieving the Value of a Form Element

When a button is clicked in a form, the data from the form is placed into the query string. The query string is sent to the page that is specified in the action attribute of the form. This page can retrieve the value of the form element by using EL, just as the edit page used EL to initialise the form element with the value from the query string.

The next listing shows the contents of Confirm.jsp, the JSP that processes the data and displays a new HTML page. It displays the value of the form parameter that was sent to it, using the EL statement `${param.hobby}`. Once the data has been placed into the query string, it can be retrieved by any JSP.

```html
<!DOCTYPE HTML>
<html>
  <head>
    <meta charset="utf-8">
    <title>Simple Confirmation Page</title>
  </head>
  <body>
    <p>The value of the hobby that was sent to
       this page is: <b>${param.hobby}</b>.
  </body>
</html>
```

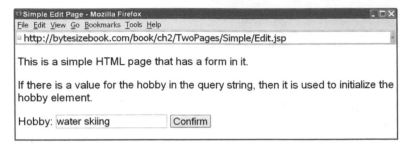

Fig. 2.2 Edit.jsp with some data entered into the hobby element

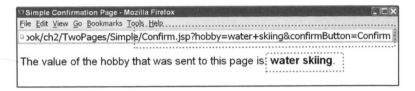

Fig. 2.3 The confirm page with data that was sent from the edit page

 Try It

http://bytesizebook.com/book/ch2/TwoPages/Simple/Edit.jsp

Enter some data into the hobby element (Fig. 2.2).

Click the confirm button and look at the URL in the browser window (Fig. 2.3). The URL is for the confirm page and contains the data that was sent from the edit page: the hobby and the button. The hobby is displayed in the browser window.

Note that

1. The URL has changed
2. The data that was entered in the first page is sent to the second page in the query string via the URL
3. The data that was entered in the first page has been displayed in the second page

2.1.2   Hidden Field Technique

There are now two JSPs: Edit.jsp and Confirm.jsp. The edit page can send data to the confirm page. The next challenge is to allow the confirm page to send the data back to the edit page (Fig. 2.4).

If you think about web pages that you have visited, you will realise that when a web page accepts information from the user, data can only be changed on one page: the data entry page. Furthermore, once data has been entered into the site, the user usually has the ability to confirm that the information is correct, before submitting the data to be processed.

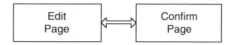

Fig. 2.4 The data that was sent to the confirm page can be returned to the edit page

This is the structure of the next example. The user can enter and edit data in the edit page, but cannot edit data in the confirm page; the confirm page will only display the data that was entered in the edit page and provide a button that will allow the user to return to the edit page to make corrections.

When accepting data from the user, it is important to validate that the data is correct. The simplest way to do this is to allow the user to confirm that the data is valid. It is essential that the page, in which the user confirms that the data is correct, does not allow the user to edit the data. In such a case, there would need to be another page for the user to validate that the new data is correct. This leads to an infinite chain of confirmation pages. It is much simpler to ask the user to confirm the data and return the user to the first page if there is an error.

First Attempt

The first attempt would be to add a form with a button to Confirm.jsp (Listing 2.2). This will allow the application to return to the edit page when the user clicks the button.

```
<!DOCTYPE HTML>
<html>
  <head>
    <meta charset="utf-8">
    <title>Simple Confirmation Page</title>
  </head>
  <body>
    <p>The value of the hobby that was sent to
       this page is: <b>${param.hobby}</b>.
    <form action="Edit.jsp">
      <p>
        If there is an error, please select <i>Edit</i>.
        <br>
        <input type="submit" name="editButton"
                             value="Edit">
    </form>
  </body>
</html>
```

Listing 2.2 A confirm page that fails to send data back to the edit page

This approach will allow the confirm page to call the edit page, but the data from the edit page will be lost.

 Try It

http://bytesizebook.com/book/ch2/TwoPages/Error/Edit.jsp

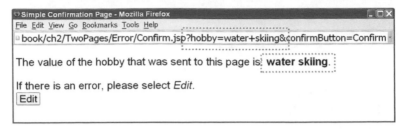

Fig. 2.5 The data is sent correctly from the edit page to the confirm page

Fig. 2.6 The data is not returned from the confirm page to the edit page

Enter a hobby and click the confirm button (Fig. 2.5). Note that the data that was entered in the edit page has been sent to the confirm page via the query string and that the data has been displayed in the JSP.

Click the edit button on the confirm page to return to the edit page (Fig. 2.6). Note that the hobby field does not have the value that was sent to the confirm page. The original data from the edit page has been lost.

Examine the URL and you will see why it failed: there is no hobby listed in the query string. The only data in the query string is the button that was clicked in the confirm page.

```
.../ch2/TwoPages/Error/Edit.jsp?editButton=Edit
```

For now, the only way to send data from one page to another is to place it in the query string. Even though the value of the hobby was sent to the confirm page, the value was not put back into the query string when control was returned to the edit page. That is the reason why the value of the hobby was lost.

Second Attempt: Hidden Fields
One way to place data into the query string is to place the data in a named element within a form. This was done when the data was sent from the edit page.

```
Hobby: <input type="text" name="hobby"
                          value="${param.hobby}">
```

In the first attempt (Listing 2.2), the confirm page did not have an input element for the hobby in its form. In order to send the hobby to another page, an input element must be added for it in the form.

However, remember that the design of this application is mimicking the design of many websites: the user should not be able to edit the data on the confirm page. If a normal text element were added to the confirm page, then the user would be able to change the data on this page. This contradicts the intended design.

The solution is to add a special form element whose value cannot be changed by the user. This is known as a *hidden* element. It is not visible in the browser, so it cannot be changed by the user. It has the same structure as a *text* element, but the *type* attribute of the form element is set to *hidden*. It will behave just like a visible element; when a button is clicked, the value from the hidden element will be added to the query string and sent to the action page.

```
<input type="hidden" name="hobby"
                     value="${param.hobby}">
```

By adding this element to the form, the Confirm.jsp page will work as planned. Note that the value to save in the hidden element is the value that was sent to this page.

```
<!DOCTYPE HTML>
<html>
  <head>
    <meta charset="utf-8">
    <title>Confirmation Page with Edit Option</title>
  </head>
  <body>
    <p>The value of the hobby that was sent to
       this page is: <strong>${param.hobby}</strong>.
    <form action="Edit.jsp">
      <p>
        If there is an error, please select <em>Edit</em>.
        <br>
        <input type="hidden" name="hobby"
                            value="${param.hobby}">
        <input type="submit" name="editButton"
                            value="Edit">
    </form>
  </body>
</html>
```

Be sure that the name of the hidden element is the same name as the original text element in the edit page. In fact, the only difference between the visible element in the edit page and the hidden element in the confirm page is the type attribute of the elements (Table 2.1).

 Try It

http://bytesizebook.com/book/ch2/TwoPages/Edit.jsp

Table 2.1 Comparison of text and hidden elements

Edit page	Hobby: `<input type="text" name="hobby" value="${param.hobby}">`
Confirm page	`<input type="hidden" name="hobby" value="${param.hobby}">`

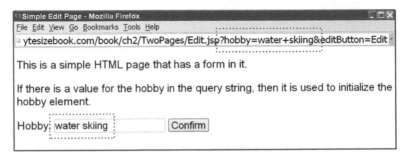

Fig. 2.7 The data is returned from the confirm page to the edit page

Enter a hobby and click the confirm button. Choose the edit button from the confirm page and return to the edit page (Fig. 2.7).

This time, it works.

1. The hobby cannot be changed on the confirm page.
2. The hobby can be sent back to the edit page.
3. The hobby appears in the query string that is sent to either page.
4. The name of the element is *hobby* regardless of whether it is the text element or the hidden element.

2.1.3 Sending Data to Either of Two Pages

The application can now pass the data back and forth between two pages and only one of the pages can change the data. This is a good start, but now there needs to be a new page that can process the user's data (Fig. 2.8).

Once the user has entered data into a website, there is usually a button that allows the user to return to the first page and edit the data. There is also a button that allows the user to confirm that the data is correct. When this button is clicked, the website processes the user's data.

To implement this design, a new page must be added to the application. This will be the process page and will have the name `Process.jsp`. At this stage of development, there is nothing to do in the process page. Eventually, this is where

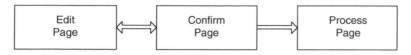

Fig. 2.8 The confirm page can send data to the edit page or the process page

the database will be accessed. For now, the process page will only echo the data that the user has entered (Listing 2.3).

```html
<!DOCTYPE HTML>
<html>
  <head>
    <meta charset="utf-8">
    <title>Process Page</title>
  </head>
  <body>
    <p>
      Thank you for your information. Your hobby
      of <strong>${param.hobby}</strong> will be added to
      our records, eventually.
    </p>
  </body>
</html>
```

Listing 2.3 The process page

The first half of the intended design has been implemented in our web application. The additional requirement is that the data from the confirm page can also be sent to the process page. This presents a problem: a form can only have one action attribute, so it can send data to only one page. The action attribute in a form can only specify one address. Even if there are multiple buttons in a form, they will all send the data to the same page.

Inefficient Solution: Adding Another Form

A solution to the problem of sending data to two different pages will be covered now, but a better technique will be revealed in the next section of the chapter. The current technique is being covered in order to demonstrate the limitations of only using JSPs to design a web application.

The solution to this problem, using JSPs, is not a pretty solution. The solution is to have two forms in the confirm page (Listing 2.4). Each form will have its own action attribute; each form will have its own button. One form will have an action that points to the edit page and the other form will have an action that points to the process page.

```
<!DOCTYPE HTML>
<html>
  <head>
    <meta charset="utf-8">
    <title>Confirmation Page with Edit/Process Options</title>
  </head>
  <body>
    <p>The value of the hobby that was sent to
       this page is: <strong>${param.hobby}</strong>
    <p>
       If there is an error, please select <em>Edit</em>,
       otherwise please select <em>Process</em>.
    <form action="Edit.jsp">
      <input type="hidden" name="hobby"
                           value="${param.hobby}">
      <input type="submit" name="editButton"
                           value="Edit">
    </form>
    <form action="Process.jsp">
      <input type="hidden" name="hobby"
                           value="${param.hobby}">
      <input type="submit" name="processButton"
                           value="Process">
    </form>
  </body>.
</html>
```

Listing 2.4 An inefficient solution that requires two forms

In order to return to the edit page, the user will click the edit button, which is in the form with the action set to the edit page. In order to confirm the data and continue to the next step, the user will click the process button, which is in the form with the action set to the process page.

Note that the hidden data must be included in each form. Imagine if there were three possible destinations: there would be three separate forms with duplicate copies of the hidden fields. Imagine if there were ten fields of data: it would not take long for this technique to become difficult to update. This is the reason why this is an inefficient technique. As a web application becomes more robust and offers the user many different options, the technique of using a separate form for each action becomes unwieldy.

Instead of having multiple forms with one button, it would be better to have one form with multiple buttons. This could be accomplished by adding Java code to the JSP or by adding Javascript to the JSP; however, this would tend to scatter the logic for the application amongst separate pages. There is a better solution that uses a separate Java program to decide which button was clicked. Such a solution will be covered in the section on controllers.

 Try It

http://bytesizebook.com/book/ch2/ThreePages/Edit.jsp

Fig. 2.9 The confirm page now has two buttons

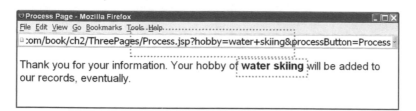

Fig. 2.10 The data can be seen in the edit page. The URL contains Edit.jsp

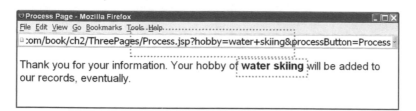

Fig. 2.11 The data can be seen in the process page. The URL contains Process.jsp

Enter data in the edit page and click the confirm button (Fig. 2.9). From the confirm page, it is possible to send the data back to the edit page (Fig. 2.10) or forward to the process page (Fig. 2.11).

This solution does have the desired effect, but it is difficult to maintain. A better solution will be discussed in the next section.

2.2   Using a Controller

A better solution to the problem of sending data to either of two pages is to use a fourth page. The idea is to use the fourth page as a control centre. In this technique, the action attribute of all the forms is set to the fourth page (Fig. 2.12). The fourth

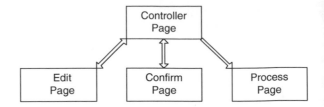

Fig. 2.12 Each page only communicates with the controller

page then decides which of the other pages to present. The fourth page will not contain any HTML code; it will only contain Java code. The fourth page is known as a *controller*.

In this technique, each page has only one form, but may have multiple buttons in a form. For example, the confirm page will have a single form with two buttons. The action attribute of the form will be set to the controller and each button will have a unique name. The controller will determine which page to display next, based upon the button that was clicked.

```
. . .
<form action="Controller.jsp">
  <p>
    <input type="hidden" name="hobby"
                         value="${param.hobby}">
    <input type="submit" name="editButton"
                         value="Edit">
    <input type="submit" name="processButton"
                         value="Process">

</form>
. . .
```

Think of a controller as a gateway on a network. Computers on the network want to be able to communicate with each other, but each computer does not want to have to know the address of all the other computers on the network. The gateway simplifies the process of communication, since each computer only has to know the location of the gateway. The gateway knows the location of all the computers on the network. Additional computers can be added to the network and only the gateway will be affected.

2.2.1 Controller Details

The controller only contains Java code. Each JSP will send its data to the controller. The controller determines which button was clicked and then forwards control to the corresponding JSP to complete the request.

The controller simplifies the way that JSPs communicate with each other. Each JSP only knows the location of the controller. The controller knows the location of all the pages. If a new page is added, then only a few pages are changed: the controller and any pages that have a button for the new page.

One of the functions of the controller is to determine what the next page is, based upon which button was clicked. All buttons should have a name. When the button is clicked, its name will be added to the query string. By inspecting the query string, the controller can determine which button was clicked.

The query string is sent to the server as part of the request from the browser. Since the controller is a JSP, it will be handled by the servlet engine. The servlet engine creates an object that encapsulates all of the information that was sent from the browser, including the query string. This object is known as the request object and has a method in it than can retrieve the value of a parameter in the query string.

The controller also received the response object from the servlet engine. All the details for communicating with the browser are encapsulated in the response object.

Based on the button that the user clicked, the controller will send the request and response objects to the correct JSP. The JSP will use the request object to access the query string. It will use the response object to send the HTML code to the browser.

The basic tasks of the controller will be implemented with Java code. In the first example, the Java code will be embedded in a JSP. Later, the Java code will be placed in a user-created servlet.

Request and Response Objects

When the servlet engine handles a JSP, it creates an object that encapsulates all the information that was sent in the request from the browser. This object is known as the *request object* and is accessible from Java code within a JSP. The class of the object is `HttpServletRequest`.

The servlet engine also creates an object that encapsulates all the information that is needed to respond to the browser. This object is known as the *response object* and is accessible from Java code within a JSP. The class of the object is `HttpServletResponse`.

Referencing Parameters

Java code cannot use the new expression language for accessing parameters. Java code must use the traditional technique of passing parameters to a method of an object. To reference a query string parameter from Java code, pass the name of the form element to the `getParameter` method of the request object.

```
request.getParameter("hobby")
```

When accessing a parameter from Java code, use `request.getParameter("xxx")`. When accessing a parameter from HTML, use the expression language `${param.xxx}`.

Testing for the Presence of a Button

The most important test in the controller is for the presence of a named button. Even if there are multiple buttons on a page, only the one that is clicked will appear in the query string. When the getParameter method is called with a button name, then either the value of the button will be returned or null will be returned. To test if a particular button was clicked, test if the value returned is not null.

```
if (request.getParameter("processButton") != null)
```

The value of the button is irrelevant to the controller; only the name of the button is important. The value of the button is what is visible on the button in the browser window; the controller does not need to know what that value is. The controller is only concerned with which button was pressed; that can be determined by looking at the name of the button.

Control Logic

The JSP indicates the next page by the name of a button. The JSP does not know the physical location of the next page. This is analogous to a gateway on a network when a computer name is used to identify a computer instead of its IP address.

The following list summarises how the JSP and the controller interact.

1. The action of each form in each JSP is set to the controller's URL.
2. In the JSPs, each submit button has been given a unique name.
3. By testing for the presence of a name, the controller can decide which page to call next. If there is no button name in the query string, then the controller will use a default page.
4. The controller knows the URL of all the JSPs that it controls.

The controller uses a nested **if** block, written in Java, to decide which page to display based on which submit button was clicked.

```
. . .
if (request.getParameter("processButton") != null)
{
   address = "Process.jsp";
}
else if (request.getParameter("confirmButton") != null)
{
   address = "Confirm.jsp";
}
else
{
   address = "Edit.jsp";
}
. . .
```

Forwarding Control to Another JSP

Once the controller has determined the address of the next JSP, it must send the request and response objects to the JSP. The request and response objects contain all of the information from the browser and all of the information for sending data back to the browser. By sending the request and response objects to the JSP, the controller is sending complete ownership of the request to the JSP. It will be the responsibility of the JSP to complete the response to the browser.

Two steps are needed in order for the controller to pass control of the request to another JSP. First, a communication channel must be created for the controller to communicate with the JSP. This channel is known as a *request dispatcher*. The request dispatcher is created for the URL of the next JSP. Second, the controller forwards the request and response objects to this dispatcher, which passes them to the JSP.

```
RequestDispatcher dispatcher =
        request.getRequestDispatcher(address);
dispatcher.forward(request, response);
```

Forwarding control to another JSP is a two-step process, just like opening a file for writing. When writing a file, the file must be opened before it can be written. When a file is opened, the actual location of the file is specified. Once the file is opened, data can be written to the file. The request dispatcher is similar: first, open the dispatcher for the address of a JSP, then use the dispatcher to send objects to the JSP.

2.2.2   JSP Controller

Controllers can be written as JSPs or as servlets. Since the controller will not contain any HTML, it is better to write it as a servlet. However, it is easier to understand a controller if it is first written as a JSP. Therefore, the general concept of a controller will be demonstrated in a JSP, then servlets will be introduced and the controller will be rewritten as a servlet. After the first example using a JSP, all controllers will be written as servlets.

Including Java Code

JSP controllers do not contain any HTML code, they only contain java code. A special syntax is used to include arbitrary Java code in a JSP. Place all the Java code between special opening and closing tags: <% and %>.

```
<%
//place a block of Java code here
%>
```

Controller Code

Listing 2.5 contains the complete JSP for the controller. Note that there is only Java code, there is no HTML.

```jsp
<%
  String address;

  if (request.getParameter("processButton") != null)
  {
    address = "Process.jsp";
  }
  else if (request.getParameter("confirmButton") != null)
  {
    address = "Confirm.jsp";
  }
  else
  {
    address = "Edit.jsp";
  }

  RequestDispatcher dispatcher =
          request.getRequestDispatcher(address);
  dispatcher.forward(request, response);
%>
```

Listing 2.5 Listing for a JSP controller

Edit Page

The edit page is the same as the one from Listing 2.1, except for the action attribute of the form.

```jsp
. . .
<form action="Controller.jsp">
. . .
```

Confirm Page

Listing 2.6 contains the confirm page that is used with a controller.

```
<!DOCTYPE HTML>
<html>
  <head>
    <meta charset="utf-8">
    <title>
      Confirmation Page with Edit/Process Options
    </title>
  </head>
  <body>
      <p>The value of the hobby that was sent to
         this page is: <strong>${param.hobby}</strong>.
      <p>
        If there is an error, please select <em>Edit</em>,
        otherwise please select <em>Process</em>.

        <form action="Controller.jsp">
          <p>
            <input type="hidden" name="hobby"
                                  value="${param.hobby}">
            <input type="submit" name="editButton"
                                  value="Edit">
            <input type="submit" name="processButton"
                                  value="Process">

      </form>
  </body>
</html>
```

Listing 2.6 Efficient solution for sending data to one of two pages

Note the following about the confirm page:
1. There are two buttons in one form.
2. The action is to the controller.
3. There is one set of hidden fields.
   This is a much cleaner solution than Listing 2.4 for sending data to one of two pages. That example had a separate form for each button and each form had to have its own set of hidden fields.

Process Page
The process page to be used with the controller is exactly the same as Listing 2.3.

 Try It

http://bytesizebook.com/book/ch2/jspController/Controller.jsp
    When the controller is accessed, the Edit.jsp is the first page displayed (Fig. 2.13) because it was set as the default in the controller, and no form button is pressed when the controller is accessed for the first time. Note that there is no query string and that the URL points to the controller.

Fig. 2.13 The first page that the controller displays is the edit page

Fig. 2.14 The confirm page with data sent from the edit page

Fig. 2.15 The edit page with data sent from the confirm page

Enter a hobby and visit each page: confirm page (Fig. 2.14), edit page (Fig. 2.15), process page (Fig. 2.16). Examine the URL and query string for each page. The URL for each page is the same.

```
.../ch2/jspController/Controller.jsp
```

The query string changes for each page. The query string will contain the name of the button that was clicked. The name of the button was chosen so that it corresponds to the actual JSP that is being displayed. For instance, when the query string contains confirmButton, the JSP being displayed is Confirm.jsp. The address of the JSP

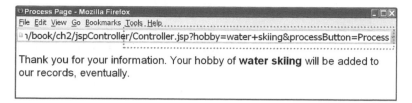

Fig. 2.16 The process page with data sent from the confirm page

does not appear in the URL because the request was made to the controller. The fact that the controller did not complete the request but forwarded it to another JSP is not visible to the browser.

There are four key points about the controller application.

1. The action attribute of each form has been set to `Controller.jsp`.
2. Each button in each form has a unique name. When a named button is clicked, its name and value will appear in the query string. If there are multiple buttons on a page, only the name and value of the button that is clicked will appear in the query string.
3. For each page, the URL contains a name and value in the query string for the button that was clicked. This name is what the controller uses to determine the next page; the value is not tested.
4. Except for the query string, the URL always remains the same, as long as the controller is called first.

2.2.3   JSPs Versus Servlets

The controller only contains Java code; there is no HTML in it. JSPs are designed to have HTML with a little bit of Java code. Whenever a JSP contains mostly Java code with very little or no HTML, then it should be written from scratch as a servlet, not as a JSP. A servlet has several advantages.

1. The servlet engine will not have to create the servlet from the JSP when it is called the first time.
2. A Java IDE can be used to develop and test the Java code. It is difficult to debug Java code that is embedded in a JSP.

Compare these to the advantages of a JSP:

1. It is easy to write HTML.
2. The servlet will be recreated whenever the JSP is modified.

The decision of using a JSP or a servlet should depend upon the mix of HTML and Java code.

1. If there is a lot of HTML with a small amount of Java, then use a JSP.
2. If there is a lot of Java with a small amount of HTML, then use a servlet.
3. If there is an equal amount of Java and HTML, then redesign your application so that it uses a controller. Place most of the Java in the controller and create separate JSPs for the HTML.

2.2.4 Controller Servlet

The same application that was just written using a JSP controller will now be rewritten using a servlet. Servlets are Java programs that extend a base class for a generic servlet. Follow these steps to write a servlet from scratch.
1. Place the servlet in a package so that its location is never left to the default implementation of the servlet engine.
2. Import the following classes.

```
import java.io.IOException;
import javax.servlet.RequestDispatcher;
import javax.servlet.ServletException;
import javax.servlet.http.HttpServlet;
import javax.servlet.http.HttpServletRequest;
import javax.servlet.http.HttpServletResponse;
```

3. Make the class public and extend it from HttpServlet. This is a wrapper for the abstract class GenericServlet. It has no functionality; it only defines all the methods that are specified in GenericServlet. To create a servlet that does something, override some methods from HttpServlet.

4. Include a method with the following signature and place the controller logic in this method.

```
protected void doGet(HttpServletRequest request,
    HttpServletResponse response)
    throws ServletException, IOException
```

JSPs for Servlet Controller
The JSPs for the servlet controller are identical to the JSPs for the JSP controller, except that the action statement in each form is to 'Controller' instead of to 'Controller.jsp'.

```
. . .
<form action="Controller">
. . .
```

Servlet Controller Code
Listing 2.7 contains the controller as a servlet. Note that the contents of the doGet method in the servlet are identical to the Java code that was inserted into the JSP controller (see Listing 2.5).

```
package ch2.servletController;

import java.io.IOException;
import javax.servlet.RequestDispatcher;
import javax.servlet.ServletException;
import javax.servlet.http.HttpServlet;
import javax.servlet.http.HttpServletRequest;
import javax.servlet.http.HttpServletResponse;

public class Controller extends HttpServlet
{

    protected void doGet(HttpServletRequest request,
        HttpServletResponse response)
        throws ServletException, IOException
    {

      String address;

      if (request.getParameter("processButton") != null)
      {
        address = "Process.jsp";
      }
      else if (request.getParameter("confirmButton") != null)
      {
        address = "Confirm.jsp";
      }
      else
      {
        address = "Edit.jsp";
      }

      RequestDispatcher dispatcher =
          request.getRequestDispatcher(address);
      dispatcher.forward(request, response);
    }
}
```

Listing 2.7 The code for the servlet controller

Servlet Location

The source file for a servlet can be anywhere, but the `.class` file must be in a subdirectory of the *classes* directory in the web application. The servlet should be in a package.

The package must agree with the subdirectory of *classes* that the servlet is in. Do not include the *classes* directory in the package statement. The *classes* directory must already be in the CLASSPATH or Java will not search it for class files.

To determine the package, start with subdirectories of the *classes* directory. If the servlet is in the *classes/store* directory, then the package will be *store*. If the servlet is in the *classes/store/hardware* directory, then the package will be *store.hardware*. See the Appendix for more information about class paths and packages.

For the current example, the directory structure must be *classes/ch2/servletController* in order to agree with a package of *ch2.servletController*.

```
package ch2.servletController;
```

The package for a Java class must agree with its location in the file system.

Servlet Identity

Every servlet has a fully qualified class name that consists of two pieces of information: the package it is in and the name of its class.

```
package ch2.servletController;
...
public class Controller extends HttpServlet
```

The fully qualified class name is the combination of the package name with the name of the class. Use a period to connect the package and the name together.

```
ch2.servletController.Controller
```

The fully qualified class name uniquely identifies the servlet. It will be used to refer to the servlet without ambiguity.

Servlet Compilation

A servlet is compiled just like any other Java program: from the command line or from an *integrated development environment* [IDE].

1. Netbeans and Eclispe are good IDEs for compiling, running and debugging servlets. Being able to debug a web application is very important. Without the support of an IDE, it would be difficult to do.
2. For command line compilation,
   (a) javac is used to compile.
   (b) Be sure that **servlet-api.jar** and the *classes* directory of your web application are in the CLASSPATH of your environment.

2.2.5   Servlet Access

As was mentioned in Chap. 1, the WEB-INF directory is not available from the web. Therefore, the *classes* subdirectory of WEB-INF is not available from the web. In that case, how can the servlet be accessed?

This is analogous to the problem of allowing a port on a computer to be accessed from the web. If a computer has a firewall, then the default HTTP port (port 80) cannot be accessed from the Internet. The firewall administrator can add an exception that allows the port to be accessed, while still restricting access to all the other ports on the computer.

Similarly, an exception for the controller can be added to the *web.xml* file. The way to create the exception is to define a URL that can be used to access the controller. Such an exception associates a `.class` file with a URL that will be accessible from the web. The exception is known as a *servlet mapping*.

Servlets are usually more powerful than JSPs; therefore, the servlet engine designers made it more difficult to access them from the web. By default, no servlets can be accessed without registering them in the *web.xml* file of the web application. There are two parts two registering a servlet: creating a short name and defining a servlet mapping.

Short Name for Servlet

Class files that are in packages have very long names. It is possible to create a short name for these long names. The short name is used internally by the servlet engine to refer to the servlet. Tags are added to the *web.xml* file to create a short name.

```
<servlet>
  <servlet-name>FirstController</servlet-name>
  <servlet-class>ch2.servletController.Controller</servlet-class>
</servlet>
```

This creates a short name of `FirstController` for the fully qualified name `ch2.servletController.Controller`. There is nothing special about the short name; it can be any name. Here is another example that creates a different short name for the same controller.

```
<servlet>
  <servlet-name>Overseer</servlet-name>
  <servlet-class>ch2.servletController.Controller</servlet-class>
</servlet>
```

Servlet Mapping

Associating a URL with a short name is known as creating a servlet mapping. The servlet mapping associates the short name for a servlet file with a URL that will be accessible from the web. The URL does not need to be an actual URL in the web application, it can be totally fictitious. The URL must begin with a slash. The slash corresponds to the root of the web application, not to the root of the web server.

```
<servlet-mapping>
  <servlet-name>FirstController</servlet-name>
  <url-pattern>/ch2/servletController/Controller</url-pattern>
</servlet-mapping>
```

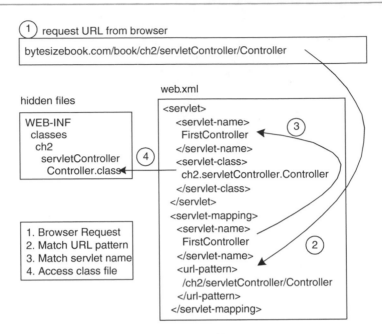

Fig. 2.17 The steps that are followed to find a class file

The servlet tag and the servlet-mapping tag both have a servlet-name tag in them. The name in the *servlet-name* tag in the servlet-mapping tag must match the name in the *servlet-name* tag in the servlet tag.

The URL pattern is used to request the servlet. The request is sent to the servlet engine, which searches the *web.xml* file for a matching pattern. If a match is found, then the servlet name is used to locate the corresponding servlet definition. The definition contains the path to the actual class file. Figure 2.17 shows the order of steps for a request for a servlet.

The URL that is chosen for the servlet can simplify the servlet. In this example, the servlet has been mapped to the same directory where the JSPs it controls are located. This makes it possible for the controller to use a simple relative reference when creating the request dispatcher for the desired JSP. Even though the JSPs and servlets are in different physical locations, the servlet mapping allows the servlet engine to treat them as though they were in the same directory.

The URL that is chosen can be an actual directory in the web application or it can be fictitious. A different servlet mapping for the same short name could be *Moe/Larry/Cheese*; however, in this case, the servlet would not be able to use relative references for the JSPs it controls.

```
<servlet-mapping>
  <servlet-name>FirstController</servlet-name>
  <url-pattern>/Moe/Larry/Cheese</url-pattern>
</servlet-mapping>
```

The URL pattern is always within the web application. The pattern **must** start with a /. This means that the URL starts from the root of the web application, not the root of the web server. If the name of the web application is book, and is running on xyz.com, then the URLs for the two servlet mappings just defined would be

```
http://xyz.com/book/ch2/servletController/Controller
http://xyz.com/book/Moe/Larry/Cheese
```

To determine what the complete URL is to access the controller, start with the URL to the web application root and append the name that is in the *url-pattern* tag.

When a request for a URL reaches the servlet engine, the servlet engine will look at the list of servlet mappings and find the short name for the servlet. Then the servlet engine will look up the fully qualified name of the servlet and call the servlet. For the above URLs, the servlet engine would call the ch2.servletController. Controller servlet.

2.2.6   Servlet Directory Structure

After creating the servlet mapping, the servlet engine will look for the servlet at the URL that was specified.

For this servlet example, the JSPs are in the /ch2/servletController subdirectory of the root of the web application. On this site, the web application is titled *book*, so the JSPs are in the directory /book/ch2/servletController.

The servlet is in a package named ch2.servletController, so it is located in the subdirectory /ch2/servletController in the *classes* directory of the web application. This directory is not visible from the web, so a servlet mapping is created for the servlet, which equates the servlet to a URL that is visible from the web.

The simplest way to implement the mapping is to equate it to the directory where the JSPs are located. This is what was done in this example. The URL pattern /ch2/servletController is relative to the root of the web application, so it is the same URL as the directory of the JSPs.

By mapping the controller to the directory where the JSPs are located, the controller can use a relative reference for the address of the next page.

```
...
else if (request.getParameter("confirmButton") != null)
{
   address = "Confirm.jsp";
}
...
```

Fig. 2.18 The structure of a
web application

The servlet mapping equates the URL
/ch2/servletController/Controller to the
class file that is in the hidden folder
/WEB-INF/classes/ch2/servletController

When a *request dispatcher* is created, the argument contains the address of the
next JSP.

```
. . .
RequestDispatcher dispatcher =
    request.getRequestDispatcher(address);
dispatcher.forward(request, response);
. . .
```

This address is similar to the *action* attribute in a form. However, the address is
limited to relative references from the current directory and relative references from
the root of the web application.
1. If the next JSP is in the directory where the controller is mapped, then only
   include the file name of the JSP.
   address="Confirm.jsp"
2. If the next JSP is not in the directory where the controller is mapped, then the JSP
   must be in another directory in the web application. The address for this JSP
   must start with / and must include the complete path from the root of the web
   application to the JSP. Do not include the name of the web application in the
   path.
   address="/ch2/servletController/Confirm.jsp";
   Figure 2.18 is a diagram of the directory structure of the web application and the
location of the JSPs and the servlet. The servlet mapping makes a logical mapping
of the servlet to the same directory as the JSPs.

  Try It

http://bytesizebook.com/book/ch2/servletController/Controller

Fig. 2.19 Listing of the directory where the controller servlet is mapped

Access the controller by appending the url-pattern to the end of the URL for the web application.

`bytesizebook.com/book/ch2/servletController/Controller`

From the browser, this application behaves exactly the same as the JSP controller example. The only difference is the URL. The URL for the controller was chosen so that the servlet appears to be in the same directory as the JSPs.

Instead of typing in the URL of the controller, type in the URL for the `servletController` directory. You will see a directory listing that contains all of the JSPs for this application. You will not see the controller in this directory (Fig. 2.19). The servlet engine has created an internal link to the controller from this directory, but the link is not visible in the browser. The only way that you know that the link exists is by accessing the controller.

2.2.7 Web Servlet Annotation

Java annotations are new in the JDK 1.5. Annotations are used to mark up the Java code. Before there were annotations, separate configuration files were used to define how a package would be initialised. With annotations, the statements that were in a configuration file can now be placed in the Java code itself. Annotations make it easier to configure a package.

Annotations start with the @ symbol. There are annotations for classes, for methods and for variables. Each annotation can have attributes that set information for the annotation. The annotation must precede what it modifies.

In the Java Servlet 3.0 specification, the servlet and servlet mapping definitions in the *web.xml* file can be replaced with an annotation in the controller. The name of the annotation is `WebServlet`. Place the annotation directly before the class definition.

Table 2.2 The key points for a servlet

doGet	This is the method that does all the work. It is similar to the _jspService method in a servlet for a JSP
HttpServlet	This is an abstract wrapper class. It has default implementations of all the abstract methods. In order to make a useful servlet, it is necessary to define at least one of these methods. In this first example, the class is defining the doGet method
HttpServletRequest	This class encapsulates the information that is sent from the browser to the server
HttpServletResponse	This class encapsulates the information that will be sent from the server back to the browser

```
import javax.servlet.annotation.WebServlet;
...
@WebServlet(
      urlPatterns={"/ch2/servletController/annotated/Controller"})
public class Controller extends HttpServlet
...
```

The WebServlet annotation has many attributes, but only one is needed to create a URL pattern for the servlet. The *urlPatterns* attribute is an array of strings. Each value in the array is a URL that can be used to access the servlet. Use the curly braces to list all the URL patterns. If there is more than one pattern for the servlet, separate each pattern with a comma.

By using the WebServlet annotation, nothing needs to be added to the *web.xml* in order to run the servlet. There are still times when tags will need to be added to the *web.xml* file for a servlet. In such cases, the WebServlet annotation must be removed from the controller. If the annotation exists for the controller, then the *web.xml* will not be accessed, even if there is information in the *web.xml* for the controller.

When possible, the remaining examples in the book will use the WebServlet annotation to simplify configuration; however, some examples will have to be implemented without the annotation.

2.2.8 Servlet Engine for a Servlet

Table 2.2 summarises the key features of a servlet.

The servlet engine handles a request for a servlet in almost the same way that it handles a request for a JSP (see Fig. 1.17). The only differences are that the name of the method that the engine calls is different and that the servlet engine will not recompile the servlet if the *.java* file changes. The servlet engine calls the *doGet* method instead of the *_jspService* method, and it is up to the developer to recompile the *.java* file whenever it changes (Fig. 2.20).

Fig. 2.20 Servlet engine handling a request for a servlet

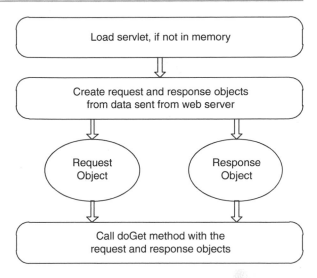

The servlet engine will not automatically reload the *.class* file when it changes. It is up to the developer to reload the web application so that a servlet will be reloaded when it is requested the next time. Some servlet engines can be configured to automatically reload when a *.class* file changes, but it is not the default behaviour of the servlet engine.

2.3 Servlets in IDEs

NetBeans and Eclipse are excellent tools for developing web applications. After creating a web project, the web application can be run from within the IDE. When this is done, Tomcat will be started, the servlet will be loaded into memory, a web browser will be opened and the default page for the web application will be displayed. Hypertext links can be added on this page that lead to the URLs of JSPs and servlets. See the Appendix for information on running servlets in these IDEs.

After building a web project, it is possible to execute servlets from it. The servlets must be placed in the appropriate source folder for the IDE. Always place servlets in packages. When the WAR file for the project is built, the source packages will be copied into the *classes* folder of the web application structure.

Once a web project has been created and tested locally, it is a simple matter to upload the web application to a remote server. Every time that a web project is built, NetBeans packages all the files that are needed for a servlet engine into a WAR archive. In Eclipse, the WAR archive must be built from File - > Export - > Web - > WAR file. A WAR archive is a zip file containing all the files for the web application. If this is uploaded to a remote server, it can be deployed without making any modifications.

2.3.1   Class Files

The *Source Packages* folder in a NetBeans project contains all the source files and packages for Java Servlets. For Eclipse, it is the *Java Resources/src* folder. All source files should be placed in packages within this folder. All of the servlet examples in this book have been placed in packages. The source folder is added to the classpath variable, so every package that is placed in this folder can be found by Java at runtime. See the Appendix for a discussion of Java packages.

Add a new package by using the Java package wizard in each IDE. In the wizard, all of the folders for a package can be created at once. For example, if there is a servlet in a package named edu.fiu.cis, then all the necessary folders for the package can be created by adding a package named edu.fiu.cis to the source folder.

In NetBeans, the <default package> is the package that has no name. In Eclipse, it is the src folder itself. Avoid using them. It is better to always place your servlets in a named package. Strange things can happen if you place servlet in the default package. The only files that should be placed here are configuration files, like those for Hibernate and Log4j.

There are wizards for creating classes and servlets in each IDE. When creating a servlet, there are two choices. An empty class file can be created. It is then up to the developer to add all the code for the servlet and to create the servlet mapping for the servlet. There is also a wizard for a servlet. When this template is used, the default methods for a servlet are defined and a servlet mapping is added to the *web.xml* file.

When the wizard is used to create a servlet, there are options for defining the servlet mapping. By using the wizard, it will not be necessary to edit the *web.xml* file to define a servlet mapping. If the template is not used to create the servlet, then the servlet definition and servlet mapping will need to be added to the *web.xml* file manually. The third option is to use annotations to define the servlet mapping.

 Try It

http://netbeans.org
or

 Try It

http://eclipse.org

If you have not already done so, download a copy of the latest NetBeans or Eclipse packages.

Add a package to the source packages folder and add a servlet to the package.

Define a servlet mapping for the servlet, so that it can be accessed from the web.

Edit the *index.jsp* page in the *Web Pages/Web Content* folder. Add a relative URL to the servlet. To make a relative URL to the servlet from this page, create a hypertext link that contains the URL pattern from the servlet mapping, except remove the leading slash from it.

Build and run the web application. The *index.jsp* page will appear in the browser. Follow the link to the servlet.

2.4   Summary

Typical web applications have an edit page, a confirm page and a process page. The edit page contains visible form elements where the user can enter information. The confirm page has two buttons: one for sending the data back to the edit page and one for sending the data to the process page. The process page shows the results of processing the user's data.

The form tag has an attribute, named *action*, which allows the form to send the data to any other page. The page could be in the current directory, in a different directory on the same server or on a different server. All the data that are in a named form element will be sent to the URL that is in the action attribute. It is important that the element has a name or it will not be added to the query string.

Only the edit page has visible form elements for the user to enter data. The confirm page only shows the data as plain text: plain text is never sent to the next page when a button is clicked. In order for the data to be sent, it must be in a named form element. There is a non-visible form element, whose type is *hidden*, that can be used to store the data that was received by the current page. When a button is clicked, the data will be sent to the next page. If the current JSP places the data that it receives into the hidden fields, then the user's data can be passed on to the next page.

Some pages in web applications need to send data to one of two pages: for example, the confirm page. There are two buttons on the confirm page: one that sends the data back to the edit page and one that sends the data onto the process page. Using a simple JSP to solve this problem requires two separate forms in the page; each form would have a separate copy of the hidden fields. Such a solution is difficult to read and modify. There is a better solution for this situation: use a separate program to determine the next page based on the button that the user clicks.

Such a program is known as a controller. Instead of hard coding the name of the next page into the action attribute, all JSPs send the data to the controller. It is important that the buttons in the forms are named, so that the controller will know which button the user clicked. The controller will calculate the URL of the next JSP and send the user's data to that page.

Controllers can be written as JSPs or as servlets. The first example of a controller was developed as a JSP; however, it is better to write the controller as a servlet, since it has no HTML in it. It is easier to debug Java code if it is in a servlet. If a page has more Java than HTML, then it should be written as a servlet, not as a JSP.

Since servlets are Java programs, the details of creating, compiling and accessing servlets were covered. Creating and compiling servlets is the same as creating and compiling any Java program. Accessing the servlet is more difficult because it must be placed in a web application. The *web.xml* file is used to create a URL mapping that can be used to access the servlet. Java annotations can also be used to define the mapping. If this URL mapping is not created in the *web.xml* file or defined by an annotation, then the servlet cannot be accessed from the web.

2.5   Chapter Review

Terms
1. Form's Action Attribute
   (a) Relative
   (b) Absolute
2. Hidden Field
3. Request and Response Objects
4. Controller
   (a) Logic
   (b) Forward
5. JSP Controller
6. Servlet Controller
7. Servlet in *web.xml*
   (a) Servlet Definition
   (b) Servlet Mapping
8. WebServlet Annotation
   (a) URL Pattern

New Java
1. HttpServletRequest
   (a) getParameter
   (b) getRequestDispatcher
2. HttpServletResponse
3. ServletException
4. RequestDispatcher
   (a) forward
5. @WebServlet(url-patterns = {"/...."})

Tags
1. JSP
   (a) ${param.element_name}
   (b) <%java code%>
2. input
   (a) hidden
3. web.xml
   (a) servlet
   (b) servlet-mapping
   (c) servlet-name
   (d) servlet-class
   (e) url-pattern

Questions

1. Assume that the data in a form is being sent to the absolute address `http://bytesizebook.com/book/ch5/persistentData/Controller`.
   (a) What is the relative reference if the absolute reference of the current page is `http://bytesizebook.com/book/ch5/persistentData/Edit.jsp`?
   (b) What is the relative reference if the absolute reference of the current page is `http://bytesizebook.com/book/index.jsp`?
   (c) What is the relative reference if the absolute reference of the current page is `http://bytesizebook.com/index.jsp`?
   (d) What is the relative reference if the absolute reference of the current page is `http://bytesizebook.com/ch5/persistentData/config-ure/Edit.jsp`?

2. How can data be entered in a form on one page and be sent to a different page?
3. How is a parameter in the query string retrieved from Java code?
4. What is the purpose of the nested **if** block in a controller?
5. Write the statements that belong in a controller that will forward the request and response to the JSP named 'Example.jsp'.
6. What are the advantages of using a JSP over a Servlet?
7. What are the advantages of using a Servlet over a JSP?
8. When is a servlet loaded into memory? How long does it remain in memory?
9. How often is the `.class` file for a servlet generated?
10. Where does the `.class` file for a servlet belong in a web application?
11. What is contained in the request object that is sent to the `doGet` method?
12. What is contained in the response object that is sent to the `doGet` method?
13. A confirmation page was covered in this chapter that could send data to one of two pages. There were two techniques discussed for achieving this. Summarise the differences between these two techniques.
14. Summarise the differences in how the Tomcat engine handles a JSP and a Servlet.
15. Assume there is a class named `MyJavaExample` in a package named `book.webdev`. Create a servlet definition and servlet mapping for this class as follows:
    (a) Create a servlet definition named `MyExample` for this class in *web.xml*.
    (b) Associate the URL `/book/webdev/MyExample` with the short name that was just created in the *web.xml*.
16. For the servlet in question 15, instead of using the *web.xml* file, use the *WebServlet* annotation to map this servlet to `/book/webdev/MyExampleAgain`.
    (a) Where does the annotation belong in the servlet definition?
    (b) If both the annotation and the *web.xml* are used to define the URL pattern, which pattern will be defined and which pattern will be ignored?

Tasks

1. Another form element is a password text box. Its type is *password*.
   ```
   <input type="password" name="secretCode">
   ```

Create a JSP that has a text box, a password text box and a button. Send the data from the form to a second JSP in which the values from the text box and the password text box are displayed.

2. Create a form with three text boxes and a button. Initialise the text elements with corresponding data from the query string. Send the data to a second page that will display the values that are sent to it. The second page should have hidden fields and a button so that the data can be sent back to the first page.

   (a) Implement this design without using a controller.

   (b) Implement this design with a JSP controller.

   (c) Implement this design with a Servlet controller. Map the controller using the *web.xml* file.

3. Create a page with three text boxes and three buttons. Create three more distinct JSPs. Each button on the first page will send the data from the form to a different page.

   (a) Implement this design with a JSP controller.

   (b) Implement this design with a Servlet controller. Map the controller with the *WebServlet* annotation.

   (c) How could this design be implemented without using a controller and without embedding Java code in the first JSP?

Java Beans and Controller Helpers

3

With the introduction of a controller servlet, it is now possible to add all the power and convenience of Java to the development process. It is possible to create auxiliary classes in the web application that will simplify development.

One of the most powerful classes that can be added to a web application is one that contains all the data that was entered by the user. All of the data from the user are available from the request object, but the request object also contains a lot of other information that is not related to the user's data. A better design is to create a new class that only contains the data. Such a class is known as a *bean*.

With the introduction of a bean, it is a simple matter to add validation to the web application. One type of validation is *default validation*. In default validation, the user's data must meet criteria. If the data does not meet the criteria, then a default value is used in place of the data that the user entered.

While servlets are very powerful tools for implementing dynamic content on the web, they do have a limitation: member variables. Member variables are useful when designing object-oriented programs, but they are dangerous to use in a servlet. In order to circumvent this limitation, an auxiliary class will be added to the web application that is created by the controller and can use member variables.

With the addition of these new classes, the servlet from Chap. 2 will be reorganised. It will still perform the same functions, but it will be redesigned to use a class for the data and a class that does the work of the controller. The JSPs for the web application will also need some minor changes.

3.1 Application: Start Example

In order to demonstrate the new features clearly, the web application from Chap. 2 will be modified with the addition of a new text element and the addition of a button on the process page that will allow the user to edit the data again.

These are the changes that will need to be made to the web application.
1. The edit page will have a new text element added.

T. Downey, *Guide to Web Development with Java: Understanding Website Creation*,
DOI 10.1007/978-1-4471-2443-6_3, © Springer-Verlag London Limited 2012

Fig. 3.1 The location of files for the start example

2. There will be an additional hidden field in the confirm page.
3. There will be a new form, hidden fields and a button on the process page.

The first controller in this chapter will be identical to the servlet controller from Chap. 2 (see Listing 2.7), except that it is in a different package.
1. For organisation, the controller for this example has been placed in a package named ch3.startExample.
2. In the *web.xml* file of the web application, the controller has been mapped to the URL /ch3/startExample/Controller.
3. The JSPs for the web application have been placed in the directory named /ch3/startExample.

Figure 3.1 shows the location of the files for the Start Example controller.
Just like the servlet controller from Chap. 2, this controller has been mapped to the directory where the JSPs are located.

```
. . .
@WebServlet(urlPatterns={"/ch3/startExample/Controller"})
public class Controller extends HttpServlet
. . .
```

The edit page is similar to Listing 2.1, but will have an additional input field for a property named *aversion*.

```
Aversion:
<input type="text" name="aversion"
                  value="${param.aversion}">
```

The confirm page is similar to Listing 2.6, but will echo the new property and have an additional hidden field for the new property.

```
The value of the aversion that was sent to
this page is: <strong>${param.aversion}</strong>
...
<input type="hidden" name="aversion"
                     value="${param.aversion}">
```

The process page is similar to Listing 2.3, but will echo the new property and will have a form with a button, for returning to the edit page, and two hidden fields.

```
Thank you for your information. Your hobby of
<strong>${param.hobby}</strong> and aversion of
<strong>${param.aversion}</strong> will be added to our
records, eventually.
...
<form action="Controller">
  <input type="hidden" name="hobby"
                       value="${param.hobby}">
  <input type="hidden" name="aversion"
                       value="${param.aversion}">
  <p>
  <input type="submit" name="editButton"
                       value="Edit">
</form>
```

3.2   Java Bean

Controllers are all very similar. They have two basic tasks: process the user data and forward the request to the next JSP. It is a good design principle to encapsulate all the data processing into a separate class.

When data is sent from a browser, it is sent as individual pieces of data. It would be easier to manipulate this data in the web application if it were all placed into one class. This class would have ways to access and modify the data and would have additional helper methods for processing the data. Such a class is known as a *bean*.

A piece of data in the bean is known as a *property*. A typical property will have an *accessor* and a *mutator*. The accessor is used to retrieve the data associated with the property and the mutator is used to store the data associated with the property. An important aspect of a property is that it hides the implementation of the data.

In the next example, each property will hide a string variable, but it could also hide an integer or a double. Properties can also encapsulate more complex data structures like lists or maps. The point of encapsulating data in a property is that when the implementation for the data changes, no other classes that use the property will need to be changed.

In a web application, the data can be accessed from the controller and the JSPs. Soon, the data will also be accessed by a database. In this type of application, it is essential to have a central class for the data that uses a standard way to retrieve the data; a bean is such a class. In the future, if the data changes, then only the bean will need to be updated, not all the classes that use the data.

The standard format of a bean requires that the names of the accessor/mutator pair have a fixed syntax.
1. The mutator will be of the form setXxx.
2. The accessor will be of the form getXxx.
3. *set* and *get* are in lowercase.
4. The first letter after set or get is uppercase. All letters after that can be uppercase or lowercase.

The accessor/mutator pair should operate on the same type.
1. The mutator has a parameter that must have the same type as the return value of the accessor.
2. The accessor returns a value that must have the same type as the parameter to the mutator.

The next listing shows a complete property named *hobby*. It makes no difference what the name of the variable is in the bean, since the variable is protected. What makes this a property is that there are methods named *getHobby* and *setHobby* that operate on the same type.

```
protected String hobby;
public void setHobby(String hobby) {
    this.hobby = hobby;
}
public String getHobby() {
    return hobby;
}
```

For a bean that is used in a web application, the names of the accessor and mutator must agree with the name of the corresponding input element from the JSP. If the accessor is *getHobby*, then the name of the element in the JSP must be *hobby*. Please note that the *H* in the accessor is uppercase, while the *h* in the name of the input element is lowercase.

Table 3.1 The relationship between the form element name and the accessor/mutator names

Element name	Accessor name	Mutator name
name="hobby"	getHobby	setHobby
name="aversion"	getAversion	setAversion

3.2.1 Creating a Data Bean

Beans should be used to store the elements coming from the form. The names of the properties in the bean should correspond with the names of the form elements in the JSPs. If the form has an input element named *hobby*, then the bean should have a property with an accessor named getHobby and a mutator named setHobby.

The bean for our web application will have two properties: hobby and aversion. These correspond to the input elements that are in the JSPs for this web application. For each input element that contains data to be processed, create a corresponding property in the bean.

Java Bean: Request Data

When encapsulating data, the first step is to recognise what the data is. In a web application, the user enters the data in form elements. In our application, all the data is entered in the edit page. A bean will be created that has properties that correspond to the input elements that are in the edit page.

```
...
Hobby:
<input type="text" name="hobby"
                    value="${param.hobby}">
<br>
Aversion:
<input type="text" name="aversion"
                    value="${param.aversion}">
...
```

There are two input elements in the edit page that contain data to be processed: hobby and aversion. Table 3.1 shows the relationship between the input elements in the form and the corresponding properties in a bean.

A bean that encapsulates the web application data will need to have properties with these accessors and mutators. The next listing contains a bean with a property for hobby and aversion. Note that in the JSP, the names are all lower case, but in the bean, the first letter after *get* or *set* is upper case. Lowercase and uppercase to be consistent with usage in the previous page.

```
package ch3.dataBean;

public class RequestData {

    protected String hobby;
    protected String aversion;

    public RequestData() {
    }

    public void setHobby(String hobby) {
        this.hobby = hobby;
    }

    public String getHobby() {
        return hobby;
    }

    public void setAversion(String aversion) {
        this.aversion = aversion;
    }

    public String getAversion() {
        return aversion;
    }
}
```

3.2.2   Using the Bean in a Web Application

Now that the bean class exists, it must be incorporated into the web application.
It must be added to the controller and accessed in the JSP.

The controller is in charge of all of the logic in the web application, so it is the
controller's responsibility to create the bean. Once the bean has been created, it
must be filled with the data from the request and placed somewhere so that the JSPs
will have access to it.

Each JSP is primarily HTML, with some data to display from the controller.
There is a special syntax used in a JSP for accessing the data from a bean.

Creating and Filling the Bean

The controller will create the bean. In this example, the name of the bean class is
RequestData, which is in the *ch3.dataBean* package.

```
RequestData data = new RequestData();
```

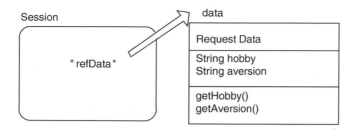

Fig. 3.2   The effect of calling getSession().setAttribute("refData", data)

The most important thing that the controller can do is to get the new data that was just sent from the user and copy it into the bean. The controller must call the mutators for the properties in the bean in order to fill them with the data from the request.

```
data.setHobby(request.getParameter("hobby"));
data.setAversion(request.getParameter("aversion"));
```

We are calling getParameter to retrieve the data from the request parameters and then calling the bean's mutators to copy the data to the bean.

Making the Bean Accessible to the JSPs

The controller is a separate class from the JSPs. The bean has been created as a local variable in the controller. The last detail to work out is how to let the JSP access this bean.

There is an object which is maintained by the servlet engine that can hold arbitrary data for the web application. This object is known as the *session*; the data in it can be accessed by the controller and by all of its JSPs. If the controller places the bean in this object, then it can be retrieved in all of the JSPs. From inside the controller, the session can be retrieved from the request with the method getSession.

Additional information can be added to the session by using the method setAttribute. This method associates a simple name with an object. In our application, it will be used to associate a name with the bean that holds the data. For example, if a new bean has already been created and named *data*, then it can be added to the session with the following statement.

```
request.getSession().setAttribute("refData", data);
```

The second parameter is the bean, which contains the data; the first parameter is an arbitrary name. Figure 3.2 is a representation of how the session is changed after a call to the setAttribute method.

There are two steps that are required to make the bean accessible to a JSP.
1. Retrieve the session object for the request with the getSession method.
2. Call the setAttribute method to associate a name with the bean.

Fig. 3.3 The location of the files for the data bean controller

3.3   Application: Data Bean

All the previous steps can now be put together to create an application that uses a bean to encapsulate the request data. In addition to these new steps, it is necessary to know the details that were introduced in Chap. 2: the location of the JSPs, the visible URL for the controller, the package of the controller and the package for the bean.

1. The JSPs for the web application have been placed in the /ch3/dataBean directory.
2. The controller has been mapped to the URL /ch3/dataBean/Controller either in the *web.xml* file or by using annotations. Note that the path in the URL is the same as the path to the JSPs. This allows the controller to use a relative reference in the address for the JSPs.
3. The controller for this example has been placed in a package named ch3. dataBean. It is not necessary that the name of the package resemble the path to the JSPs. This was done just as an organisational tool. By keeping the package and the path similar, it is easier to remember that they correspond to the same servlet.
4. The bean is in the same package as the controller.
   Figure 3.3 shows the location of the files for the Data Bean controller.

3.3.1   Mapping: Data Bean

The URL mapping for the controller can be set with either the *web.xml* or with annotations.

The location of the controller and the location of the JSPs are needed in order to create the servlet definition and the servlet mapping in the *web.xml* file.

```
. . .
<servlet>
    <servlet-name>ControllerBean</servlet-name>
    <servlet-class>ch3.dataBean.Controller</servlet-class>
</servlet>
<servlet-mapping>
    <servlet-name>ControllerBean</servlet-name>
    <url-pattern>/ch3/dataBean/Controller</url-pattern>
</servlet-mapping>
. . .
```

The location of the JSPs is needed in order to define the mapping using an annotation. The location of the servlet is not needed, since the annotation is located in the physical file for the controller.

```
. . .
@WebServlet(urlPatterns={"/ch3/dataBean/Controller"})
public class Controller extends HttpServlet
. . .
```

3.3.2   Controller: Data Bean

There are now five tasks that a controller performs. In Listing 3.1, identify the sections of code that implement these five tasks.
1. Creating the bean
2. Making the bean accessible to the JSPs
3. Copying the request parameters into the bean
4. Decoding the button name into an address
5. Forwarding the request and response to the JSP

```java
package ch3.dataBean;

import java.io.IOException;
import javax.servlet.RequestDispatcher;
import javax.servlet.ServletException;
import javax.servlet.annotation.WebServlet;
import javax.servlet.http.HttpServlet;
import javax.servlet.http.HttpServletRequest;
import javax.servlet.http.HttpServletResponse;

@WebServlet(urlPatterns={"/ch3/dataBean/Controller"})
public class Controller extends HttpServlet
{

  protected void doGet(HttpServletRequest request,
      HttpServletResponse response)
        throws ServletException, IOException
  {
    RequestData data = new RequestData();
    request.getSession().setAttribute("refData", data);

    data.setHobby(request.getParameter("hobby"));
    data.setAversion(request.getParameter("aversion"));

    String address;

    if (request.getParameter("processButton") != null)
    {
      address = "Process.jsp";
    }
    else if (request.getParameter("confirmButton") != null)
    {
      address = "Confirm.jsp";
    }
    else
    {
      address = "Edit.jsp";
    }

    RequestDispatcher dispatcher =
        request.getRequestDispatcher(address);
    dispatcher.forward(request, response);
  }
}
```

Listing 3.1 A controller that uses a data bean

3.3.3   Accessing the Bean in the JSP

All the details for adding a bean to the controller have been covered. The controller has even made the bean available to the JSPs. The last step is for the JSPs to access the data.

Table 3.2 EL statements and the equivalent Java code

EL statement in JSP	Equivalent Java in controller
${refData.hobby}	data.getHobby()
${refData.aversion}	data.getAversion()

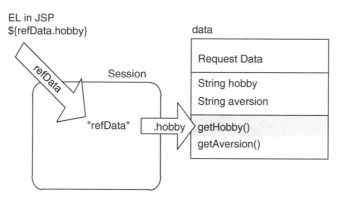

Fig. 3.4 ${refData.hobby} accesses data.getHobby() in controller

In a JSP, EL can be used to access the bean that was stored in the session. The bean is accessed by the name that was used in the call to the setAttribute method in the controller. In our example, the name *refData* was used by the controller when adding the bean to the session. The bean was added to the session with the call to setAttribute.

```
request.getSession().setAttribute("refData", data);
```

The second parameter is the bean, which contains the data; the first parameter is an arbitrary name. Place the name in an EL statement and the bean will be retrieved. Do not use quotes around the name in the EL statement.

```
${refData}
```

In addition to accessing the entire bean, EL can access every public accessor that is in the bean. The servlet engine translates all EL statements into Java code. Table 3.2 shows the equivalent Java code for the EL statements in the edit page. Figure 3.4 demonstrates how the EL in the JSP can access the public accessor from the bean.

3.3.4 JSPs: Data Bean

All references to the data should use the bean and not the request parameters. This is possible since all the data from the query string was copied into the bean in the controller. In the JSPs, replace all occurrences of ${param.hobby} with ${refData.hobby} and ${param.aversion} with ${refData.aversion}.

In the edit page, use the bean to initialise the input elements with any data that was passed in the query string.

```
Hobby:
<input type="text" name="hobby"
                   value="${refData.hobby}">
<br>
Aversion:
<input type="text" name="aversion"
                   value="${refData.aversion}">
```

In the Confirm and Process pages, use the bean to retrieve the values for the hobby and aversion that were sent in the query string.

```
The value of the hobby that was sent to
this page is: <strong>${refData.hobby}</strong>
<br>
The value of the aversions that was sent to
this page is: <strong>${refData.aversion}</strong>
```

Use the bean to initialise the hidden elements with any data that was passed in the query string.

```
<input type="hidden" name="hobby"
                     value="${refData.hobby}">
<input type="hidden" name="aversion"
                     value="${refData.aversion}">
```

The purpose of the bean is to encapsulate the data for the web application. In the controller, all the request data from the query string was copied to the bean. Once the data is in the bean, all references to the data should use the bean. In the JSPs, all references to the request parameters should be replaced with references to the bean.

 Try It

http://bytesizebook.com/book/ch3/dataBean/Controller

This application does not look any different from the one developed in Chap. 2. However, it is implemented with a bean.

3.4   Application: Default Validation

So far, there has not been much of a motivation for using a bean other than demonstrating the advanced features of Java. However, a bean is a powerful class. The bean can be enhanced to validate that the user has entered some data. This will use default validation.

Default validation is used to fill in fields with default values, if the user leaves out some data. This is not the most powerful way to do validation, but it is simple and offers a good introduction to two topics at once: validation and enhancing the bean.

A new bean and controller will be created to demonstrate default validation. In order to keep the code organised better, each new controller and bean will be created in a new package. If the JSPs are changed, then they will also be placed in a new directory, while the names of the JSPs will remain the same: Edit.jsp, Confirm.jsp and Process.jsp. If the JSPs are the same as another example, then those JSPs will be used.

3.4.1 Java Bean: Default Validation

This bean is similar to the first example, but the accessors now do default validation. For each property, a helper method has been added that will test if the user has entered data into the input field. If the data is empty, then a default value will be supplied.

For example, there is a helper method in the bean that tests if the hobby element is valid. A simple validation is used: the hobby cannot be null or empty.

```
. . .
public boolean isValidHobby() {
  return hobby != null && !hobby.trim().equals("");
}
. . .
```

This helper method is called by the accessor for the hobby property. If the hobby does not pass the validation, then the accessor will return a default string instead of null or empty. If the hobby passes the validation, then the value that the user entered will be returned by the accessor.

```
. . .
public String getHobby() {
  if (isValidHobby()) {
    return hobby;
  }
  return "No Hobby";
}
. . .
```

A similar helper method has been added for the aversion property, which is called from the accessor for the aversion.

The validation has been placed in the accessor, but it could easily have been placed in the mutator. It is a matter of personal preference. If the validation is done in the mutator, then the actual value that the user entered will be lost. By placing the validation in the accessor, the user's invalid data is still in the bean. It is conceivable that the validation test could change and that an invalid value today could become a valid value tomorrow. Because of this, I prefer to place the validation in the accessor.

3.4.2   Controller: Default Validation

The only differences between the controller for this example and the *Data Bean* controller of Listing 3.1 are the name of the bean, the URL for the controller and the name of the package. Since nothing has changed in this example as far as the JSPs are concerned, this controller will use the same JSPs that were used in the last example.

The next listing shows the part of the controller that has changed. Note that the URL for the JSP must include a path. This is necessary because the controller is being mapped to /ch3/defaultValidate/Controller, while the JSPs are the ones from the previous application and are already located in the /ch3/dataBean folder.

```
. . .
String address;
if (request.getParameter("processButton") != null)
{
    address = "/ch3/dataBean/Process.jsp";
}
else if (request.getParameter("confirmButton") != null)
{
    address = "/ch3/dataBean/Confirm.jsp";
}
else
{
    address = "/ch3/dataBean/Edit.jsp";
}
. . .
```

Note that the name of the web application is not included in the URL. Web applications can only forward to URLs that are within the web application, so the name of the web application is always assumed and should not be included in the URL that is used to forward to a JSP.

The URL pattern for the servlet does not correspond to a physical directory in the web application, but this is irrelevant. The URL can still be used to access the controller. The servlet engine will intercept the URL for the controller and route it to the correct location. This demonstrates the point that the URL pattern can be any string at all.

```
. . .
@WebServlet(urlPatterns={"/ch3/defaultValidate/Controller"})
public class Controller extends HttpServlet {
    . . .
```

Figure 3.5 shows the location of the files for the Data Bean controller. There are no new JSPs for this example; it uses the JSPs from the previous example.

By making a few modifications to the bean and minor modifications to the controller, the web application now does default validation. This is a simple example of how a bean is the perfect place for extending the capabilities of the web application.

Fig. 3.5   The location of the files for the default validate controller

 Try It

http://bytesizebook.com/book/ch3/defaultValidate/Controller

This application will supply default values if the user leaves either input field empty.

When the application starts, the default values have already been supplied by the bean. Erase the values that are there and click the confirm button. You will see that on the next page, the default values have been provided by the bean again.

3.5   Member Variables in Servlets

In object-oriented design, member variables are powerful tools. By using member variables, the number of parameters that must be passed to methods can be reduced. Member variables also allow for encapsulation of data: access to the underlying variable can be limited through the use of methods. However, using member variables in servlets is dangerous and can lead to bugs.

3.5.1   Threads

Consider the process of filling out a form on a website: the user visits a website that has a form; the user fills in the data on the form; the user clicks the submit button on

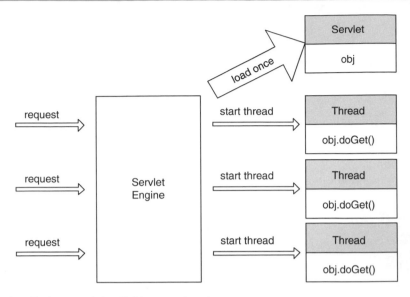

Fig. 3.6 Each request is handled in a new thread

Table 3.3 Requests compared to an exam

Student	Servlet engine
A student asks the teacher for a test	A request is sent to the servlet engine
A student receives the test paper	A thread is started for each request
Each student works on the exam	The thread processes the doGet method of the servlet

the form. If there were multiple requests at the same time, then the server would process each set of data independently: the data from one request would not be mixed up with the data from another. The server ensures that the data is processed independently by using *threads*. A thread is like a separate process on the computer: each thread runs independently of all other threads. Each request to a web application creates a new thread on the server (Fig. 3.6).

Multiple requests to a web application are like students taking a midterm exam (Table 3.3).

Each student is like a separate thread performing the same steps on different data.

3.5.2   The Problem with Member Variables

After a servlet is called for the first time, the servlet engine will load the servlet into memory and execute it. The servlet will stay in memory until the servlet engine is stopped or restarted. Member variables exist as long as the servlet is in memory.

Table 3.4 Two threads executing the same commands

Thread A	Thread B
A1 read x	B1 read x
A2 increment	B2 increment
A3 write x	B3 write x

When a request is received from a browser, the server starts a new thread to handle the request. As soon as the request has been handled, the thread is released. The thread is created by the servlet engine and has access to the servlet's member variables. The member variables exist before the thread starts and will continue to exist after the thread has ended.

Member variables in the servlet can be accessed by all of the threads. If two threads attempt to save a value to a member variable, only the value written by the last thread will be stored.

Continuing the analogy of the midterm exam, using a member variable is like writing an answer on the board in the front of the room. This might not seem like a bad idea until you realise that the board can only hold one answer to each question; only the response of the last student who answers the question will be recorded. Only the last student who writes the answer on the board will receive credit for that question.

The problem with member variables makes them dangerous to use in a servlet. Think of member variables in a servlet as being more like static variables in a simple Java program. Because of this, it is better to avoid using member variables in a servlet.

It is possible that the simple example of $x = x + 1$ can return the wrong result if enough simultaneous requests are made. Consider the steps that are taken by a computer in order to complete this task.
1. Read x from memory into the CPU.
2. Increment the value in the CPU by 1.
3. Write the value to x from the CPU back to memory.

Consider two different requests, A and B. Each would try to increment x, and the steps from Table 3.4 would be needed.

Assuming that both threads are being executed on the same processor, all that is guaranteed is that request A performs these tasks in the order A1, A2, A3, and that request B performs these tasks in the order B1, B2, B3. However, there is no rule that states that request A will complete all of its steps before request B begins its steps. Since the two requests are in different threads, it is up to the CPU to schedule time for each request.

The CPU might perform these steps in the order A1, A2, B1, B2, A3, B3. In this case, both requests will wind up with the same value for x, since they both read the value of x before either request writes the new value of x. It is important to understand that arithmetic only occurs in the CPU, and that the results need to be written back to memory. Table 3.5 shows the values of x as it is changed by each thread.

Both threads incremented x and both threads received the same value for x. This is the type of error that occurs when member variables are used incorrectly in a servlet.

Table 3.5 The values of
shared variable x

Step	Value in CPU	Value in x
A1: read x	0	0
A2: incr x	1	0
B1: read x	0	0
B2: incr x	1	0
A3: write x	1	1
B3: write x	1	1

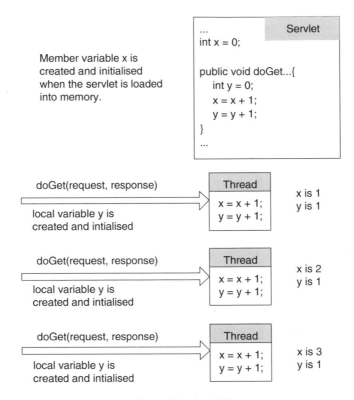

Fig. 3.7 How a servlet processes member and local variables

In an actual case, this error happened in a chat program. From time to time, the comments made by one user would be attributed to a different user. This occurred because the user name was being stored in a member variable. If enough people were online at the same time, the error would occur.

3.5.3   Local Versus Member Variables

If two users on different machines access the servlet at the same time, then each one will have its own doGet running in its own thread. Variables that are local to the doGet procedure are private variables that cannot be accessed by a different thread. However, member variables are shared by all the threads.

Consider a controller that has a member variable x. Assume that the doGet method has a local variable y. If the doGet method increments both x and y, then what values will they have after three requests have been made?

Figure 3.7 demonstrates how these variables will be changed. Each new request will create a separate thread to run the doGet method. Each thread will have its own local copy of the variable y. There will only be one instance of the variable x, and each thread will access that one instance. The value of x after three requests will be 3. The value of y for each request will be 1.

The servlet is loaded and executed by the servlet engine the first time the servlet is called. After that, the servlet resides in memory and handles requests from browsers. Each request is handled in a different thread. This means that the member variables of the servlet are created and initialised when the servlet is first loaded and executed. Each request will share the member variables. Local variables inside the doGet method are created each time the method is called.

3.6   Application: Shared Variable Error

Programmers must resist the desire to create member variables in servlets to avoid passing parameters to methods. Even though object-oriented design promotes the use of member variables, it can cause intermittent errors when used in a servlet.

It is difficult to create an example that always produces incorrect answers, but with enough requests, most servlets that use member variables will have errors. Of course, it is possible to use member variables if the intent is to share data across all requests. In this case, care must be taken to synchronize all access to the shared variable. This example demonstrates that something as simple as adding 1 to a shared variable can produce incorrect answers.

3.6.1   Controller: Shared Variable Error

The controller for this application is very simple. It always transfers control to the same JSP. The only work that it performs is to increment a member variable by 1. In order to cause an error each time a request is processed, the work has been placed in a helper method.

```
. . .
protected void doGet(HttpServletRequest request,
                        HttpServletResponse response)
throws ServletException, IOException {

    String address = "/ch3/sharedVariable/Edit.jsp";

    incrementSharedVariable();

    request.setAttribute("accessCount", accessCount);
    request.getRequestDispatcher(address)
        .forward(request, response);
}
. . .
```

Describing the error is easier than causing the error in a servlet. Such an error will only occur if two requests are made very close to each other. Usually, this will occur in a servlet that receives many requests. There is a low probability that this error will occur, but, with enough requests, it can happen.

There is a static method in the thread class that tells the CPU to stop processing the current thread for a period of time. The result of this is that the CPU will allow other threads to run and then will return to this thread after the specified time has elapsed. The name of this method is sleep. By using it, we can force the CPU to stop processing the current thread and to start processing another thread. It is not possible to know which thread will be selected by the CPU; however, if we put the current thread to sleep for a long enough time, then we can be assured that the CPU will access all other threads before returning to this one.

In this example, the value of the shared variable is copied into a local, private variable; the local variable is then incremented and the thread is put to sleep; the thread copies the local variable back to the shared variable when it wakes up.

This mimics the action of the thread copying the value of a variable into the CPU, the thread incrementing the value and being interrupted by the CPU and the thread writing the value in the CPU back to memory when it regains control.

The advantage of doing this is to be able to set the length of time that the thread sleeps. Instead of losing control for a few milliseconds, we can force the thread to sleep for many seconds. This will give us slow humans the ability to cause this error every time.

```
. . .
public int accessCount = 0;
. . .
public void incrementSharedVariable() {
    int temp = accessCount;
    temp++;
    System.out.println(temp);
    try {
      Thread.sleep(3000);
    } catch (java.lang.InterruptedException ie) {

    }
    accessCount = temp;
}
. . .
```

If two threads are started within a few seconds of each other, this arrangement will force the execution of the statements similar to what was outlined above: A1, A2, B1, B2, A3, B3. To see the effect, open two browsers and execute the servlet in each one. Be sure to start both requests to the servlet within a few seconds of each other. It is important that this is done in two different brands of browsers since the servlet engine will only allow one thread per browser brand.

 Try It

http://bytesizebook.com/book/ch3/sharedVariable/error/Controller
    Open two different browsers, not just two instances of the same browser, as Tomcat does not allocate a new thread to the same servlet from the same browser. After doing this, you will see that both instances display the same number, even though both of them were incrementing the same shared variable.

Synchronizing
There are two solutions to this problem: synchronize access to the shared variable and avoid using member variables in servlets. The simpler solution is to avoid using member variables in servlets; however, it is possible to avoid this problem by using a synchronization block.

```
. . .
public void incrementSharedVariable() {
    synchronized (this) {
        int temp = accessCount;
        temp++;
        System.out.println(temp);
        try {
          Thread.sleep(3000);
        } catch (java.lang.InterruptedException ie) {
        }
        accessCount = temp;
    }
}
. . .
```

A synchronization block forces the CPU to give the thread all the time it needs to complete the block, without being interrupted. It is best to keep the synchronized block as short as possible so that the CPU is not limited in how it allocates time segments to threads. By synchronizing the access to the shared variable, there is no error.

This was an example where the programmer wanted to have shared access to a member variable. In this case, synchronization fixed the error. However, there are very few instances where shared access to a member variable is needed.

Even with synchronization, never place the request object in a member variable in a servlet; otherwise all active threads will have access to the parameters of the thread that set the member variable last. This would be a bad idea if this were an application for Swiss bank accounts.

 Try It

http://bytesizebook.com/book/ch3/sharedVariable/Controller

Open two different browsers, not just two instances of the same browser, as Tomcat does not allocate a new thread to the same servlet from the same browser. After doing this, you will see that both instances display different numbers.

Note that the requests take longer to complete. Instead of taking around 3 seconds to complete both requests, it now takes 6 seconds. The CPU must allow the thread to sleep and wake up before it gives access to the second thread. This is another reason for not using synchronized, shared variables in servlets.

When to Use Member Variables in Servlets

The simple answer to the question is to never use member variables in servlets. There will never be synchronization issues if there are no member variables in servlets.

Another way to answer the question of using member variables is to ask the question, "Should this data be shared amongst **all** requests?" If the answer is "Yes", then it is safe to use a synchronized member variable. If the answer is "No", then use local variables inside methods and pass the data to other methods via parameters.

3.7   Reorganising the Controller

Member variables are useful; it would be nice to be able to use them in a controller. For instance, controllers communicate with the browser through the request and response objects. Any helper method that needs to know information about the request or that needs to add information to the response would need to have these objects passed to it as parameters. It would be easier to place these two objects into member variables, so that they could be accessed by every method in the controller.

The problem with member variables is only limited to classes that extend *HttpServlet*. However, member variables can be used in every class that does not extend *HttpServlet*. For this reason, a helper class will be created that will be used to store the request and response objects. This helper class can have helper methods too. These helper methods will have direct access to the request and response objects.

Fig. 3.8 ControllerHelper
will inherit from HelperBase

Even a `doGet` method can be added to the helper class, so that the controller only needs to call `doGet` in the helper.

The helper class should also have a reference to the servlet that it is helping. Even though the helper will do all the work, the servlet receives the initial request from the servlet engine. Sometimes, it will be necessary to retrieve information about the servlet when processing a request, like initialisation parameters. An additional member variable for the servlet class will be added to the helper.

In addition to the request, response and servlet objects, the helper class will have a member variable for the bean that contains all of the user's data. This will make it easier for the controller to process the data. A helper method named `getData` will be added so that the data in the bean can be accessed from the JSPs using EL.

From now on, whenever a controller is created, a helper class will also be created. Most of the work that could be done in the controller will be done in the helper class, instead. It will be easier to do the work of the controller in the helper class because of the member variables.

There are two types of variables that can be added to the helper class. Some of the variables that are added are not specific for a controller, but are common to all controllers. For example, the request, response and servlet objects have the same structure for all controllers. On the other hand, some variables are unique to a controller, like the bean that encapsulates the request data.

This is a perfect place to use inheritance. Those variables that are common to all controllers can be placed in a base class, while the ones that are specific to a controller will be placed in a class that extends the base class. The base class will be called `HelperBase` and the extended class will typically be called `ControllerHelper`.

Figure 3.8 shows the relationship between the two classes, the member variables in each and the helper methods in each.

3.7.1 Creating the Helper Base

The helper base will contain the member variables that are common to all controllers, like the request, response and servlet objects. These objects have the same

structure regardless of the controller that is using them. Helper methods will be
added to the class to facilitate access to these variables.

There needs to be a helper method that sets the request, response and servlet
objects. These should be set as soon as the helper base is created. The most logical
place to set them is in the constructor for the helper base class. The helper base will
not have a default constructor; it will only have a constructor that has parameters for
the request and response objects. Whenever a new helper base object is constructed,
the current request, response and servlet objects will need to be passed to the
constructor.

```
package ch3.reorganised;

import javax.servlet.http.HttpServlet;
import javax.servlet.http.HttpServletRequest;
import javax.servlet.http.HttpServletResponse;

public class HelperBase {

    protected HttpServletRequest request;
    protected HttpServletResponse response;
    protected HttpServlet servlet;

    public HelperBase(HttpServlet servlet,
                      HttpServletRequest request,
                      HttpServletResponse response) {
        this.servlet = servlet;
        this.request = request;
        this.response = response;
    }

}
```

For the current example, the helper base class will be placed in the same package
as the controller. In the future, as more features are added to the helper base class, it
will be placed in a more centrally located package.

3.7.2   Creating the Controller Helper

The main motivation for using a controller helper is to be able to use member variables. There are two types of member variables: those that are created in the controller helper and those that are created in the helper base.

The controller helper will be placed into the session. This means that the member
variables in it can be made visible to the session. In order to make a member variable
visible from the session, an accessor for the variable needs to be added to the controller

helper. The member variables in the controller helper can be accessed from a JSP just like the member variables in a bean are accessed: by using an accessor.

The controller helper will do all the work for the controller. The controller will still receive the request from the browser, but will then delegate the work to the controller helper. For this reason, the controller helper will have a doGet method that does all the work that the controller used to do. The controller will only create the controller helper and call its doGet method.

Controller Helper Variables

The controller helper will contain variables that are specific to the current controller, like the bean that contains the request data. The bean will have a different structure for each controller, since each bean will contain different properties that encapsulate the data that the user enters. For this reason, it cannot be placed in the HelperBase. In the future, additional member variables will be added to the controller helper.

```
protected RequestDataDefault data;
```

Initialise Helper Base Variables

The controller helper must initialise all of its variables. Since the controller helper will extend the helper base, it must initialise the request, response and servlet variables that are stored in the base class. The constructor for the controller helper will have parameters for the request, response and servlet objects. The constructor must call the base class constructor with these parameters. The call to super(servlet, request, response) must be the first statement in the constructor. The call to the base constructor will set the values of the request and response objects in the helper base class. The controller helper must also initialise the bean.

```
public ControllerHelper(HttpServlet servlet,
                        HttpServletRequest request,
                        HttpServletResponse response) {
    super(servlet, request, response);
    data = new RequestDataDefault();
}
```

Making Variables Visible from the Session

There needs to be a helper method that allows the data to be retrieved from the JSPs, using EL. Remember that EL statements are translated into calls to accessors, so there should be an accessor in the controller helper that returns the bean. This accessor only needs to return the type Object because the EL uses reflection to determine the methods an object has. Without this method, the bean would not be accessible from the JSPs.

```
public Object getData() {
    return data;
}
```

Doing the Work of the Controller

The `ControllerHelper` will also have a `doGet` method that is similar to the code that has been in previous controllers. It does not need the request, response and servlet objects passed to it, since it can access them directly from the helper base class.

Five basic steps were performed by the `doGet` method in the servlet controller from Listing 2.7: create the bean, make the bean accessible, fill the bean, translate the button name and forward to the next page.

This method does not need to create a bean, since the bean has been added to the controller helper as a member variable and is created when the controller helper is constructed.

Instead of placing the bean in the session, the controller helper will place itself in the session. In conjunction with the `getData` accessor, the bean will still be accessible from the JSPs.

The remaining steps for a controller are performed just like the previous controller.

```
public void doGet()
    throws ServletException, IOException
{
    request.getSession().setAttribute("helper", this);

    data.setHobby(request.getParameter("hobby"));
    data.setAversion(request.getParameter("aversion"));

    String address;

    if (request.getParameter("processButton") != null)
    {
        address = "Process.jsp";
    }
    else if (request.getParameter("confirmButton") != nu
    {
        address = "Confirm.jsp";
    }
    else
    {
        address = "Edit.jsp";
    }

    RequestDispatcher dispatcher =
        request.getRequestDispatcher(address);
    dispatcher.forward(request, response);
}
```

Complete Controller Helper

The next listing shows the complete code for a simple controller helper. It is using the bean from the *DefaultValidate* application – the controller helper has imported the class for the bean. The JSPs for the application will be rewritten in the next section. Since a relative reference is being used in the address for the JSP, it is assumed that the controller will be mapped to the directory that contains the JSPs.

```java
package ch3.reorganised;

import java.io.IOException;
import javax.servlet.RequestDispatcher;
import javax.servlet.ServletException;
import javax.servlet.http.HttpServletRequest;
import javax.servlet.http.HttpServletResponse;

import ch3.defaultValidate.RequestDataDefault;
import javax.servlet.http.HttpServlet;
public class ControllerHelper extends HelperBase {

  protected RequestDataDefault data;

  public ControllerHelper(HttpServlet servlet,
                          HttpServletRequest request,
                          HttpServletResponse response) {
    super(servlet, request, response);
    data = new RequestDataDefault();
  }

  public Object getData() {
    return data;
  }

  public void doGet()
      throws ServletException, IOException
  {
    request.getSession().setAttribute("helper", this);

    data.setHobby(request.getParameter("hobby"));
    data.setAversion(request.getParameter("aversion"));

    String address;

    if (request.getParameter("processButton") != null)
    {
      address = "Process.jsp";
    }
    else if (request.getParameter("confirmButton") != null)
    {
      address = "Confirm.jsp";
    }
    else
    {
      address = "Edit.jsp";
    }

    RequestDispatcher dispatcher =
        request.getRequestDispatcher(address);
    dispatcher.forward(request, response);
  }

}
```

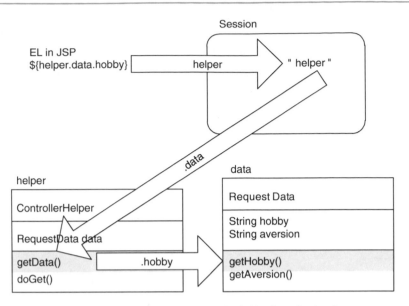

Fig. 3.9 EL statement that uses the helper to access the hobby from the data bean

The controller helper looks very similar to the controller from previous examples. At this point, there does not seem to be a justification for going to all of this trouble. However, this reorganisation will simplify the implementation of features that will be added to the controller.

3.7.3   JSPs: Reorganised Controller

The only difference between the JSPs for this example and the JSPs from the previous example is how the data is retrieved from the session. The servlet controller from earlier in the chapter placed the bean in the session and accessed the bean from the JSP. The current example placed the controller helper into the session. This requires an extra step to access the data.

The controller helper is added to the session under the name of *helper*. Any public accessors in the controller helper can be accessed from the JSP using EL. In particular, the getData accessor can be accessed from the bean as ${helper.data}. This will return the bean that contains the data.

Once the bean is accessible, then all its public accessors are accessible. In particular, the getHobby accessor could be called to retrieve the hobby that the user entered. The EL statement that would do this is ${helper.data.hobby} (Fig. 3.9).

To modify the JSPs for this example, replace all ${refData.hobby} with ${helper.data.hobby} and replace all ${refData.aversion} with ${helper.data.aversion}.

In the edit page, use the helper to access the bean, then access the bean to initialise the input elements with any data that was passed in the query string.

In the confirm and process pages, use the helper to access the bean, then access the bean to retrieve the values for the hobby and aversion that were sent in the query string.

```
Hobby:
<input type="text" name="hobby"
                   value="${helper.data.hobby}">
<br>
Aversion:
<input type="text" name="aversion"
                   value="${helper.data.aversion}">
```

In the confirm and process pages, use the helper to access the bean, then access the bean to initialise the hidden elements with any data that was passed in the query string.

```
<input type="hidden" name="hobby"
                     value="${helper.data.hobby}">
<input type="hidden" name="aversion"
                     value="${helper.data.aversion}">
```

3.7.4   Controller: Reorganised Controller

The last detail is to modify the controller so that it uses the controller helper. The controller only has to construct a controller helper and call its doGet method.

```
package ch3.reorganised;

import java.io.IOException;
import javax.servlet.ServletException;
import javax.servlet.annotation.WebServlet;
import javax.servlet.http.HttpServlet;
import javax.servlet.http.HttpServletRequest;
import javax.servlet.http.HttpServletResponse;

@WebServlet(urlPatterns={"/ch3/reorganised/Controller"})
public class Controller extends HttpServlet {

    public void doGet(HttpServletRequest request,
                      HttpServletResponse response)
    throws ServletException, IOException {
        ControllerHelper helper =
            new ControllerHelper(this, request, response);
        helper.doGet();
    }
}
```

Fig. 3.10 The location of files for the reorganised controller

3.8   Application: Reorganised Controller

With the above modifications, the *Default Validate* application can be rewritten. The
HelperBase, ControllerHelper and Controller were developed in the
last three sections. All the Java files have been placed in a package named ch3 .
reorganised (Fig. 3.10).

The controller has been mapped to the URL */ch3/reorganised/Controller*,
which is the directory where the JSPs have been placed. Even though the controller
is using a helper, the controller is still the class that is visible from the web,
because it is the class that extends *HttpServlet*. The controller helper, helper base
and bean classes should not be added to the *web.xml* file and should not be
annotated with WebServlet. They are not visible from the web, so they do not
need a URL pattern.

```
. . .
@WebServlet(urlPatterns={"/ch3/reorganised/Controller"})
public class Controller extends HttpServlet {
. . .
```

 Try It

http://bytesizebook.com/book/ch3/reorganised/Controller

This controller behaves exactly like the *DefaultValidate* controller. The only difference is that the controller has been reorganised using a controller helper class and a helper base class.

3.9   Model, View, Controller

There are three major components in a web application: the bean, the JSPs and the controller. These components are known as the *Model, View, Controller* (MVC).

Model
The model defines the data that will be used in the application. It also defines the operations that can be performed on the data. In a web application, the bean is the model.

View
The view displays the data to the user. The view does not do any of the processing of the data, it only presents the data. There are usually multiple views in an application. In a web application, each JSP is a separate view.

Controller
The controller is the program that ties the views and the models together. In a web application, the controller servlet is the controller.

The model is where the data processing will be done. The most important aspect of a web application is data processing. The model encapsulates the data and all the methods that work on it.

The controller is important because it is the program that is handling the request from the browser and sending a response back to the server. The controller will delegate responsibility to the model whenever it can.

The views are simple. They contain HTML and a few directives to display the data from the model. It is best not to add code to the view.

3.10   Summary

This chapter introduced Java beans, which are used to encapsulate the data that is sent from a request. The basic structure of a bean was covered, as well as how a bean can be incorporated into a web application. To demonstrate the power of a bean, the additional feature of default validation was added.

One of the shortcomings of a servlet is the problem with using member variables. This restriction goes against one of the basic concepts of object-oriented design. This problem was discussed in detail and two solutions to the problem were offered: avoid using member variables or use synchronization blocks. Synchronization blocks should only be used when data needs to be shared amongst all requests. For most situations, member variables should be avoided in servlets.

A helper class was introduced that can use member variables to simplify the tasks of the controller. The helper class contained a member variable for the bean that encapsulates the request data. A base class was introduced for member variables that are the same for all controllers. The first variables that were added to this class were for the request and response objects. Together, these classes allow easy access to all the objects that are needed in an application.

In the future, every controller will have a controller helper that is extended from the base class. All request and response processing will be done in the helper class.

The addition of the bean to a web application adds the final component of the MVC structure. The model is the bean, the views are the JSPs and the controller is the servlet that extends HttpServlet.

3.11   Chapter Review

Terms
1. Java Bean
2. Property
3. Accessor
4. Mutator
5. Session
6. Copy Request Parameters
7. Default Validation
8. Default Value
9. Variables
    (a) Member
    (b) Local
10. Thread
11. Synchronization
12. Controller Helper
    (a) Member Variables
13. Helper Base
    (a) Member Variables
14. MVC

New Java
1. request.getSession().setAttribute
2. super
3. synchronized

Tags
1. ${param.name}
2. ${refData.property}
3. ${helper.bean.property}

Questions

1. When discussing threads, the steps A1, A2, A3 must execute in order, and the steps B1, B2, B3 must execute in order. However, there is no restriction on how the A steps relate to the B steps. Other than the sequence A1, A2, B1, B2, A3, B3 explained above, what other sequences will cause both threads to obtain a value of 1 for x?
2. What would be the name of the mutator and accessor in a bean for form elements with the following names?
   (a) fun
   (b) moreFun
   (c) tOoMuChFuN
   (d) wAYTOOMUCHFUN
3. What would be the name of the form element that would correspond with the following accessors in a bean?
   (a) getBetter
   (b) getOutOfHere
   (c) getOFFMYCLOUD
4. What methods in the helper and the bean are called when the EL statement ${helper.data.hobby} is executed?
5. What determines if a member variable should be declared in the helper base or in the controller helper?
6. What method must be added to the controller helper in order to allow a member variable to be accessed from a JSP?

Tasks

1. Create a bean that encapsulates the data in a form with elements named name, city and country.
   (a) Add default values to the accessors for city and two-letter country code. Use a city and country of your choice for the default values. Use the default values if user leaves the city or the country blank.
   (b) Change the validation in the last question so that the country must be GB, US or DE. If the country is GB, then the city must be London, Oxford or Leeds. If the country is US, then the city must be New York, Los Angeles or Miami. If the country is DE, then the city must be Berlin, Frankfurt or Baden-Baden. Add additional countries and cities of your choice. If the country is not valid, then choose a default country and city. If the country is valid, but the city is not valid, choose a default city for that country.
2. In a servlet:
   (a) Write the statements that will add a bean named preferences to the session attributes.
   (b) Write the statements that will copy the request parameters into a bean object named fruit that has properties named apples and bananas with data from the query string. Assume that the form elements in the query string have the same names as the bean properties.

3. In a JSP:
   (a) Write the EL statements that will display the values of the query string parameters named bookName and bookAuthor.
   (b) Write the EL statements that will display the values of session attributes named salesManager and accountant.
   (c) Write the EL statements that will display the values of the bean properties named car and boat. Assume that the bean has been added to the session attributes with the name vehicles.
   (d) Write the EL statements that will display the values of the bean properties named car and boat. Assume that the bean has been added to the helper and that the helper has been added to the session attributes with the name "helper". Assume that there is a getData method in the helper that returns the bean.
4. Create a new controller application that accepts the data from question 1. Create a bean and a controller helper for this application. Use the helper base class from the book.

Enhancing the Controller

4

The previous chapter introduced the idea of a helper class that has easy access to all the objects that are used in a controller application: the bean, the request, the response. This chapter builds on this framework and adds features to the helper class and its base class.

Many tasks are common to all controller applications. These tasks include specifying the location of the JSPs, eliminating hidden fields, filling a bean, using a logger and decoding a button name into an address. Other common capabilities will be added to the controller application in future chapters.

Some of these tasks require specific information about the current controller application, so they will be added to the controller helper class. Others are common to all controller applications, so they will be added to the helper base class.

Up until now, all the features that have been used are part of the normal servlet engine. From now on, additional features will be added to the servlet engine by including *Java Archive* (JAR) files. JAR files are actually *zip* archives with the extension *.jar* that can be read by the *Java Virtual Machine* (JVM). Typically, a developer who wants to add a feature to the servlet engine will package all the necessary class files in a JAR. Then, anyone who wants to incorporate the new feature into the servlet engine only has to place the JAR into a specific directory in the web application where the servlet engine can find it. This directory is the *lib* subdirectory of the WEB-INF directory.

4.1 Logging in Web Applications

When debugging a Java application, it can be useful to display error messages when some exception fires. A standard technique is to use System.out.

```
System.out.println("Something bad happened");
```

T. Downey, *Guide to Web Development with Java: Understanding Website Creation*,
DOI 10.1007/978-1-4471-2443-6_4, © Springer-Verlag London Limited 2012

In a servlet, this is not a very useful technique. In a typical Java application, System.out is routed to the monitor, so the error will display on the current monitor. However, a servlet is not connected to a monitor; it is run by the servlet engine. The servlet engine is not connected to a monitor either; the servlet engine routes System.out to a log file that is owned by the system administrator and cannot be accessed by a typical developer.

Instead of using System.out, it is better to create a log file that the developer can read.

4.1.1   Logging with Log4j

There is a package named Log4j that can be used to open and write to a log file. To implement it, add the following jar file to the *lib* directory of the web application. This file can be downloaded from *http://bytesizebook.com/jar* or the most recent version of the JAR can be retrieved from *http://logging.apache.org/log4j/docs/ download.html*. Choose the stable branch 1.2. The current stable release is 1.2.16.

```
log4j-1.2.16.jar
```

One of the nicest features of a Log4j logger is that an error message can be given an error level. The log file also has a level; it will only record error messages that have the same level or more a severe level. Those messages that have a less severe error level will not be written to the log file. This feature allows the developer to add error messages that will only display when trying to trace an error. By changing the level of the log file to a more severe level, the less severe messages will not be written to the log file.

There are five error levels for a log file: Level.FATAL, Level.ERROR, Level.WARN, Level.INFO, Level.DEBUG. These error levels range from the level that records the fewest number of messages to the level that records the highest number of messages.

There are five error methods that a logger can use to write to a log file: fatal(), error(), warn(), info(), debug(). For each of these methods, a message will be written to the file, only if the level of the log file includes that type of message. For instance, warn() will only write to the log file if the level of the log file is Level.WARN, Level.INFO or Level.DEBUG; debug() will only write to the log file if the level of the file is Level.DEBUG (Table 4.1).

The fatal error message can never be ignored; it will always be written to the log file. The other error messages can be ignored, depending on the level of the file.

Think of error messages in a new way. Instead of just one type of error message, there are now five. To take full advantage of this, categorise messages while programming. As the need for an error message arises, decide if the message indicates a fundamental problem in the program, or if the message is just to help debug the program. Think of the warn, info and debug messages as three different types of debugging messages. Think of the fatal and error messages as critical messages that indicate something is wrong with the program.

Table 4.1 The relationship between error messages and file levels

File level	Error messages
Level.FATAL	Fatal
Level.ERROR	Fatal, error
Level.WARN	Fatal, error, warn
Level.INFO	Fatal, error, warn, info
Level.DEBUG	Fatal, error, warn, info, debug

4.1.2 Configuring Log4j

There are many ways to configure Log4j; one way is to use an initialisation servlet. An initialisation servlet is different from a normal servlet. The initialisation servlet should only have its code executed once. It should never be called by the user; it should only be called by the servlet engine. To prevent users from executing the servlet, it will not have a `doGet` method.

Log File Location

One advantage of using a servlet to initialise Log4j is that the location of the actual log file can be specified using a relative reference from the root of the current web application. This allows the log file to be made portable; whenever the web application is deployed, the log file will be deployed with it. In order to retrieve the path to the root of the web application on the current computer, use the methods `getServletContext().getRealPath()`.

The log file should never be placed in a location that can be viewed from the web. By placing the log file in the WEB-INF directory, it cannot be accessed from the web. Use the following command to specify that the log file is located in a file named *error.log* located in the *logs* subdirectory of WEB-INF. Be sure that the file already exists and is writable by the servlet engine.

```
getServletContext().getRealPath("/WEB-INF/logs/error.log")
```

In order to make the logger even more portable, the path to the log file will be passed to the servlet instead of hard-coding the path in the Java code. The `web.xml` file can be used to declare an initialisation parameter for the servlet.

Initialisation Parameters in web.xml

The purpose of initialisation parameters is to be able to change values for the controller without having to recompile and redeploy the servlet. By using an initialisation parameter for the location of the log file, the file can be moved or renamed without having to recompile the servlet.

There is an attribute to the `WebServlet` annotation for declaring and initialising an initialisation parameter; however, in order to change the value of the parameter, the actual controller file would need to be edited and recompiled. For this reason, any servlet that uses an initialisation parameter will not use the `WebServlet` annotation for declaring the URL pattern for the servlet. All servlets that have an initialisation parameter will use the *web.xml* file to declare the parameter.

It is not possible to define some configuration details for a servlet in the
WebServlet annotation and define other details for the same servlet in the
web.xml file. Either all the configuration for the servlet is in the WebServlet
annotation or it is in the *web.xml* file. Servlets that have an initialisation parameter
will use the *web.xml* file for all of its configuration; the WebServlet annotation
will not be used at all.

The servlet tag has already been used in the web.xml file to define the servlet. Initialisation parameters are added to this tag using an init-param tag.

The init-param tag has two nested tags. Define the name of the initialisation
parameter with the param-name tag. Define the value of the parameter with the
param-value tag.

Add a parameter named logPath to the servlet tag. It will have a value of
/WEB-INF/logs/error.log. This is the path to the log file. It can be changed
to any path, but it will always be relative to the location of the web application.

```
...
  <servlet>
      <servlet-name>Log4jInitServlet</servlet-name>
      <servlet-class>shared.InitLog4j</servlet-class>
      <init-param>
          <param-name>logPath</param-name>
          <param-value>/WEB-INF/logs/error.log</param-value>
      </init-param>
      <load-on-startup>1</load-on-startup>
  </servlet>
...
```

Reading Initialisation Parameters

The value of an initialisation parameter is retrieved from a servlet using the
getInitParameter method of the servlet. This method returns a string. Since
the path to the log file is a string, no data conversion is needed when reading the
parameter.

```
String initPath = getInitParameter("logPath");
```

If the logPath parameter in the *web.xml* is not null, then it will be used to set
the value of the path to the log file. If it is null, then a default path will be used.

```
String initPath = getInitParameter("logPath");
String logPath = "/WEB-INF/logs/error.log";
if (initPath != null) logPath = initPath;
```

Loggers

Log4j uses a class named Logger to encapsulate the process of writing messages
to a log file. There could be many different loggers that write to the same log file.

In web applications that use many different packages, it is common that many loggers will write to one log file.

There is a default logger that should be initialised when using Log4j. This logger is known as the root logger. This logger is always available. This is the logger that will record all messages that are written to any other logger. This is the only logger that needs to be defined. By defining the root logger, all messages from all packages can be recorded.

Once Log4j has been initialised, any application can retrieve a logger and write to it. The logger can be given a name so that different parts of the same application can write to the same logger.

Helper Methods

To simplify the initialisation of Log4j, two helper methods will be created. One helper method is used to open the actual file that will contain the error messages. The other helper method will configure the object that is used to write to the file.

In order to associate an actual file with the logger, there is a class named `Appender`. An appender is created with the name of the file that will hold the error messages and the pattern to be used for each message.

The name of the file will be passed to the method. The name will be translated into a path that is relative to the root of the web application. The pattern can include many things, like the date, the method that threw the error, the error message, etc.

```
private FileAppender getAppender(String fileName) {
  RollingFileAppender appender = null;
  try {
    appender = new RollingFileAppender(
        new PatternLayout("%-5p %c %t%n%29d - %m%n"),
        getServletContext().getRealPath(fileName),
        true);
    appender.setMaxBackupIndex(5);
    appender.setMaxFileSize("1MB");
  } catch (IOException ex) {
    System.out.println(
        "Could not create appender for "
        + fileName + ":"
        + ex.getMessage());
  }
  return appender;
}
```

To initialise a logger, retrieve the logger from Log4j, using the static methods `Logger.getLogger(name)` or `Logger.getRootLogger()`. These will create the logger or return it if it had been created already. Log4j keeps track of all the loggers that have been opened.

The next steps are to set the level and the appender. A helper method has been added to the servlet for these steps.

```
private void initLogger(String name,
                        FileAppender appender,
                        Level level)
{
  Logger logger;
  if (name == null) {
    logger = Logger.getRootLogger();
  } else {
    logger = Logger.getLogger(name);
  }
  logger.setLevel(level);
  logger.addAppender(appender);
  logger.info("Starting " + logger.getName());
}
```

Init Method

In each servlet, there is a method that is executed when it is loaded into memory: init. Servlets are loaded into memory by the servlet engine when they are accessed for the first time. They remain in memory until the web application shuts down. Whenever an action needs to be executed once, then it can be placed in the init method.

With the aid of the helper methods, it is a simple matter to configure the root logger. By passing a null value as the first parameter, the helper method will create the root logger.

```
FileAppender appender = getAppender(logPath);
if (appender == null) return;
initLogger(null, appender, Level.ERROR);
```

It is also possible to define additional loggers that can be configured differently from the root logger. By using separate loggers, it is possible to limit the number of messages from one logger, while allowing many messages from another.

For instance, in a later section of the chapter, a new package will be introduced that automates copying the request parameters to the bean. A separate logger could be opened for this package with a different level. This new logger could be set to Level.DEBUG, while the root logger is set to Level.ERROR. The new package could generate a lot of information that could be useful while debugging, and the other packages in the web application would only write error messages to the log file.

```java
public void init() {
  String initPath = getInitParameter("logPath");
  String logPath = "/WEB-INF/logs/error.log";
  if (initPath != null) logPath = initPath;
  FileAppender appender = getAppender(logPath);
  if (appender == null) return;
  initLogger(null, appender, Level.ERROR);
  initLogger("org.apache.commmons.beanutils",
             appender, Level.DEBUG);
}
```

Initialisation Servlet

Putting all this together yields the initialisation servlet for Log4j. This servlet has been placed in the *shared* package. This is a package that will be used throughout the book that will contain classes that will be used by many different controllers. The complete InitLog4j servlet can be found in the Appendix.

```java
package shared;

import java.io.IOException;
import javax.servlet.http.HttpServlet;
import org.apache.log4j.FileAppender;
import org.apache.log4j.Level;
import org.apache.log4j.Logger;
import org.apache.log4j.PatternLayout;
import org.apache.log4j.RollingFileAppender;

public class InitLog4j extends HttpServlet {

  public void init() {
      ...
  }

  private FileAppender getAppender(String fileName) {
      ...
  }

  private void initLogger(String name,
                          FileAppender appender,
                          Level level)
  {
      ...
  }
}
```

Since this servlet does not have a doGet method, there is no way to call it from the web. The servlet needs to be called by the web application when the web application starts. This can be accomplished by modifying the web.xml.

There is a tag named load-on-startup that tells the servlet engine to start the associated servlet whenever the web application starts. Add this tag to the servlet definition for the Log4j initialisation servlet. The initialisation parameter containing the path to the log file is also added to the servlet tag. All of these are added to the same servlet tag in the web.xml file. Do not create multiple servlet tags for one servlet.

```
. . .
  <servlet>
      <servlet-name>Log4jInitServlet</servlet-name>
      <servlet-class>shared.InitLog4j</servlet-class>
      <init-param>
          <param-name>logPath</param-name>
          <param-value>/WEB-INF/logs/error.log</param-value>
      </init-param>
      <load-on-startup>1</load-on-startup>
  </servlet>
. . .
```

By removing the doGet method from the servlet, adding an init method and configuring the servlet to load when the servlet engine starts, the initialisation servlet will only be run once and cannot be accessed by the user. No servlet mapping will be created for the initialisation servlet.

4.1.3   Retrieving the Logger

The helper base class has been renamed to HelperBaseCh4 and has been placed in the *shared* package. Each of the next three chapters will add features to the helper base, so there will be a distinct helper base for each chapter: HelperBaseCh4, HelperBaseCh5 and HelperBaseCh6. They have been placed into the *shared* package because they do not contain specific details for any controller helper and can be accessed from any package.

A variable for a logger will be added to the application. Since the logger is the same for all controllers, it will be placed in the helper base class. It will be declared as a member variable that will be initialised when the helper base class is created. The helper base class now has four member variables: servlet, request, response, logger (Fig. 4.1). Each is initialised in the constructor.

To initialise the logger, call the static method Logger.getLogger with an arbitrary name. This will create a new logger that is inherited from the root logger, so it will use the same appender that the root logger uses. Instead of

Fig. 4.1 Add the logger to
the helper base class

```
HelperBase

HttpServletRequest request
HttpServletResponse response
Logger logger
```

hard-coding the name of the logger in the helper base class, an initialisation
parameter will be used. If the initialisation parameter is null, then a default
name will be used.

```
...
String logName = "bytesizebook.webdev";
String initName = servlet.getInitParameter("logName");
if (initName != null) logName = initName;
...
```

Since this is the helper base class and the helper base class is not a servlet, it does
not have a servlet tag in the web.xml file. The helper base class will be shared by
many servlets, so the initialisation parameter should be added to the servlet tag for
the servlet for the application. The helper base class can access the servlet parameters from the servlet member variable.

To override the default level of the logger, call the setLevel method. Instead
of hard-coding the level of the logger in the helper base class, an initialisation
parameter will be used. If the initialisation parameter is null, then the level will not
be changed. Since the getInitParameter method returns a string, the parameter will need to be parsed to a value in the Level enumeration. If the parameter
does not contain a valid string for the Level enumeration, then the level will default
to DEBUG.

```
...
Level logLevel = Level.DEBUG;
String strLevel = servlet.getInitParameter("logLevel");
if (strLevel != null) {
    logLevel = Level.toLevel(strLevel);
}
...
```

A helper method will be used to read these two parameters and to set the name
and level of the logger. This method belongs in the helper base and should be called
from the helper base constructor.

```
. . .
public HelperBaseCh4(
          HttpServlet servlet,
          HttpServletRequest request,
          HttpServletResponse response) {
      this.servlet = servlet;
      this.request = request;
      this.response = response;
      initLogger();
}

protected void initLogger() {
      String logName = "bytesizebook.webdev";
      String initName = servlet.getInitParameter("logName");
      if (initName != null) logName = initName;

      Level logLevel = Level.DEBUG;
      String strLevel = servlet.getInitParameter("logLevel");
      if (strLevel != null) {
          logLevel = Level.toLevel(strLevel);
      }
. . .
```

Once it is retrieved into a member variable, the logger can be accessed from any method in the controller helper and helper base classes. There are five methods to write errors with a specific level:
1. logger.debug("message")
2. logger.info("message")
3. logger.warn("message")
4. logger.error("message")
5. logger.fatal("message")

Use these to write a message with a given severity level to the log file. Only those messages that have the same or higher severity as the level of the logger will be written to the file.

The remaining examples in the book will regularly use the logger to write error messages to the log file.

4.1.4   Adding a Logger in the Bean

Only the controller helper and helper base class can access the logger member variable. Other classes in the application will not have access to the logger member variable; however, all other classes do have the ability to create loggers and initialise them just like the helper base class did.
1. Declare a member variable for a logger.
2. Call getLogger to initialise the logger.
3. Call setLevel to set the level of the logger.
4. Use the fatal, error, warn, info, debug messages.

For example, the following code shows how to create a logger in the bean class.

```
. . .
protected Logger logger;

public RequestDataWithLogger() {
    logger = Logger.getLogger("bytesizebook.webdev");
    logger.setLevel(Level.DEBUG);
    logger.info("Setting logger in bean.");
}
. . .
```

4.2   Eliminating Hidden Fields

In the *reorganised controller* example from Chap. 3, the controller helper is saved
in the session and can be accessed from a JSP using the EL statement of
`${helper}`. The controller helper has a member variable for the bean that contains the user's data. Because there is also a `getData` method, the data in the bean
can also be retrieved in a JSP using the EL statement of `${helper.data}`. The
fact that the helper is in the session has an added benefit: the JSPs no longer need
hidden fields to pass data from one page to the next.

The session attributes exist as long as the user does not close the browser and continues to interact with the controller. The information that is in the controller helper is
available for the JSPs to access. Furthermore, the information will still be available the
next time the controller is called during the same session. The controller helper for the
next request only needs to retrieve the data that is in the session (Fig. 4.2).

Consider how the data is stored in the session and retrieved from the session.
1. The controller helper has a bean that contains the data that was entered by the user.
2. The controller helper writes itself to the session so that the JSPs can access it.
   The data bean can also be accessed.
3. The hidden fields were used to store this data and send it back to the application
   when a form button was clicked.
4. The data that is in the session was used to initialise the values in the hidden
   fields. This means that the data that the hidden fields are sending back to the
   controller is identical to the data that is already in the session.
5. Since the data is in the session and the session exists from request to request, the
   hidden fields are no longer needed.
6. The controller helper for the next request can retrieve the data from the session
   instead of from the query string.

4.2.1   Retrieving Data from the Session

Each time a new request is made, the controller helper is added to the session.
If there is already a controller helper in the session, then it should be retrieved and

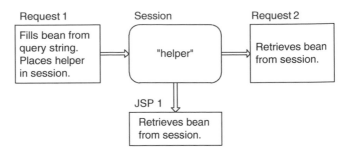

Fig. 4.2 The data is always available from the session

its data should be copied into the current controller helper. A method will be added to the helper base class to do this: addHelperToSession. Every time this method is called, the current controller helper will be saved in the session. This method will have two parameters that control how the session is accessed.

There maybe times when the application creates a new helper, but does not want to retrieve the previous one from the session. For this reason, the method will have a parameter that will control if the old helper in the session is accessed. If it is not accessed, then the data from the previous helper will not be copied into the current helper.

There maybe times when helpers from different applications are saved in the session at the same time. To allow this, there is an additional parameter to the addHelperToSession method that specifies the name that is used to save the object in the session.

Helper Base: Eliminating Hidden Fields
Three modifications need to be made to the helper base class to eliminate the need for hidden fields.

If there is a controller helper in the session with the correct name, then its values will be copied to the current helper. This requires an additional method named copyFromSession. This method should not be defined in the base class, since it needs to know the names of all the properties in the bean. For this reason, it is declared as an abstract method in the base class; this will force the derived class to define it.

```
protected abstract void copyFromSession(Object helper);
```

Through polymorphism, the copyFromSession method in the derived class will be called at runtime, even though the call is made from a method in the base class. By having an abstract method in the class, the helper base will have to be declared as an abstract class.

```
public abstract class HelperBaseCh4 {
        . . .
}
```

The next listing contains the code for the `addHelperToSession` method that checks the session for previous data and adds the current helper to the session. There are two parameters to this method: the name to use to retrieve the data and a parameter that indicates if any previous data in the session should initialise the current helper. The method makes a polymorphic call to the `copyFrom-Session` method, which will be resolved at runtime to a method in the derived controller helper.

```
. . .
public void addHelperToSession(String name,
        SessionData state) {
    if (SessionData.READ == state) {
        Object sessionObj =
                request.getSession().getAttribute(name);
        if (sessionObj != null) {
            copyFromSession(sessionObj);
        }
    }
    request.getSession().setAttribute(name, this);
}
. . .
```

The first parameter to this method is a string that identifies the object that is placed in the session. This name should be unique. If the same name is used for different controllers that are running at the same time, then each controller will erase the data from the other controller. By having unique names, more than one object can be stored in the session. Each controller would use its name to retrieve its object from the session.

With that said, all of the controller helpers in this book will always use the name *helper* for the session object. The reason for this is that each controller that is developed is an extension of the controllers before it. These controllers are not intended to run at the same time. If these controllers were designed to run at the same time, then each one should use a different name when adding data to the session.

The second parameter to this method is an enumeration type named `SessionData` and has the values READ and IGNORE (Fig. 4.3). When the old helper in the session should be used to initialise the current helper, call `addHelperToSession` with the value `SessionData.READ`. If this is the start of a new request and the old session helper should not be used to initialise the current helper, then call `addHelperToSession` with the value `SessionData.IGNORE`.

Fig. 4.3 The `Session`
`Data` enumeration

Fig. 4.4 The `copyFrom`
`Session` method is defined
in the helper base and
controller helper

Controller Helper: Eliminating Hidden Fields

There are two modifications to the controller helper to eliminate the need for hidden
fields. The `copyFromSession` method is defined and the `doGet` method must
be modified so that it always updates the session with itself and checks the session
for old data.

The `copyFromSession` method must be defined in every controller helper
that extends the helper base class. The helper base is now an abstract class. Every
class that extends it must implement its abstract method. The helper base and controller helper class diagrams are listed in Fig. 4.4. Both classes define the `copy-`
`FromSession` method. In the base class, it is an abstract method. In the extended
class, it must be implemented.

For example, the controller that will be developed in this chapter defines a
`copyFromSession` method that sets the bean for the controller helper to the
bean that was found in the session.

```
public void copyFromSession(Object sessionHelper) {
    if (sessionHelper.getClass() == this.getClass()) {
        data = ((ControllerHelper)sessionHelper).data;
    }
}
```

It is necessary to test that the controller helper that is in the session has the same
type of the controller helper for the current application. It is possible that there is a

helper from a previous application in the session that was stored with the same name as the helper for the current application. By testing the type, a class cast exception is avoided.

The doGet method in the controller helper will be modified to call the addHelperToSession method. It should be called every time a request is made so that any previous values can be retrieved and to add the current bean to the session. For now, call this method with SessionData.READ.

```
. . .
public void doGet()
   throws ServletException, IOException
{
   addHelperToSession("helper", SessionData.READ);
. . .
```

By calling this method for each request, the JSPs no longer need to have hidden fields. This simplifies the JSPs. However, hidden fields still have an advantage over the session data: hidden fields never expire. There may be times when a hidden field will be more useful than using the session.

The session must be used cautiously. Servlet engines do not maintain a session forever. Thirty minutes is a typical time for an idle session to remain active. After that time, the servlet engine will delete the data from the session. Before processing data that is in the session, it is recommended to check that the data still exists. If the data no longer exists, then the session has expired and the user should be redirected to a page where the data can be entered again.

4.3   Specifying the Location of the JSPs

In the *data bean* controller, from Chap. 3, the JSPs were in a directory that was visible from the web and the controller was mapped to that directory; a relative reference could be used to specify the address of the JSPs, since the controller was mapped to the same directory.

```
if (request.getParameter("processButton") != null)
{
   address = "Process.jsp";
}
else if (request.getParameter("confirmButton") != null)
{
   address = "Confirm.jsp";
}
else
{
   address = "Edit.jsp";
}
```

Fig. 4.5 The
jspLocation method is
added to the controller helper

ControllerHelper
RequestData data
doGet() getData() copyFromSession() jspLocation()

In the *default validate* controller, from Chap. 3, the JSPs were in a visible directory that was different from the directory where the controller was mapped; a path had to be added to the address of the JSP, since the controller was not mapped to the directory of the JSPs.

```
if (request.getParameter("processButton") != null)
{
   address = "/ch3/dataBean/Process.jsp";
}
else if (request.getParameter("confirmButton") != null)
{
   address = "/ch3/dataBean/Confirm.jsp";
}
else
{
   address = "/ch3/dataBean/Edit.jsp";
}
```

In this example, if the location of the JSPs were changed, this would require modifying several lines of code. A more efficient solution is to encapsulate the path to the JSPs in a helper method. By adding a method to the bean that generates the location of the JSPs, it is easy to modify the application in the future if the JSPs are moved (Fig. 4.5).

The method has one parameter that is the file name of the next JSP. The method will append this name to the path of the JSPs. By adding the path in a separate method, it will be easier to move the JSPs in the future.

```
protected String jspLocation(String page) {
   return "/ch3/dataBean/" + page;
}
```

The path should not include the name of the web application. The controller cannot access paths outside the web application, so the name of the web application is assumed.

The address of each JSP that is used in the bean must use this method to generate the address of the JSP.

```
if (request.getParameter("processButton") != null)
{
    address = jspLocation("Process.jsp");
}
else if (request.getParameter("confirmButton") != null)
{
    address = jspLocation("Confirm.jsp");
}
else
{
    address = jspLocation("Edit.jsp)";
}
```

In the future, if the location of the JSPs is changed, then only the return value of this method needs to be changed in order to update the controller helper.

Let us see how to use this method when the JSPs are in a visible directory, a hidden directory and the same physical directory as the controller.

4.3.1   JSPs in the Directory Where the Controller Is Mapped

If the JSPs are in a visible directory and the controller is mapped to that directory, then return the parameter that was passed to the jspLocation method.

```
protected String jspLocation(String page) {
    return page;
}
```

This will look for the JSP in the same directory where the controller is mapped.

The controller's *.class* file is not visible from the web, which is why a servlet mapping is created in the *web.xml* for the controller. The servlet mapping defines a URL that is visible from the web that can be used to access the controller. If the directory of this URL is also a physical directory in the web application, then the JSPs can be placed in that directory and a relative reference can be used to specify the URL of the JSPs. This is the technique that has been used for all controllers before the *default validate* controller (Table 4.2).

In each case, the path that was used in the URL pattern for the controller is the same as the path to the edit page. Since the directory for the servlet mapping and the directory for the JSPs are the same, the URL of the JSP can be specified by using the name of the JSP only.

Table 4.2 The relationship between the servlet mapping and the location of the JSPs

URL pattern	JSP location
/ch2/servletController/Controller	/ch2/servletController/Edit.jsp
/ch3/startExample/Controller	/ch3/startExample/Edit.jsp
/ch3/dataBean/Controller	/ch3/dataBean/Edit.jsp

4.3.2   JSPs in a Different Visible Directory

If the JSPs are in a visible directory, but not in the same directory as where the controller is mapped, then append the name of the page to the path to the JSPs. This path must start with a slash, which represents the root of the web application. Do not include the name of the web application in the path.

For example, in the *default validate* controller, the controller was mapped to the URL /ch3/defaultValidate/Controller, but the JSPs were located in the /ch3/dataBean/ directory. The method would return the following path:

```
protected String jspLocation(String page) {
    return "/ch3/dataBean/" + page;
}
```

4.3.3   JSPs in a Hidden Directory

If the JSPs are not in a visible directory, then it will always be necessary to return the full path to the JSPs.

The WEB-INF directory cannot be accessed from the web. By placing the JSPs in this directory, they cannot be accessed directly from the web; they can only be accessed through the servlet. The servlet has access to all the files and directories in the web application.

For example, if the JSPs are located in WEB-INF as

```
WEB-INF/ch3/defaultValidateHidden/Edit.jsp
WEB-INF/ch3/defaultValidateHidden/Confirm.jsp
WEB-INF/ch3/defaultValidateHidden/Process.jsp
```

then they cannot be accessed from the web. However, by setting the base path to /WEB-INF/ch3/dataBean/in the *jspLocation* method, the servlet will be able to access the JSPs.

```
protected String jspLocation(String page) {
    return "/WEB-INF/ch3/defaultValidateHidden/" + page;
}
```

4.3.4   JSPs in the Controller's Directory

We can take this concept one step further and place the JSPs in the same physical directory as the controller.

```
protected String jspLocation(String page) {
  return "/WEB-INF/classes/ch3/defaultValidateHidden/" + page;
}
```

This has advantages and disadvantages. One advantage is that applications will be easier to develop. It will not be necessary to change to different directories to edit the files that are in the application. One disadvantage is that if there are JSP developers and servlet developers, then they would each have access to all the files. This might not be acceptable. It might be better to place the JSPs in one directory and the servlet in another directory.

4.3.5   Where Should JSPs Be Located?

By creating the *jspLocation* method in the controller, it is easy to modify the location of the JSPs. However, this raises the question of where the JSPs should be placed. The answer to this question depends on your development needs.

Single Developer
If there is only one developer who is maintaining the JSPs and the controller, then it is easier to place the JSPs in the same directory as the controller's *.class* file. This is the approach that will be used for the remainder of this book.

HTML Developer and Controller Developer
If there are separate developers for HTML and for the controller, then the JSPs should be kept in a separate directory from the controller's *.class* file. This would allow the system administrator to allow different access permissions to the different directories.

Visible Versus Hidden
It is recommended to have the JSPs in a hidden directory. The intent of the controller is that all requests should be made to the controller and that the controller will forward the request to the proper JSP. If the JSPs are in a directory that is visible from the web, then it would be possible for a user to circumvent the controller and access the pages directly; this could result in unexpected results.

4.4   Controller Logic

Every controller needs to translate the button that the user clicked into the address for the next JSP. Each controller has a series of nested *if* statements that do this translation.

```
...
if (request.getParameter("processButton") != null)
{
  address = "Process.jsp";
}
else if (request.getParameter("confirmButton") != null)
{
  address = "Confirm.jsp";
}
else
{
  address = "Edit.jsp";
}
...
```

This is the logic for the simplest controller. However, in addition to calculating the next address, there will usually be tasks to perform when different buttons are clicked. The following listing is an example of a more complicated controller:

```
if (request.getParameter("processButton") != null)
{
  hibernateHelper.updateDB(data);
  request.setAttribute(
      "database",
      hibernateHelper.getListData(RequestData.class));
  address = jspLocation("Process.jsp");
}
else if (request.getParameter("confirmButton") != null)
{
  fillBeanFromRequest(data);
  String address;
  if (isValid(data)) {
    address = jspLocation("Confirm.jsp");
  } else {
    address = jspLocation("Edit.jsp");
  }
}
else
{
  address = jspLocation("Edit.jsp");
}
```

A more organised solution would be to write a separate method for each button. In the method, the next address would be calculated and the tasks for that button would be executed (Listing 4.1).

```java
public String processMethod() {
  hibernateHelper.updateDB(data);
  request.setAttribute(
      "database",
      hibernateHelper.getListData(RequestData.class));
  return jspLocation("Process.jsp");
}

public String confirmMethod() {
  fillBeanFromRequest(data);
  String address;
  if (isValid(data)) {
      address = "Confirm.jsp";
  } else {
      address = "Edit.jsp";
  }
  return jspLocation(address);
}

public String editMethod() {
  return jspLocation("Edit.jsp");
}

protected void doGet()
throws ServletException, java.io.IOException
{
  addHelperToSession("helper", SessionData.READ);

  if (request.getParameter("processButton") != null)
  {
    address = processMethod();
  }
  else if (request.getParameter("confirmButton") != null)
  {
    address = confirmMethod();
  }
  else
  {
    address = editMethod();
  }

  request.getRequestDispatcher(address)
      .forward(request, response);
}
```

Listing 4.1 A more organised controller helper

4.4.1   Decoding Button Names

Java annotations were introduced in Chap. 1. Extending Listing 4.1 and using
annotations, it is now possible to automate the nested **if** block and place it into the
helper base class. The idea is to mark each method with an annotation that associates the name of the button with the method and to replace the nested **if** block with
a call to a method that loops through the button names in the annotations, looking
for the one that matches the user's choice.

```
@ButtonMethod(buttonName="processButton")
public String processMethod() {
  hibernateHelper.updateDB(data);
  request.setAttribute(
      "database",
      hibernateHelper.getListData(RequestData.class);
  return jspLocation("Process.jsp");
}

@ButtonMethod(buttonName="confirmButton")
public String confirmMethod() {
  fillBeanFromRequest(data);
  String address;
  if (isValid(data)) {
    address = "Confirm.jsp";
  } else {
    address = "Edit.jsp";
  }
  return jspLocation(address);
}

@ButtonMethod(buttonName="editButton", isDefault=true)
public String editMethod() {
  return jspLocation("Edit.jsp");
}

protected void doGet()
throws ServletException, java.io.IOException {
  addHelperToSession("helper", SessionData.READ);

  String address = executeButtonMethod();

  request.getRequestDispatcher(address)
      .forward(request, response);
}
```

The annotations must precede the method that they modify. The annotations contain information about the method. In this example, the annotation is @Button Method. The intent of the annotation is to associate the name of a button with the method, so that the method can be called whenever that button is clicked. The exe-cuteButtonMethod will determine which method to call.

Two attributes can be included in the annotation: *buttonName* and *isDefault*. Set the *buttonName* attribute to the name that appears in the form element in the JSP for the button. The name of the button in the form element must agree with the *button-Name* attribute.

For example, the following form element is a submit button with a name of *confirmButton*.

```
<input type="submit" name="confirmButton"
                    value="Confirm">
```

In order to associate the above button with a method in the controller helper, annotate a method with the ButtonMethod annotation and set the value of the *buttonName* attribute to *confirmButton*.

```
@ButtonMethod(buttonName="confirmButton")
public String confirmMethod() {
      . . .
}
```

Set the *isDefault* attribute to the Boolean value *true* if this is the method that should be called when no button has been clicked. One of the button methods should be marked as the default. Do not include *true* in quotes, it must be a Boolean value.

4.4.2   Executing the Correct Button Method

The work of calling the correct method is relegated to the helper base class. A new method named executeButtonMethod will be added to the helper base class (Fig. 4.6).

Reflection is used to retrieve all the methods in the controller helper and look for those that are marked with the ButtonMethod annotation. If an annotated method is found and its ButtonName attribute is found in the query string parameters, then the method is executed. The essential details are contained in the next listing.

The innermost **if** should look familiar. It is testing for the presence of a button name in the query string. This is exactly what the nested **if** in the first controller did. This method automates this by using a loop. In order to handle a new button in the

Fig. 4.6 The `execute`
`ButtonMethod` method is
added to the helper base class

HelperBase
HttpServletRequest request HttpServletResponse response Logger logger
abstract copyFromSession() addHelperToSession() executeButtonMethod()

controller helper, all that is needed is an annotated method that performs the tasks
for that button.

```
Method[] methods =  clazz.getDeclaredMethods();
for(Method method : methods) {
  ButtonMethod annotation =
      method.getAnnotation(ButtonMethod.class);
  if(annotation != null) {
    if (request.getParameter(annotation.buttonName())
           != null)
    {
      result = invokeButtonMethod(method);
      break;
    }
  }
}
```

4.5   Filling a Bean

In all controllers up to this point, the mutators for each property in the bean needed
to be called in order to copy the data from the request into the bean.

```
data.setHobby(request.getParameter("hobby"));
data.setAversion(request.getParameter("aversion"));
```

Wouldn't it be nice if someone would write a Java package that would automate
this process?

There is an extension to Java that allows all the information from the request to
be sent to the bean. This extension will call the mutators automatically.

It is important that the name of the form element corresponds to the name of the
mutator. To determine what the name of the form element should be, take the name

Table 4.3 The form element
name corresponds to the name
of the mutator

Element name	Mutator
value	setValue
longName	setLongName

of the mutator and remove the word *set*, then change the first letter to lowercase. If the names do not correspond correctly, then the data will not be copied from the request to the bean.

Table 4.3 shows the relationship between the name of a form element and the name of the corresponding mutator.

In order to have the mutators called automatically for all data that are in the query string, include the following JAR files into the *lib* directory of the web application. These can be downloaded from *http://bytesizebook.com/jar*, or the latest versions can be downloaded from *http://jakarta.apache.org/commons/*.

```
commons-collections-3.2.1.jar
commons-logging-1.1.1.jar
commons-beanutils-1.8.3.jar
```

The magical method that calls all the mutators is named populate and is located in the org.apache.beanutils.BeanUtils package. It has two parameters: the bean to fill and a map that contains the data from the query string.

```
org.apache.commons.beanutils.BeanUtils.
        populate(data, request.getParameterMap());
```

The method can throw several exceptions, so it is best to place the call inside a method that can catch any errors.

```
public void fillBeanFromRequest(Object data) {
    try {
        org.apache.commons.beanutils.BeanUtils.
                populate(data, request.getParameterMap());
    } catch (IllegalAccessException iae) {
        logger.error("Populate - Illegal Access.", iae);
    } catch (InvocationTargetException ite) {
        logger.error("Populate - Invocation Target.", ite);
    }
}
```

Fig. 4.7 The fillBean
FromRequest method is
added to the helper base class

HelperBase
HttpServletRequest request HttpServletResponse response Logger logger
abstract copyFromSession() addHelperToSession() executeButtonMethod() fillBeanFromRequest()

If there is an exception, a message is written to the logger. In addition to these messages, if BeanUtils encounters an error, it will also write a message to the log file via its own logger org.apache.commons.beanutils.ConvertUtils. This logger was also declared in the *InitLog4j* servlet.

This method receives the data as an Object. This means that the method does not have access to any specific information about the bean. All that this method knows is that an object has been passed to it. For this reason, the method can be added to the helper base class (Fig. 4.7).

Now that the session is being used to retrieve previous values entered by the user, the values from the request only need to be added to the bean when the values change. In other words, the only time that this method needs to be called is when there are visible form elements that can be changed by the user. In the current example, this only happens when the user clicks the button named *confirmButton*. Using annotations, the only method that needs to call fillBeanFromRequest is the method that corresponds to the confirm button. No other pages have visible form elements.

```
@ButtonMethod(buttonName="confirmButton")
public String confirmMethod() {
    fillBeanFromRequest(data);
    return jspLocation("Confirm.jsp");
}
```

4.6   Application: Enhanced Controller

All of the above enhancements will now be combined into a controller application.
1. The controller and controller helper classes will be placed in the *ch4.enhanced* package.
2. The JSPs will be placed in the same directory as the controller.

Fig. 4.8 The location of files for the enhanced controller

3. It makes no difference what the URL pattern is for the controller, since the controller specifies the path to the JSPs. For simplicity, the controller has been mapped to */ch4/enhanced/Controller*.
4. Classes that are shared by many controllers have been placed in the *shared* package.

   Figure 4.8 shows the directory structure and file locations for this application.

4.6.1   JSPs: Enhanced Controller

The JSPs are similar to the JSPs from the *reorganised controller* in Chap. 3, except all of the hidden fields have been removed from the process and confirm pages. All the JSPs have been placed in the controller's directory.

4.6.2   ControllerHelper: Enhanced Controller

The controller helper is extended from the helper base class from this chapter. The complete listing for the helper base class for Chap. 4 is in the Appendix. The controller helper will do the following:
1. Use a bean to encapsulate the data from the user.
2. Use a logger to record any errors.
3. Eliminate hidden fields.
4. Use a method to specify that the JSPs are in the same directory as the controller.
5. Use annotations to execute a method based on the button the user clicked.
6. Automatically copy the query string data into the bean.
   The complete listing of the controller helper is in Listing 4.2.

```java
package ch4.enhanced;

import java.io.IOException;
import javax.servlet.http.HttpServletRequest;
import javax.servlet.http.HttpServletResponse;
import javax.servlet.ServletException;
import shared.ButtonMethod;
import shared.HelperBaseCh4;

import ch3.defaultValidate.RequestDataDefault;
import javax.servlet.http.HttpServlet;

public class ControllerHelper extends HelperBaseCh4 {

    private RequestDataDefault data;

    public ControllerHelper(
            HttpServlet servlet,
            HttpServletRequest request,
            HttpServletResponse response) {
        super(servlet, request, response);
        data = new RequestDataDefault();
    }

    public Object getData() {
        return data;
    }
```

```java
public void copyFromSession(Object sessionHelper) {
  if (sessionHelper.getClass() == this.getClass()) {
    data = ((ControllerHelper)sessionHelper).data;
  }
}

protected String jspLocation(String page) {
  return "/WEB-INF/classes/ch4/enhanced/" + page;
}

@ButtonMethod(buttonName="editButton", isDefault=true)
public String editMethod() {
  return jspLocation("Edit.jsp");
}

@ButtonMethod(buttonName="confirmButton")
public String confirmMethod() {
  fillBeanFromRequest(data);
  return jspLocation("Confirm.jsp");
}

@ButtonMethod(buttonName="processButton")
public String processMethod() {
  return jspLocation("Process.jsp");
}

@Override
public void doGet()
  throws ServletException, IOException
{
  addHelperToSession("helper", SessionData.READ);

  String address = executeButtonMethod();

  request.getRequestDispatcher(address)
      .forward(request, response);
}
}
```

Listing 4.2 Enhanced Controller Helper

The application uses the bean that was developed in the *default validate* controller, `RequestDataDefault`. The class for the bean is imported so that it is easier to reference the class.

The `ButtonMethod` class is needed to annotate the methods that are associated with button names. This class will be used by all controllers that are developed later in the book. It has been placed in a package named *shared*. This package will be used to hold classes that might be used by all controllers. The HelperBaseCh4 class has also been added to the *shared* package, as it can be used by all controllers. Both of these classes have been imported in the controller helper.

The `jspLocation` method returns the full path for each JSP. This means that the JSPs for this application can easily be moved to any location, including the physical directory of the controller. If the JSPs are moved under the WEB-INF folder, then they cannot be accessed directly from the web; only the controller will have access to them.

Each button that the user can click has a corresponding method that has been annotated with the name of the button. The edit method has also been set as the default method, in the case that the user does not click a button.

The `copyFromSession` method is the implementation of the abstract method that was declared in the helper base class. The `copyFromSession` method is needed to copy session information into the current controller helper. There is only one member variable in the controller helper that needs to be copied. The parameter is passed as an object, so it must be cast to the type of the current class in order to access the data variable. If the parameter is not the correct type, then the data in the session will be ignored.

4.6.3   Controller: Enhanced Controller

The controller is simplified; it only needs to create the controller helper and call its `doGet` method (Listing 4.3).

```
package ch4.enhanced;

import java.io.IOException;
import javax.servlet.ServletException;
import javax.servlet.http.HttpServlet;
import javax.servlet.http.HttpServletRequest;
import javax.servlet.http.HttpServletResponse;

public class Controller extends HttpServlet {

    protected void doGet(HttpServletRequest request,
                         HttpServletResponse response)
    throws ServletException, IOException {
        ControllerHelper helper =
            new ControllerHelper(this, request, response);
        helper.doGet();
    }
}
```

Listing 4.3 Enhanced Controller

Since the servlet has the `logName` and `logLevel` initialisation parameters, it will be configured using the *web.xml* file. The *web.xml* will contain the servlet definition, servlet mapping and initialisation parameters. To change the name and level, edit the `web.xml` file, then restart the web application. The new values will be read when the web application is reloaded.

```xml
<servlet>
    <servlet-name>Ch4Enhanced</servlet-name>
    <servlet-class>ch4.enhanced.Controller</servlet-class>
    <init-param>
        <param-name>logName</param-name>
        <param-value>bytesizebook.webdev.ch4</param-value>
    </init-param>
    <init-param>
        <param-name>logLevel</param-name>
        <param-value>INFO</param-value>
    </init-param>
</servlet>
<servlet-mapping>
    <servlet-name>Ch4Enhanced</servlet-name>
    <url-pattern>/ch4/enhanced/Controller</url-pattern>
</servlet-mapping>
```

 Try It

http://bytesizebook.com/book/ch4/enhanced/Controller

This application looks the same as the others, but it is now using a controller helper.

4.7   Libraries in IDEs

NetBeans and Eclipse use different techniques to add JAR files to the project. NetBeans uses links to JAR files that already exist on the computer, while Eclipse must have the actual JAR files added to the project. NetBeans manages the JAR files from within the IDE, but the JAR files must be added to the project from outside the Eclipse IDE. When a project is built, all the JAR files are copied into the corresponding *lib* directory of the web application structure. See the Appendix for detailed instructions on adding JAR files to each IDE.

4.8   Summary

Additional packages can be added to a web application by adding JAR files to its library. As a first example, the Log4j package was added to the application and a logger was used to record errors.

Initialisation parameters allow the application to be reconfigured without having to recompile the servlet. The location, level and name of the logger were all added as initialisation parameters. Many aspects of how the application uses a logger can be configured without recompiling the servlet. If a servlet has an initialisation parameter, then the servlet will be configured in the *web.xml* file, not in the `WebServlet` annotation. The whole point of an initialisation parameter is to be able to make changes without recompiling; this is not possible if the parameter is defined in the `WebServlet` annotation in the controller.

From now on, all controllers will have a helper class to facilitate performing the controller's tasks. All controller applications perform similar tasks. Some of these tasks use objects that are the same for all controllers; these objects can be stored in the base class. Other tasks require the details of the current application; these belong in the helper class. In this chapter, many of these common tasks were explored.

There are tasks that are common to all controllers: creating a logger, eliminating hidden fields, automating the controller logic and filling the bean. These tasks have been implemented so that they do not access any of the individual data members of the bean, so they can be placed in the base class. All controller helpers that are extended from the base class will have access to these features. The base class has been placed in the *shared* package, so that all future controller helpers can have access to it.

The tasks that require the knowledge of the current application are specifying the location of the JSPs and copying the data from one bean to another. The `copy-FromSession` method is needed so that hidden fields can be eliminated; the data from the session must be copied into the current bean. These tasks were added to the controller helper.

4.9   Chapter Review

Terms
1. Logger
2. Logger Path
3. Logger Name
4. Initialisation Parameter
    (a) Defining
    (b) Reading
5. Logger Initialisation Servlet
6. Session
7. Annotations
8. ButtonMethod Annotation
    (a) buttonName
    (b) isDefault
9. Filling a Bean

New Java
1. init
2. Logger.getLogger

3. Logger.fatal
4. Logger.error
5. Logger.warn
6. Logger.info
7. Logger.debug
8. Level.FATAL
9. Level.ERROR
10. Level.WARN
11. Level.INFO
12. Level.DEBUG
13. addHelperToSession(name, SessionData)
14. copyFromSession
15. jspLocation
16. executeButtonMethod
17. request.getParameter(btnMethod.buttonName()) ! = null
18. fillBeanFromRequest
19. Enumerations
    (a) SessionData {READ, IGNORE}

Tags
1. load-on-startup
2. init-param
3. param-name
4. param-value

Questions
1. How are additional packages added to a web application?
2. List all the error messages that will be written to an error file that has a level of Level.INFO.
3. List the file levels that will accept an info error message.
4. Explain how the level of the logger controls the number of messages that are written to the log file.
5. Explain how hidden fields can be removed from an application.
6. Explain why the *web.xml* file is used to define initialisation parameters instead of using the *WebServlet* annotation.
7. What should jspLocation return if the JSPs are located in the directory where the servlet is mapped?
8. What should jspLocation return if the JSPs are located in the same directory as the servlet class?
9. Explain why a method is added to the controller helper that returns the path to a JSP.
10. Explain what the parameters to addHelperToSession do.
11. Why is copyFromSession a separate method in the controller helper and not in the helper base?

12. Explain what the `ButtonMethod` annotation does. Explain what the parameters do.
13. Explain what `executeButtonMethod` does.
14. Write the Java code that will test if the button named *confirmButton* is in the query string.
15. Write the Java code that will copy the data from the query string into the bean.

Tasks

1. Use a logger, named *com.bytesizebook.test*, to write five different messages to the log file. Each message should have a different error level.
2. For the *InitLog4j* servlet, look up the PatternLayout class and investigate the constructor. Determine what each character means in the layout. Devise a new layout for your error messages.
3. Change the location of the log for the InitLog4j servlet. Do not modify the servlet code, only modify the *web.xml* file.
4. Implement the *enhanced controller* in your own web application. Modify the JSPs to use your own fields, with names other than *hobby* and *aversion*. Create a bean that corresponds to your data. Modify the controller helper so that it uses your bean and your data.
    (a) Change the default name and level of the logger for the controller helper. Do not modify the controller helper, only modify the *web.xml* file.
    (b) Add a logger to the bean.
    (c) Write warn, info and debug messages in the controller helper and the bean.
    (d) Set the level of the logger in the bean to a different level than the logger in the controller helper. Compare the types of messages that are sent to the logger from each class.

Hibernate

5

Two very important processes are needed in any website: data validation and data persistence. Both of these can be automated with a package named Hibernate.

Default validation was introduced in Chap. 3. Required validation will be introduced in this chapter. Hibernate can validate strings, numeric data and collections. String validation is so important that there is a part of standard Java that can simplify it: regular expressions. Hibernate will use regular expressions to perform sophisticated required validation on string data. Numeric validation is much simpler than string validation. Hibernate can test for numeric minimums, maximums and ranges. Hibernate also has tests for collections, such as the size of the collection and if the collection is empty.

Data persistence is the process of saving data to a database. Hibernate makes this a simple task by letting the developer work only with the bean and not with SQL statements. When data is retrieved from the database, it will be in the form of a collection of beans.

5.1 Required Validation

Default validation is used to supply a value for a property for which the user provided an invalid value. It is up to the developer to choose a reasonable default value, because not all properties have an obvious default. An area code could have a default value of the local area code, but a bank account number does not have a good default value. In the latter case, it is better to inform the user that something is missing and allow the user to supply the missing data; this is known as *required validation*.

In our application, if there is invalid data, then the user will remain on the edit page. Only when all the data are valid can the user proceed to the confirm page (Fig. 5.1).

Required validation should be done every time the user enters new data. It should also be done before data is entered into a database. Since the session is being used to store data, there is the possibility that the session expires and all the data are lost. In such a case, it would be a mistake to enter empty data into the database.

T. Downey, *Guide to Web Development with Java: Understanding Website Creation*,
DOI 10.1007/978-1-4471-2443-6_5, © Springer-Verlag London Limited 2012

Fig. 5.1 The application will
remain on the edit page until
valid data is entered

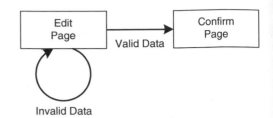

One of the most powerful tools for performing required validation on string data is regular expressions.

5.1.1 Regular Expressions

Validation is such a common task that there is an entire language dedicated to declaring patterns that can be used to test the format of a string. This language is known as *regular expressions*. Regular expressions are strings that contain wildcards, special characters and escape sequences. For example, a regular expression can be used to test if a string is a valid zip code, user identification number (ID) or social security number (SSN). A regular expression can also be used to test if a string matches an integer or a double, but this can be done more easily by parsing the string to the desired type and catching an exception if the parsing fails.

A sequence of regular expression characters is known as a pattern. The following patterns can be used to test for a valid zip code, SSN and user ID, respectively.

Zip Code: \d{5}(?:-\d{4})?
SSN: \d{3}(-?)\d{2}\1\d{4}
User ID: [a-zA-Z]{3,5}[a-zA-Z0-9]?\d{2}

These probably look very strange and cryptic now, but soon they will be very clear.

Character Classes
Square brackets define a *character class*. The character class pattern will match any single character that is in the brackets. For instance, the class [xyz] will match *x*, *y* or *z*, but only one of them. If the class starts with ^, then it will match all characters that are not listed inside the brackets.

A hyphen can be used to include a range of characters: [a-z] will match any lowercase letter. More than one hyphen can be used: [a-zA-Z] will match any letter. The order of letters is based on the ASCII numbering system for characters. This means that [a-Z] (lowercase *a* - uppercase *Z*) will not match any letters because lowercase *a* has a higher ASCII number than uppercase *Z*. [A-z] will match all letters, but will also match some additional symbols, since the symbols [\]^_` have ASCII numbers between capital *Z* and lower *a*.

Table 5.1 Special character classes

Character class	Meaning
.	Any character, except line terminators
\d	A digit: [0–9]
\D	A non-digit: [^0-9]
\s	A whitespace character: [\t\n\x0B\f\r]
\S	A non-whitespace character: [^\s]
\w	A word character: [a-zA-Z_0-9]
\W	A non-word character: [^\w]

[abc] a, b or c (simple class)

[^abc] Any character except a, b or c (negation)

[a-zA-Z] a through z or A through Z, inclusive (range)

Predefined Character Classes

Some character classes are used so often that there are special characters and escape sequences for them. Table 5.1 lists the special classes with their meaning.

Escaping Special Characters

There are times when a special character needs to be treated as a normal character. Use a \ before the special character to treat it as a normal character. For example, to match a period in a URL, use the \ before the period: index\.jsp. Without the \, the expression . would match any character, not just the period.

Alternatively, many special characters lose their special meaning when placed inside the square brackets. The pattern index[.]jsp would also match the period in a URL. The \ does not lose its special meaning inside square brackets: [\d] still matches a digit; it does not match a slash or a d.

Alternation

Character classes allow for the selection of a single character, but do not allow for the choice amongst different words. In this case, the operator | is used to indicate alternation. For example, yes|no would match the word *yes* or the word *no*. This can be extended for as many choices as are needed: yes|no|maybe will match the word *yes*, *no* or *maybe*, but only one of them.

Grouping and Capturing

It is possible to use parentheses to group several patterns into one pattern. There are two types of parentheses: (pattern) and (?:pattern). The first type will capture what was matched inside the parentheses; the second is non-capturing and is only used for grouping.

If the capturing parentheses are used, then the pattern that was matched can be retrieved later in the regular expression. Retrieve a captured value with \1 .. \9. The number refers to the order that the parentheses in the regular expression were

Table 5.2 Repetition symbols

Repetition symbol	Meaning
*	Matches zero or more occurrences of the preceding pattern. This means that the preceding pattern might not be in the pattern or it might appear repeatedly in sequence
?	Matches zero or one occurrence of the preceding pattern. This means that if the pattern is in the string, then it appears once, but that it might not be there at all
+	Matches one or more occurrences. This is like *, except that the pattern must appear at least once
{m,n}	Specifies a range of times that the pattern can repeat. It will appear at least *m* times in sequence, but no more than *n* times. The character ? is the same as {0,1}
{m}	Specifies that the preceding pattern will match exactly *m* times
{m, }	Specifies that the preceding pattern will match at least *m* times. The character * is the same as {0,}. The character + is the same as {1,}

evaluated. Up to nine different patterns can be captured and accessed in a regular expression.

If the string *abyes3* were matched against the pattern [a-z]([a-z]) (yes|no)\d, then \1 would be *b* and \2 would be *yes*.

Ignoring Case

It is possible to ignore the case of the letters that are being tested. For example, if the word *yes* is a valid response, then all variations of case should also be accepted, like *YES* and *Yes*. Entering all the possible combinations could be done like [yY] [eE][sS], but there is an easier way. If the regular expression starts with the symbols (?i), then the case of the response will not be considered. The expression (?i)yes|no is the same as [yY][eE][sS]|[Nn][Oo].

Repetition

Table 5.2 lists special characters and operators that indicate that the previous pattern could be repeated or that the previous pattern is optional.

A group can then have repetition sequences applied to it. For example, (a[0-5] b)+ will match *ab*, *a0b*, *a1b*, *a5ba0ba4b* and many more.

The repetition symbol only applies to the preceding symbol or group. The patterns ab+ and (ab)+ are very different: ab+ matches the letter a followed by one or more letters b; (ab)+ matches one or more occurrences of the two-letter sequence ab.

Examples Explained

It is now possible to explain the meaning of the patterns that were mentioned at the start of this section. Three patterns were introduced: one for a zip code, one for a social security number and one for a user identification number.

A zip code has two formats: five digits or five digits, a hyphen and four more digits. The pattern for the zip code was `\d{5}(?:-\d{4})?`. This indicates that the pattern starts with five digits. The 5 within the braces indicates that the previous pattern should match five times. The previous pattern is a digit. Together, this means that there should be five digits.

A non-capturing parenthesis is used to group the next part of the pattern. The question mark at the end of the closing parenthesis indicates that the entire group is optional. The pattern within the group is a hyphen followed by four digits.

A social security number is nine digits. Typically, the digits are written in two different ways: as nine digits or as three digits, a hyphen, four digits, another hyphen and four more digits.

The pattern for the social security number was `\d{3}(-?)\d{2}\1\d{4}`. The pattern starts with three digits. After the first three digits, there is a capturing group. Whatever matches inside the parentheses will be remembered and can be recalled later in the pattern as `\1`. Inside the group is an optional hyphen.

The next part of the pattern matches two more digits. After the digits is the symbol for the grouped pattern from earlier in the regular expression: `\1`. Whatever was matched earlier must be matched again. If a hyphen was used earlier in the expression, then a hyphen must be used here. If a hyphen was not matched earlier, then a hyphen cannot be entered here. The last part of the pattern matches four more digits.

The use of the capturing group is very powerful. This guarantees that there are either two hyphens in the correct places or there are no hyphens. The placement of the `?` is very important: try to determine what would happen if the pattern used `(-)?` instead of `(-?)`.

An example of a user identification number might be from three to five letters followed by three digits or three to six letters followed by two digits. A simple solution would be to use alternation and define two separate patterns:

```
[a-zA-Z]{3,5}\d{3}|[a-zA-Z]{3,6}\d{2}.
```

However, both of these patterns begin and end with the same sequences, the only difference being the character where letters become digits. By placing an optional character that can be a letter or a digit at this point, the pattern can be rewritten as follows:

```
[a-zA-Z]{3,5}[a-zA-Z0-9]?\d{2}.
```

When writing regular expressions in Java, each `\` character must be written as double backslashes, `\\`. In a traditional regular expression, there would only be one backslash, but in Java there must be two. This is necessary so that the escape sequence is passed to the regular expression and not intercepted by Java. Escape sequences in Java are one backlash character. So it is necessary to escape the escape in order for Java to ignore something like `\d`. If you leave the `\d` in a pattern, Java will complain that it is an illegal escape sequence. By placing a backslash before the escape sequence, Java will translate the \ \ into a single \ and send it to the regular expression.

 Try It

http://bytesizebook.com/book/ch5/TestRegEx
     This servlet tests several strings to see if they match the above patterns. It is also possible to enter a string and test it against any of these patterns.

5.1.2   Hibernate Validation

Required validation is such a common task that someone has gone to all the trouble to create a package that automates the process. This package is named *Hibernate*.
     It is not part of the standard servlet engine, so the following JAR files must be placed in the *lib* directory of the web application in order to enable Hibernate. Download these from http://hibernate.org or from the book's website.

```
hibernate-validator-4.2.0.Final.jar
slf4j-api-1.6.1.jar
validation-api-1.0.0.GA.jar
hibernate-validator-annotation-processor-4.2.0.Final.jar
```

NetBeans 6 and newer versions have a library that contains most of the files that are needed for Hibernate. This library does not contain the latest version of the Hibernate JAR files. In order to guarantee that the examples from the book work properly, it is better to download the JAR files listed above.
     Hibernate can be configured with a separate file or with Java annotations. Java annotations will be used in this book. Java annotations were introduced in the last chapter.

Hibernate Annotations for Validation
Using annotations, it is a simple task to mark some methods as requiring validation. The methods to mark are the accessors. There are annotations to validate objects, strings, numbers and collections. More than one annotation can be placed on an accessor.
     All of these annotations have an optional attribute named message that defines the error message that will be generated if the validation fails. Each annotation has a default message already defined. In many cases, the default message is sufficient, but in other cases, the default message can be confusing. In those instances, it is better to define a more helpful error message.
     The @NotNull annotation can be used to validate any accessor that returns an object. It validates that the accessor does not return null. The default message is 'cannot be null'. Do not use it on properties for primitive types, like *int* and *double*.
     The @Pattern annotation should only be used on string properties. It has a required attribute named regex that is a regular expression. If the complete string

returned from the accessor matches the regular expression, then the property is valid, otherwise it is invalid.

The default message for the `Pattern` annotation is 'must match `regex`', where `regex` is replaced with the actual regular expression. In this case, it is better to define a more helpful message.

By default, the entire string must match the regular expression. If the regular expression only needs to match a substring, then the characters . * can be added to the beginning and end of the pattern. The . * at the start indicates that there can be any other characters before the pattern. The . * at the end means there can be other characters after the pattern.

There are three annotations that can be used with accessors that return numbers: @Min, @Max, @Range. Both the `Min` and `Max` annotations have an attribute named `value`. The `Range` annotation has two attributes named `min` and `max`. All three have the obvious default message. The values for all three attributes can only be integers; it is not possible to set a minimum or maximum of 2.5.

There are annotations for collections that will be covered in Chap. 6.

Annotating a Bean for Validation

In the bean from the last chapter, the only validation that will be needed is that the hobby and aversion cannot be null or empty. Each accessor will have the `Pattern` and `NotNull` annotations. To be non-empty, a test can be made for a non-space character anywhere in the string. The pattern . * \ \ S . * will match any characters, followed by a non-space character, followed by more characters. The characters before and after the non-space character are optional. The double-backslash is needed in the expression because the string is being written in a Java file.

The default error message will be used for the `NotNull` annotation and a new message will be defined for the `Pattern` annotation.

```
@Pattern(regexp="c.*\\S.*", message="cannot be empty")
public String getHobby() {
    return hobby;
}

public void setAversion(String aversion) {
    this.aversion = aversion;
}

@Pattern(regexp="d.*\\S.*", message="cannot be empty")
@NotNull
```

Both of these annotations must be valid in order for the property to be valid. If there is more than one annotation for validation on the accessor, then the validation for the property is the logical AND of the result of each validation.

Place these annotations in the bean directly before the accessor for each property that is being validated.

```
import javax.validation.constraints.NotNull;
import javax.validation.constraints.Pattern;
...
public void setHobby(String hobby) {
    this.hobby = hobby;
}

@NotNull
@Pattern(regexp="c.*\\S.*", message="cannot be empty")
public String getHobby() {
    return hobby;
}

public void setAversion(String aversion) {
    this.aversion = aversion;
}

@Pattern(regexp="d.*\\S.*", message="cannot be empty")
@NotNull
public String getAversion() {
    return aversion;
}
...
```

An additional property will be added to the bean for an integer property. This property will be validated to be in the range of one to seven. Both the Min and Max annotations will be used, so that different error messages can be displayed if the value is too small or too large.

```
@Min(value=1,
    message="must be greater than 1, if this is a hobby.")
@Max(value=7,
    message="cannot be greater than 7. A week only has 7 days.")
```

It is not necessary to validate that the value entered by the user is an integer, since the BeanUtils package will automatically parse the input as an integer. If the user enters a non-integer value, then the property will be given the value of zero. By calling the fillBeanFromRequest method from the last chapter, the parsing of integer and double properties will be done automatically. If possible, omit zero from the valid range, so that bad input from the user can be detected.

Place these annotations in the bean directly before the accessor for the numeric property. Do not use the NotNull annotation on numeric properties.

```
import javax.validation.constraints.Max;
import javax.validation.constraints.Min;
...
protected int daysPerWeek;
@Min(value=1,
     message="must be greater than 1, if this is a hobby.")
@Max(value=7,
     message="cannot be greater than 7. A week only has 7 days.")
public int getDaysPerWeek() {
    return daysPerWeek;
}

public void setDaysPerWeek(int daysPerWeek) {
    this.daysPerWeek = daysPerWeek;
}
...
```

Creating the Error Messages

When using required validation, it is important to be able to display an error message for any data that is invalid. It is a simple task to create an array of these messages using Hibernate.

The class that performs the validations is `Validator`. Only one instance of the validator is needed. It is created from a `ValidatorFactory` object. Only one instance of the validator factory is needed. These objects will be added as static members in the helper base class.

```
protected static final ValidatorFactory validatorFactory
        = Validation.buildDefaultValidatorFactory();
protected static final Validator validator
        = validatorFactory.getValidator();
```

Each message that Hibernate generates is of a type named `Constraint Violation`. This type has properties for the name of the property that generated the error and the message that was created.

An array of validation messages is created by calling the validator's `validate` method and passing it the bean to be validated. The method returns a set of constraint violations.

```
Set<ConstraintViolation<Object>> violations =
        validator.validate(data);
```

For each annotated property in the bean, if the user enters invalid data, then an error message for it will be placed in the set.

5.1.3   Implementing Required Validation

The array of validation messages that is created by Hibernate does not lend itself to easy access in a JSP. In order to find the error message for a property, a linear search would

Fig. 5.2 The error map and
methods are added to the
helper base class

HelperBase
HttpServletRequest request HttpServletResponse response Logger logger Map errorMap
abstract copyFromSession() addHelperToSession() executeButtonMethod() fillBeanFromRequest() setErrors() getErrors() isValid()

Fig. 5.3 A symbol for a
school on a topographic map

need to be performed. It would be better if there were direct access to the errors, so that
the error for a property could be retrieved using the name of the property. To this end, the
interface to the error messages will be enhanced. A map named errorMap will be
created from the array of validation messages. A map can be accessed using a string
instead of an integer. This map will be used by the JSPs to access the error messages.

In order to make the error messages more accessible, the following will be added
to the helper base class:

1. errorMap
2. setErrors()
3. isValid()
4. getErrors()
5. clearErrors()

None of these changes requires knowledge of the specific application, so all the
features will be added to the helper base class in the shared package (Fig. 5.2).
The helper base class for this chapter is named HelperBaseCh5 and can be found
in the Appendix.

java.util.Map

What is a map?

Think of a map of a city: it contains symbols that represent real things. For
instance, on a map, Fig. 5.3 represents a school. It is just a symbol, but if you live
near the school, then seeing the symbol on the map will bring the actual school into

your awareness. There are other symbols for parks, railroad tracks, etc. So, a map is a collection of simple symbols that represent other objects.

In Java, there is a data structure that is called a Map. It is called a Map because it is like a map. In the Map, one object can be associated with another object. Usually, a simple object is associated with a more complicated object. In this way, the more complicated object can be retrieved using the simple object.

We have already seen something similar to a Map; when the controller helper places itself into the session, it is placed into a data structure like a Map.

```
request.getSession().setAttribute("helper", this);
```

The session has a method named setAttribute that associates a simple object with a more complicated object: the string helper is associated with the object this. In the JSP, the more complicated object can be retrieved by using the simpler object.

```
${helper}
```

From a JSP, EL can be used to access the complicated object that was placed into the session. By using the string helper, the EL statement can retrieve the object this.

The Java Map is contained in the package java.util. It has two primary methods: put and get. The method put is used to associate one object, known as a key, with another object, known as a value. The method get is used to retrieve the value by passing it a key.

A Map is an interface: it cannot be instantiated. In order to create a Map, it is necessary to create one of the concrete classes that implement the Map interface. One such class is HashMap: it implements the Map interface using a hash table.

When creating a Map, generics from Java 1.5 should be used. The type of the key and the type of the value should be indicated when the Map is created. This allows values to be retrieved from the Map without casting them and allows for syntax checking.

As an example, a Map will be instantiated, a bean will be instantiated, the bean will be placed in the map and the bean will be retrieved from the map. The Map will have a key that is a string and a value that is a bean.

```
java.util.Map<String, MyBean> myMap
    = new java.util.HashMap<String, MyBean>();
MyBean bean = new MyBean();
myMap.put("theBean", bean);
MyBean anotherBean = myMap.get("theBean");
```

A Map is like a database: a simple key is used to retrieve a complicated value. All of the complicated data can be saved in one collection and can be retrieved easily.

errorMap

A map will be added to the helper base class that will associate the name of a property with the error message for that property. The map can be used for random access into the error messages. By using the map, it will be easy to retrieve one error message at a time in the JSP.

```
java.util.Map<String, String> errorMap =
         new java.util.HashMap<String, String>();
```

This map will be filled from within the setErrors method, described next.

setErrors

The setErrors method sets the validation messages and fills the error map. The first part of the method sets the validation messages, as was explained above. The second half of the method creates the error map by looping through the array of messages and adding an entry to the map. The property name is used as the key to the map and the error message is the value in the map. It is important to clear the old error map and only fill the map if there are validation messages.

```
public void setErrors(Object data) {

    Set<ConstraintViolation<Object>> violations =
            validator.validate(data);

    errorMap.clear();
    if (!violations.isEmpty()) {
        for(ConstraintViolation<Object> msg : violations) {
            PathImpl value = (PathImpl) msg.getPropertyPath();
            errorMap.put((String) value.getLeafNode().getName(),
                         msg.getMessage());
        }
    }
}
```

The ConstraintViolation class has accessors for retrieving the property name and the value for a message. These methods cannot be accessed from a JSP, which is why they are being used to add values to the error map. As will be seen shortly, any map can be accessed easily from a JSP.

isValid

The isValid method will return true if all the validations succeed; otherwise it will return false. This is the method that must be called in order to do required validation. It will set the error messages and the error map, by calling setErrors, and return a **Boolean** value indicating if there are any errors. If the error map is empty, then there are no errors, so the data must be valid.

```
public boolean isValid(Object data) {
    setErrors(data);
    return errorMap.isEmpty();
}
```

getErrors

The getErrors method will return the error map variable so that the errors can be retrieved in a JSP. The errorMap has been added as a member variable to the helper base class. In order for the errors to be accessible from the JSP, there must be an accessor that returns it. This method is only called from JSPs that use EL to retrieve error messages.

```java
public java.util.Map getErrors() {
    return errorMap;
}
```

clearErrors

The clearErrors method will clear all the messages from the error map. Most of the time, this method does not need to be called, since the error map is cleared every time that setErrors is called. This method will be useful when only some of the fields are gathered and validated on one page and the remaining fields are gathered and validated on a second page. Call this method before the second page displays, so the user will not see error messages when the page loads.

```java
public void clearErrors() {
    if (errorMap != null) {
        errorMap.clear();
    }
}
```

Setting the Error Messages

Required validation should be done every time the user enters new data. In our application, this happens when the user clicks the confirm button on the edit page. Required validation should be done in the controller helper in the method that corresponds to the confirm button.

```java
@ButtonMethod(buttonName="confirmButton")
public String confirmMethod() {
    fillBeanFromRequest(data);
    String address;
    if (isValid(data)) {
        address = jspLocation("Confirm.jsp");
    } else {
        address = jspLocation("Edit.jsp");
    }
    return address;
}
```

Call isValid in this method to test if the data is valid and return a different address based on the result. If the data is valid, return the address of the confirm page; otherwise, return the address of the edit page. In this way, the user cannot proceed to the confirm page until the data is valid.

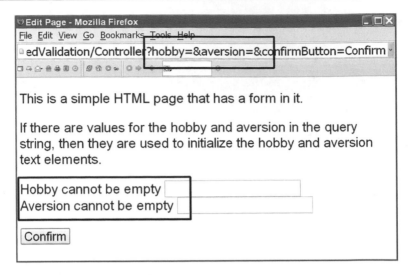

Fig. 5.4 A JSP can access the error in the error map

This is an example where the confirm page should not be in a directory that is accessible by the user. If it were, then a user would be able to call the confirm page directly, thereby circumventing the validation.

The method `isValid` indicates if the data is valid, but it also creates the array of validation messages and the error map. If `isValid` is not called, then the error messages will not be created.

Retrieving Error Messages

The error messages can be retrieved from the edit page using EL. Since there is a method named `getErrors` in the helper, it can be accessed from the JSP as `${helper.errors}`. This returns a map. An individual message in a map can be retrieved by placing the name of the property in quotes inside square brackets as `${helper.errors["hobby"]}` or by using the dot notation as `${helper.errors.hobby}`.

```
Hobby ${helper.errors.hobby}
<input type="text" name="hobby"
                   value="${helper.data.hobby}">
<br>
Aversion ${helper.errors.aversion}
<input type="text" name="aversion"
                   value="${helper.data.aversion}">
<br>
Days per week for practicing hobby ${helper.errors.daysPerWeek}
<input type="text" name="daysPerWeek"
                   value="${helper.data.daysPerWeek}">
```

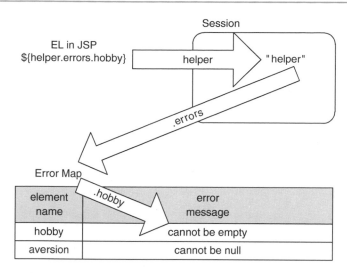

Fig. 5.5   Accessing an error message from a JSP

If isValid is not called, then all of these references to the error messages will return null, which will be displayed as an empty string by EL. If isValid is called and there is an error for the hobby property, then the reference will return the error message for the hobby (Fig. 5.4). The message that is displayed is the message that was defined in the annotation for the hobby accessor in the bean.

Figure 5.5 shows how EL can be used to access an error message from a JSP.

5.2   Application: Required Validation

An application that performs required validation can be created by incorporating the above changes into our application.

Bean
The bean will have the validation annotations added to the accessors for the hobby and aversion.

Helper Base
The helper base class, in the shared package, will have the error map and the methods for the interface to the errors added to it. The complete helper base class for Chap. 5 can be found in the Appendix.

Controller Helper
The controller helper will modify the code in the method for the confirm button. The method will test if the data is valid and will set the address of the next page

accordingly. The controller helper will also set the path of the JSPs to be the same as the folder that contains the controller's class.

Controller
The controller is like the controller from the last chapter.

JSPs
The edit page will have the EL statements added for the error messages. The confirm and process pages do not change.

Location and Mapping
The controller and controller helper will be in the same package. The JSPs will be in the same folder as the controller. Since the controller helper will specify the location of the JSPs, the controller can be mapped to any URL.

  Try It

http://bytesizebook.com/book/ch5/requiredValidation/Controller
    Leave the hobby and aversion empty and you will not be able to proceed beyond the edit page. If one field is empty, then one error message appears. If both fields are empty, then both error messages appear.

5.3   POST Requests

If the user is entering personal data, like a bank account number, there is a small problem with the application: the bank account number will be saved in the URL in the history file of the browser. This means that any other user of the computer could see the user's bank account by browsing through the history file. Now, if the password were also entered, then there is a big problem. There is a simple way to fix this problem.

5.3.1   POST Versus GET

Up to this point, every servlet has used one type of request: GET. This is the default type of request. Whenever a hypertext link is followed or a URL is typed into the location box of a window, then a GET request is made. However, when a button on a form is clicked, there is a choice of request types: GET or POST. The POST request is identical to a GET request, except for the location of the data from the form.

Format of GET Requests
A GET request sends the data from the form via the URL. Until now, every form has used this method to send data to the server. Below is an example of a GET request from the edit page from Chap. 3.

```
GET /?hobby=hiking&confirmButton=Confirm HTTP/1.1
Host: tim.cs.fiu.edu:9000
User-Agent: Mozilla/5.0 (Windows; U; ...
Accept: image/png,image/jpeg,image/gif,text/css,*/*
Accept-Language: en,es;q=0.8,fr;q=0.5,en-us;q=0.3
Accept-Encoding: gzip,deflate
Accept-Charset: ISO-8859-1,utf-8;q=0.7,*;q=0.7
Keep-Alive: 300
Connection: keep-alive
Referer: http://localhost:8085/book/ch5/request_get.jsp
```

Many request headers provide information about the browser that made the request. The data from the form has been placed in the URL in the first line of the request.

Format of POST Requests

A POST request sends the data from the form as part of the request. When POST is used, the data will not appear in the URL, but will be attached to the end of the request.

```
POST / HTTP/1.1
Host: tim.cs.fiu.edu:9000
User-Agent: Mozilla/5.0 (Windows; U; ...
Accept: image/png,image/jpeg,image/gif,text/css,*/*
Accept-Language: en,es;q=0.8,fr;q=0.5,en-us;q=0.3
Accept-Encoding: gzip,deflate
Accept-Charset: ISO-8859-1,utf-8;q=0.7,*;q=0.7
Keep-Alive: 300
Connection: keep-alive
Referer: http://localhost:8085/book/ch5/request_post.jsp
Content-Type: application/x-www-form-urlencoded
Content-Length: 34

hobby=hiking&confirmButton=Confirm
```

The headers are mostly the same as for a GET request, except that there are two additional ones: Content-Type and Content-Length. These extra headers indicate the type and amount of additional content that follows the headers. The data from the form is formatted the same way as in a GET request. The only difference is that the data follows the request headers after a blank line.

What does the word *post* mean? It means *to send*, but it also means *after*. That is a precise definition of a POST request: it posts the data post the request.

Method Attribute

The method of a form can be changed to POST by adding the method attribute to the opening form tag. If the method of a form is set to POST, then all buttons clicked in that form will generate POST requests to the server.

```
<form method="POST" action="Controller">
  <p>
    If there are values for the hobby and aversion
    in the query string, then they are used to
    initialize the hobby and aversion text elements.
  <p>
    Hobby ${helper.errors.hobby}
    <input type="text" name="hobby"
                        value="${helper.data.hobby}">
    <br>
    Aversion ${helper.errors.aversion}
    <input type="text" name="aversion"
                        value="${helper.data.aversion}">
    <br>
    Days per week for practicing hobby ${helper.errors.daysPerWeek}
    <input type="text" name="daysPerWeek"
                        value="${helper.data.daysPerWeek}">
  <p>
    <input type="submit" name="confirmButton"
                         value="Confirm">
</form>
```

This is the same form that was used in the *required validation* example, except that the method has been changed to POST.

Motivation for POST

The only other difference between the GET and the POST is how they are created.
1. There are three ways that a GET request is generated.
   (a) The user types a URL into the browser.
   (b) The user follows a hypertext link.
   (c) The user clicks a button in a form whose method is GET.
2. A POST request is only generated when the user clicks a button on a form whose method is POST.

The fact that POST can only be generated as a result of clicking a button on a form allows the conclusion that if a POST request is made, it cannot be the first access to the application. The first access would be made by following a hypertext link or by typing a URL into the location box of a browser; instead of these techniques use a GET request.

There are several reasons for using POST:

Hides Data
The data from a POST request cannot be seen in the URL. This is useful when the data contains a password.

More Data
There is no limit to the amount of data that can be transmitted using a POST request. A file can be opened to store all the data from a POST request; as more data is received over the network, the data can be written to the file. GET requests always have a limit to the amount of data that can be sent, because there is a limited amount of space for storing the URL.

Controller
doGet() doPost()

ControllerHelper
RequestData data
doGet() getData() copyFromSession() jspLocation() doPost()

Fig. 5.6 The controller and controller helper classes have a doPost method

More Secure
Since the data is not in the URL, the data will not be saved in the browser's history file. Since an unlimited amount of data can be sent, there is no danger of hacking the server by a buffer overrun attack.

Handling POST
In a servlet, there is another method that can be overridden: doPost. It has the exact same signature as the doGet method. It will be called if a form changes its method to POST and submits data to the servlet.

```
public class Controller extends HttpServlet {

    protected void doGet(HttpServletRequest request,
                         HttpServletResponse response)
    throws IOException, ServletException {
      ...
    }

    protected void doPost(HttpServletRequest request,
                          HttpServletResponse response)
    throws IOException, ServletException {
      ...
    }
}
```

A doPost method will be added to the controller, too. Like its doGet method, this will be called from the controller. Since the request and response objects are already declared in the helper base, this method does not need any parameters.

```
public void doPost()
  throws ServletException, java.io.IOException
{
      ...
}
```

Figure 5.6 demonstrates that the controller and controller helper classes will each have a doPost method.

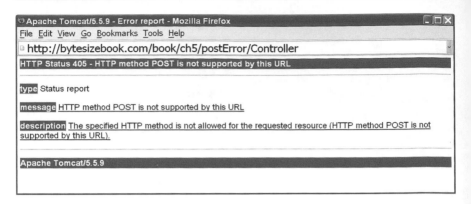

Fig. 5.7 An error will occur if the doPost method is not created

5.4   Application: POST Controller

The *required validation* example will be redesigned using doGet and doPost.
Just as the doGet method was handled, the controller will defer the doPost
method to the controller helper. In the controller helper, these methods will be
designed to perform different tasks: the doPost method will behave exactly like
the doGet method from the previous example; the doGet method will handle all
GET requests like they are the first request to the controller. The JSPs will be modified so that all forms use the POST method.

5.4.1 Controller: POST Controller

A new method will be added to the controller: doPost. It has the exact same signature as the doGet method. To be consistent with how the doGet method is
handled, the controller will defer the doPost to the controller helper.

```
protected void doPost(HttpServletRequest request,
                      HttpServletResponse response)
throws IOException, ServletException {
    ControllerHelper helper =
        new ControllerHelper(this, request, response);
    helper.doPost();
}
```

If a controller does not handle the doPost method, then an error will be generated
whenever a POST request is made (Fig. 5.7).

A similar error would occur if a GET request was made and there was not a doGet method.

5.4.2   ControllerHelper: POST Controller

If all the forms in an application use the POST method, then the doGet and doPost methods can perform different tasks in the web application. The doGet method can be used to show the welcome page only. Such a technique could be used if the user had to log into the site using a username and password. The doPost method can be used to process the user's data that has been entered via a form. Since the only way that a POST request can be made is from a form, the developer can assume that the user has entered data already.

doPost

The doPost method will perform all the same tasks as the previous doGet method: check for data in the session; execute the method for the button; forward to the next JSP. Except for the name of the method, this is identical to the previous doGet method.

```
public void doPost()
   throws ServletException, java.io.IOException
{
   addHelperToSession("helper", SessionData.READ);

   String address = executeButtonMethod();

   request.getRequestDispatcher(address)
      .forward(request, response);
}
```

doGet

The doGet method will assume this is the first access to the application: it will **not** check if there is previous data in the session when placing the bean in the session, and it will **always** display the edit page.

Since this is being treated as a first request to the application, the data in the session should be ignored. In the call to addHelperToSession, set the second parameter to SessionData.IGNORE; the current controller helper will be added to the session, but any previous data will not be read from the session.

```
public void doGet()
  throws ServletException, java.io.IOException
{
  addHelperToSession("helper", SessionData.IGNORE);

  String address = editMethod();

  request.getRequestDispatcher(address)
      .forward(request, response);
}
```

Many websites will give the user the opportunity to start over. Whenever I book an airline reservation, I will look for several different options. The site that I use allows me to click a button to start over. When I do that, all of the previous flight information that I obtained is removed, so that I can begin a new search.

The simplest way to implement such a feature is to use a GET request when all the old information should be ignored and to use a POST request when information should be carried from request to request.

5.4.3   JSPs: Updating the JSPs with POST

The final change to be made is to change all the form elements in the JSPs so that they use the POST method.

```
<form method="POST" action="Controller">
```

It is important that all of the form tags use the POST method. If one is omitted, then the user will be redirected to the edit page, regardless of the button that is clicked. The only time a form should use the GET method is when all the old data should be ignored and new data is to be entered into the edit page.

 Try It

http://bytesizebook.com/book/ch5/postServlet/Controller

Note that as you navigate from page to page, the URL does not change but the data is still transmitted to each page. Instead of placing the data in the URL, like a GET request does, the POST request adds it to the end of the request from the browser.

Next, instead of clicking a button, click in the URL window in the browser and hit the enter key: you will always be taken to the edit page and the old data will be destroyed.

5.5   Saving a Bean to a Database

The next feature that will be added to the servlet engine will be the ability to save a bean to a relational database. The package that will be used is Hibernate. We have already seen how Hibernate can be used to validate input; now it will be used to save data to a database.

Structured Query Language (SQL) is a standard language for accessing a relational database. The details of SQL are beyond the scope of this book, so this would seem to indicate that accessing a relational database from our web application would not be possible. However, there is Hibernate! The beauty of Hibernate is that a relational database that uses SQL can be accessed without learning SQL.

Hibernate focuses on the data. If a bean is sent to Hibernate, it will generate all the SQL statements to save the bean in the database. Hibernate can also generate all the SQL for creating the database tables from a bean. Hibernate can also take a bean and update it in the database or remove it entirely. By creating a bean in a web application, most of the work of saving it to a database can be handled by Hibernate without knowing one statement of SQL.

5.5.1   Hibernate JAR Files

Saving data to a database is a complex process, so it stands to reason that a lot of JAR files will need to be added to the servlet engine in order to enable this feature. As of Hibernate 3.6.7, the JAR files that are needed at runtime are listed in Table 5.3. With the Hibernate distribution, there are optional JAR files for the cache, SAX parser, etc. View the README file in the *lib* directory of the Hibernate distribution for more information. Hibernate can be downloaded from *http://hibernate.org*. All of the JAR files listed below can also be obtained from *http://bytesizebook.com*.

From Table 5.3, the following have already been added for features that were used in Chap. 4:

commons-collections-3.2.1.jar
commons-logging-1.1.1.jar
log4j-1.2.16.jar
slf4j-api-1.6.1.jar

In addition to these files, it is also necessary to have a JAR file for the type of database that will be accessed. In this book, we will use the following JAR for MySQL:

mysql-connector-java-5.0.8-bi.n.jar

Table 5.3 JAR files needed for Hibernate

antlr-2.7.6.jar	c3p0-0.9.0.jar
cglib-2.2.jar	commons-logging-1.1.1.jar
commons-collections-3.2.1.jar	
dom4j-1.6.1.jar	hibernate3.jar
hibernate-jpa-2.0-api-1.0.1.Final.jar	javassist.jar
jdbc2_0-stdext.jar	jta-1.1.jar
log4j-1.2.16.jar	slf4j-api-1.6.1.jar

A short section in the Appendix contains instructions on how to log onto a MySQL server and view the tables that Hibernate creates. While it is not necessary to do this, it is informative to see all the work that Hibernate is doing.

ZIP Files

The JAR files for all the web applications in the book have been placed into two ZIP files that can be downloaded from *http://bytesizebook.com*. One file contains the Hibernate-related JAR files. The other file contains the non-Hibernate-related JAR files. Both JAR files should be unpacked in the *lib* directory of the web application.

1. http://bytesizebook.com/jar/hibernate.zip
2. http://bytesizebook.com/jar/non-hibernate.zip

5.5.2 Hibernate Persistence: Configuration

It is also necessary to configure Hibernate. There are several options for configuring Hibernate, which can be used individually or they can be combined. Two of the options are to use Java or to use XML.

1. Each of the configuration options can be defined inside a Java program. For the first example, this is the technique that will be used, so that none of the details for Hibernate are hidden in some other configuration file.
2. An XML file can be created. Each property has its own XML tag. Such a file of properties is placed in the class path of the web application and the file will be read automatically when Hibernate is configured.

Programmatic Configuration

One common mistake when using configuration files is placing them in the wrong location. When this happens, the configuration could be correct, but the program cannot find the file. To a novice, it will look like the configuration is wrong. For this reason, the first example will configure Hibernate in the controller helper, where there is no possible problem of finding the configuration directives. Once the initialisation works, it will be a simple matter to move the code into a separate configuration file.

There is a Java class named `Properties` that implements the `Map` interface. The key and value must be strings. This class is used to set the configuration for Hibernate.

Fig. 5.8 The `Hibernate`
`Helper` class

HibernateHelper
static closeFactory() static createTable() static getFactory() static getListData() static initSessionFactory() static updateDb()

The following properties are used to configure Hibernate. The first set will be the same for everyone connecting to the MySQL database. The second set of properties contain the URL, username and password for accessing the database. These must be updated with your information.

```
Properties props = new Properties();
props.setProperty("hibernate.dialect",
        "org.hibernate.dialect.MySQLDialect");
props.setProperty("hibernate.connection.driver_class",
        "com.mysql.jdbc.Driver");
props.setProperty("hibernate.c3p0.min_size", "1");
props.setProperty("hibernate.c3p0.max_size", "5");
props.setProperty("hibernate.c3p0.timeout", "300");
props.setProperty("hibernate.c3p0.max_statements",
        "50");
props.setProperty("hibernate.c3p0.idle_test_period",
        "300");

props.setProperty("hibernate.connection.url",
        "jdbc:mysql://SERVER:PORT/DATABASE");
props.setProperty("hibernate.connection.username",
        "USERNAME");
props.setProperty("hibernate.connection.password",
        "PASSWORD");
```

These statements will be placed in a method named `initHibernate` in the controller helper.

HibernateHelper Class

There are many methods that are used to access Hibernate. All of these methods have been encapsulated into a helper class named `HibernateHelper` (Fig. 5.8). The complete listing of this class is in the Appendix. There are methods for initialising, closing, saving, deleting, etc. This helper class can be downloaded from *http://bytesizebook.com*. It should be placed into a package named `shared`.

These methods are exactly the same for all web applications, except for the names of the tables that are accessed. A helper class has been created that contains all of these methods. Since they are the same for all web applications, they have been created as static methods. Whenever a method is to be called that uses Hibernate, the method will be in the Hibernate helper class.

The method for initialising Hibernate is `initSessionFactory`. It has two parameters: the initialisation properties and the class object for the bean. Since these two parameters may change from web application to web application, the call to this method should be made from the controller helper.

```
HibernateHelper.initSessionFactory(
        props,
        RequestDataPersistent.class);
```

If there are multiple tables in the servlet, they can all be sent to the method by adding a new argument for each.

```
initSessionFactory(props,
                    table1.class,
                    table2.class,
                    table3.class);
```

The Hibernate helper class maintains a list of database tables that can be accessed by Hibernate. Whenever `initSessionFactory` is called, the class objects are added to the list if they are not already in it. If one is added to the list, then Hibernate is closed and reinitialised. If the class objects are already in the list, then Hibernate already has the ability to access them, so no initialisation needs to be done.

If there is an error when initialising the session factory, then a `Hibernate Exception` will be thrown. This is a runtime exception, so a `try ... catch` block is not needed.

Creating the SQL Tables

Hibernate has the ability to create a table in the database from your bean. This is amazing: no SQL needs to be coded in order to create the table. This is controlled by an additional property.

Whenever the tables are recreated, the data in them is erased. Therefore, this property should usually not be included, so that the data in the database does not get erased. It should only be added when the structure of the bean has changed, so that the table will be recreated to match the new structure. However, adding statements to the controller, recompiling, removing statements and recompiling is a recipe for a disaster. There are three solutions for avoiding this unhappy situation.

1. Manually create the database tables in MySQL before running the servlet the first time.
2. Add the property to a separate XML file, when the tables need to be created. The next time the servlet engine starts, it will read the value of this property from the file and create the tables. Remove the property from the XML file after the servlet is running.

3. Add an initialisation parameter to the *web.xml* file and read it during servlet initialisation. Conditionally include the property whenever the initialisation parameter is true.

I prefer the third choice: use the *web.xml* file. By using the *web.xml* file, the initialisation parameter is written in code, so there is no question of forgetting its syntax. It is easy to remember the syntax of the parameter in the *web.xml* file: it will be either `true` or `false`.

Initialisation Parameter in web.xml

An initialisation parameter named `create` will be added to the `servlet` tag in the *web.xml* file (Listing 5.1). It will have a value of `true` or `false`. If the value is set to `true`, then the controller will add the property for creating the database tables when Hibernate is configured. All other values will be interpreted to mean that the tables should not be created.

```
<servlet>
  <servlet-name>PersistentController</servlet-name>
  <servlet-class>ch5.persistentData.Controller</servlet-class>
  <init-param>
    <param-name>create</param-name>
    <param-value>false</param-value>
  </init-param>
</servlet>
<servlet-mapping>
  <servlet-name>PersistentController</servlet-name>
  <url-pattern>/ch5/persistentData/Controller</url-pattern>
</servlet-mapping>
```

Listing 5.1   The servlet definition and mapping for the persistent controller

Reading Initialisation Parameters

The value of an initialisation parameter is retrieved from a servlet using the `get-InitParameter` method of the servlet. This method returns a string, so the value must be cast to **Boolean** in order to store it in a variable.

```
boolean create =
        Boolean.parseBoolean(servlet.getInitParameter("create"));
```

If the `create` parameter in the *web.xml* is set to `true`, then the Boolean variable will be set to `true`. If the parameter does not exist or has any value except `true`, then the variable will be set to `false`.

Conditionally Creating the Tables

After reading the initialisation parameter from the *web.xml* file, the Boolean variable can be used to conditionally call a method from the Hibernate helper that will create the table. In this method, the additional property for creating the table will be added to the other properties that initialise Hibernate. The developer does not need to remember what the property is. By including a `true` value in the *web.xml* file, the table will be created. The method that creates the table has the exact same parameters as the `initSessionFactory` method.

```
if (create) {
    HibernateHelper.createTable(
            props,
            RequestDataPersistent.class);
}
```

If there is an error when initialising the session factory, then a `Hibernate Exception` will be thrown. This is a runtime exception, so a `try ... catch` block is not needed.

Set the initialisation parameter to `true` and restart the web application. The tables will be recreated. Afterwards, reset the parameter to `false`, so that the next time the web application is restarted, the tables will not be recreated and the new data will not be lost.

If there are multiple tables in the servlet that need to be created, they can all be sent to the method by adding a new argument for each class.

```
createTable(props,
            table1.class,
            table2.class,
            table3.class);
```

Initialising Hibernate in the Controller Helper

The controller helper will declare a public method that encapsulates all the commands to initialise Hibernate: setting the necessary properties, conditionally creating the table and calling the `initSessionFactory` method.

The method will be declared as static so it can be called without creating an instance of the controller helper. Since this is a static method, it does not have access to the servlet member variable in the controller helper; therefore, it will have the servlet passed as a parameter, so it can access the initialisation parameters for the servlet.

The method will read a **Boolean** initialisation parameter for the servlet. The Boolean parameter indicates whether the tables should be created in the database.

```
static public void initHibernate(HttpServlet servlet) {
    Properties props = new Properties();
    props.setProperty("hibernate.dialect",
            "org.hibernate.dialect.MySQLDialect");
    props.setProperty("hibernate.connection.driver_class",
            "com.mysql.jdbc.Driver");
    props.setProperty("hibernate.c3p0.min_size", "1");
    props.setProperty("hibernate.c3p0.max_size", "5");
    props.setProperty("hibernate.c3p0.timeout", "300");
    props.setProperty("hibernate.c3p0.max_statements",
            "50");
    props.setProperty("hibernate.c3p0.idle_test_period",
            "300");

    props.setProperty("hibernate.connection.url",
            "jdbc:mysql://SERVER:PORT/DATABASE");
    props.setProperty("hibernate.connection.username",
            "USERNAME");
    props.setProperty("hibernate.connection.password",
            "PASSWORD");

    boolean create =
            Boolean.parseBoolean(servlet.getInitParameter("create"));
    if (create) {
        HibernateHelper.createTable(
                props,
                RequestDataPersistent.class);
    }

    HibernateHelper.initSessionFactory(
            props,
            RequestDataPersistent.class);
}
```

Using init in the Controller

Hibernate is initialised with many properties, like username and password. These properties should be set once, when the servlet is first loaded into memory. Recall from the *Log4j* servlet in Chap. 4 that the init method in a servlet is executed when it is loaded into memory. An init method will be added to the controller (Fig. 5.9).

In the method, call the static initHibernate method from the controller helper. Pass the current servlet as a parameter to the method, so the helper has access to the initialisation parameters for the servlet. By calling the method from init, the initialisation will only occur once.

Since the method that initialises Hibernate was declared as a static method in the controller helper, it can be called from the controller without having to instantiate a controller helper object.

```
public void init() {
    ControllerHelper.initHibernate(this);
}
```

Fig. 5.9 An init method is
added to the controller

Controller
doGet() doPost() init()

5.5.3   Closing Hibernate

Closing Hibernate is imperative. If the web application closes without releasing the
resources that Hibernate uses, there will be a memory leak in the servlet engine. The
`closeFactory` method has been added to the Hibernate helper class to close
Hibernate.

```
static public void closeFactory() {
      ...
}
```

The difficult part is to know when to call this method. Each servlet in the web
application uses the same static helper class to make connections to the database
server. If one servlet closes Hibernate, this means that it will be closed for all
servlets.

Since the Hibernate helper class only has static members and methods, the class
will exist until the web application is stopped. Static variables will not be garbage
collected until the class is removed from memory. There is no method that is called
when a class is removed from memory. However, it is possible to detect when the
web application is stopped.

There is an interface named `ServletContextListener` that has two methods that will be called when the web application starts and when the web application
stops. By adding a class to the web application that implements the interface and
configuring the *web.xml* file to call this class, Hibernate can be closed when the web
application is stopped.

This is also the place for the web application to close any other resources that it
is using. In addition to closing Hibernate, the web application should deregister the
SQL drivers it is using.

```
try {
  Enumeration<Driver> enumer = DriverManager.getDrivers();
  while (enumer.hasMoreElements()) {
    DriverManager.deregisterDriver(enumer.nextElement());
  }
} catch (java.sql.SQLException se) {
  se.printStackTrace();
}
```

Servlet Context Listener

The context listener interface only has two methods: one that is called when the web application starts and one that is called when the web application stops. Define a class that implements this interface. There is nothing to do when the web application starts, but close Hibernate when the web application stops. By closing Hibernate when the web application stops, all the resources for Hibernate will be released.

```java
package shared;

import java.sql.Driver;
import java.sql.DriverManager;
import java.util.Enumeration;
import javax.servlet.ServletContextEvent;
import javax.servlet.ServletContextListener;
import javax.servlet.annotation.WebListener;

@WebListener
public class WebappListener implements ServletContextListener {
    public void contextInitialized(ServletContextEvent sce)
    {}

    public void contextDestroyed(ServletContextEvent sce)
    {
        try {
            Enumeration<Driver> enumer = DriverManager.getDrivers();
            while (enumer.hasMoreElements()) {
                DriverManager.deregisterDriver(enumer.nextElement());
            }
        } catch (java.sql.SQLException se) {
            se.printStackTrace();
        }
        shared.HibernateHelper.closeFactory();
    }
}
```

Calling the Listener

The context listener must be called by the servlet engine when the web application starts. This is done by adding some tags to the *web.xml* file. The only parameter that is needed is the class for the above listener class.

```xml
<listener>
    <listener-class>shared.WebappListener</listener-class>
</listener>
```

In the Java Servlet 3.0 specification, the *WebListener* annotation can be placed on the listener class. The annotation replaces the need for the listener tag in the *web.xml* file.

```java
@WebListener
public class WebappListener implements ServletContextListener {
```

Fig. 5.10 A table has columns
and rows

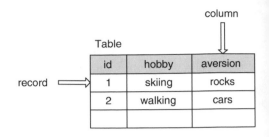

When the web application starts, it will load the listener class into memory and call the `contextInitialized` method. The listener class will remain in memory as long as the web application is running. When the web application receives a command to stop, it will first call the `contextDestroyed` method.

5.5.4   Persistent Annotations

Hibernate operates through beans. Hibernate will create the table in the database based on the structure of the bean. Most of the information that Hibernate needs can be derived from the standard structure of the bean, but there are a few details that have to be configured. These additional details could be added to a separate configuration file, but Hibernate supports annotations from Java 1.5. By using annotations, the additional configuration parameters can be placed in the bean class. The advantage of this is that the configuration information is physically located next to what it modifies.

A table in a database is organised in columns, just like a table in a spreadsheet. By default, a column will be created for each property that is in the bean. Each row in the table represents all the data for one bean object (Fig. 5.10).

The tables that are based upon a bean need a column that identifies each row uniquely. In other words, the value that is stored in that column is different for each row in the table. For instance, a student ID or a bank account number would be examples of such a column. This column is known as a *primary key*.

Once the primary key for a row has been created, it is important that it never changes. For this reason, it is better to create a separate column that has nothing to do with the data that is being entered by the user. Most relational databases have the ability to generate a primary key automatically. By allowing the database to manage the primary key, there is never a concern that two rows in the database will have the same value for the primary key. Hibernate has annotations for declaring the primary key.

There are four annotations that are used to give Hibernate additional information about the structure of the table that it creates for the bean.

1. @Entity
2. @Id
3. @GeneratedValue
4. @Transient

Creating a Separate Table

The @Entity annotation precedes the definition of the bean class. It indicates that the class will be represented in the database as a separate table. The name of the table in the database will be the same as the name of the bean class. Although it is not required for the examples in this book, it is recommended that an entity class implements the java.io.serializable interface. There are no methods to define for this interface.

```
...
import javax.persistence.Entity;
...
@Entity
public class RequestDataPersistent
        implements Serializable
```

This annotation is located in the javax.persistence package.

Creating a Primary Key

For the primary key, add a Long field with mutators and accessors. Use the @Id annotation to mark it as the primary key. The mutator is made private to limit how the field is modified. Only the database should change the value of this field.

Our examples will not always have a primary key like an account number or student ID, so we will have the database manage the field. The database will create a unique value for each new row that is added to the table; this is controlled with the @GeneratedValue annotation.

```
import javax.persistence.Id;
import javax.persistence.GeneratedValue;
...
protected Long id;

@Id
@GeneratedValue
public Long getId() { return id; }

private void setId(Long id) { this.id = id; }
...
```

The @GeneratedValue annotation is telling the database to assign numbers to the ID and to be sure that they are unique. This precedes the accessor for the primary key of the table. It indicates that the database will generate the primary key when a row is added to the database.

Both of these annotations are located in the javax.persistence package.

PersistentBase Class

All of the beans that are marked with the Entity annotation should have a primary key. For all such examples in this book, the primary key will be generated by the database, by inserting the above code into the bean. As a convenience, there is a base class named `PersistentBase` that contains this annotated property. Instead of typing the above code into the bean, if the bean extends this class, then the primary key will be created for it.

```
...
@Entity
public class RequestDataPersistent
        extends shared.PersistentBase
        implements Serializable
...
```

A bean should not define a primary key and implement persistentBase. The data will not be saved properly if both are defined.

Transient Fields

By default, every property in the bean that has an accessor will have a column created for it in the database table. There will be situations where a property does not need to be saved in the database. In such cases, if the property is preceded by the @ `Transient` annotation, then Hibernate will not create a column in the table for the property and will ignore the property when the bean is saved to the table.

Any method name that begins with *is* or *get* and has no parameters is considered an accessor, and Hibernate will try to create a column for it and try to save it to the database.

As an example of a field that does not need to be saved in the table, consider the `isValidHobby` method from the *default validation* example in Chap. 3. This is an accessor, since it begins with *is* and has no parameters, but it should not be saved to the database. Hopefully, the only data that is saved to the database is valid. If this method is in a bean that is being saved to a database, then it should be marked as transient.

```
...
import javax.persistence.Transient
...
@Transient
public boolean isValidHobby() {
   return hobby != null && !hobby.trim().equals("");
}
```

This annotation is located in the `javax.persistence` package.

5.5.5   Accessing the Database

Hibernate uses sessions and transactions to manage the access to the database. A session in Hibernate is used to connect to the database. Sessions are obtained from the session factory that was created in `initSessionFactory`. A transaction is used to update data in the database.

In its simplest format, the way that the database is accessed is to obtain a session, obtain a transaction, do the work in the database, send the transaction to the database and close the session. The following code saves a bean to the database.

```
Session session = null;
try {
    session = sessionFactory.openSession();
    Transaction tx = session.beginTransaction();

    session.saveOrUpdate(obj);

    tx.commit();
} finally {
    if (session != null) {
        session.close();
    }
}
```

The details of the session and transaction are the same, regardless of the type of work that is being done in the database: retrieving, saving, deleting. Retrieving and saving data will be covered in this chapter; deleting data will be covered in Chap. 7.

There are separate helper methods in the Hibernate helper class that manage the session for each operation that accesses the database: `getListData`, `updateDB`, `removeDB`. The details of each are similar to the above code and can be found in the listing of the Hibernate helper class in the Appendix. The methods `getListData` and `updateDB` will be covered in this chapter. The method `removeDB` will be covered in Chap. 7.

There may be situations where the helper methods in the Hibernate helper class are too limiting. For these situations, there is an accessor for the session factory in the Hibernate helper class. Any database operations can be handled from within a block of code such as the following:

```
Session session;
try {
    session = HibernateHelper.getFactory();
    Transaction tx = session.beginTransaction();

    operation1();
    operation2();
    operation3();

    tx.commit();
} finally {
    session.close();
}
```

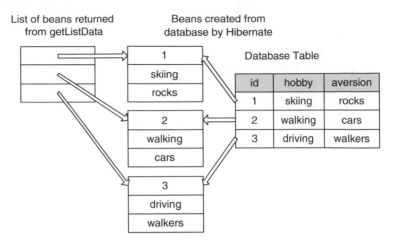

Fig. 5.11 A collection of beans is created by Hibernate

Retrieving Data

Data is retrieved from a table using the `getListData` method. The method returns a collection of beans. Each bean contains the data from one row in the database table (Fig. 5.11). Hibernate generates a bean for each row in the database and places them into a collection. This collection is returned from the method.

This method is overloaded several times in the Hibernate helper class. One version accepts a parameter that is the class object for the bean class. Since this method will be called from the controller helper, the simplest way to retrieve the class object of the bean is from the bean itself: `data.getClass()`.

```
java.util.List list =
          HibernateHelper.getListData(data.getClass());
```

This call to the method returns a list of beans. Each bean in the list represents a row from the table.

Saving Data

The method to save data to the database is `updateDB`, which has a parameter that is the bean containing the data to save. Since this will be called from the controller helper, the bean object to save will be named `data`.

```
HibernateHelper.updateDB(data);
```

Hibernate will determine the type of the bean by using reflection. From the type of the bean, Hibernate will determine the name of the table in the database.

If the bean had been retrieved from the database, then it will replace the data that is in the database. If the bean was not retrieved from the database, then it will be added to the database, even if there is duplicate data in the database. As long as the primary key is null, the bean will be added as a new row in the table. Hibernate uses the primary key to determine if a row has been saved to the database. This is a major reason for allowing Hibernate to manage the primary key.

5.5.6   Making Data Available

Once the data has been retrieved from the database, it needs to be displayed in a JSP. Whether the collection of beans that is retrieved from the database contains all the rows or just some of the rows, the collection must be made available for JSPs, and the JSPs must be able to display this data in a readable format.

Placing Data in the Request

The getListData method is used to retrieve data from the database; however, the data will not be available to the JSPs. So far, the only way that an object will be accessible from a JSP is to add it to the session or to add an accessor for it in the controller helper.

The list of rows from the database should not be added to the controller helper as a member variable. Once it is in the controller helper, it would be passed from request to request via the session. This is a waste of resources, since the data is already saved in the database.

The list of rows should not be added directly to the session for the same reason. Furthermore, objects that have been retrieved from the database and then stored directly in the session may cause thread death in the web application.

There is a third way to make an object accessible in a JSP. Arbitrary objects can be placed in the request object by the controller helper and retrieved by the JSPs, just like the session object. However, the request object is destroyed when the request is finished. This will avoid the problem of thread death.

Objects are added to the request object similarly to how they are added to the session. Set an attribute in the request object for the collection that was retrieved from the call to getListData.

```
java.util.List list =
        HibernateHelper.getListData(data.getClass());
request.setAttribute("database", list);
```

Displaying Data in the JSP

Request attributes are retrieved in the JSP the same way that session attributes are retrieved. If the attribute was set with the name *database*, then it can be retrieved using EL as ${database}. Note that this is not part of the helper: it is a separate object stored in the request.

The only complication is that this is a collection of data and a loop will be needed to access all the individual beans in the collection. There are two ways that loops can be added to a JSP: using Java and using HTML. In order to separate Java coding from HTML presentation as much as possible, the ability to loop will be added to the JSP using custom HTML tags.

It is a good design principle to reduce the amount of Java code that is exposed in a JSP. The chief justification is so that a nonprogrammer could maintain the JSPs. If there is Java code embedded in a JSP, then there is always the possibility of an exception. If the JSP throws an exception, then a stack trace will be displayed to the user. Such a page would not instill much confidence in your site by the user. The less Java code that is being maintained by a nonprogrammer means the less chance of seeing a stack trace.

Another strong reason for not placing Java code in a JSP is so that the application logic is not scattered amongst many different files. When it is time to change the logic of an application, it is preferable to have the code in as few different files as possible.

Looping in a JSP

Using HTML to loop in a JSP means that custom HTML tags must be created. Wouldn't it be nice if someone would create a package of custom tags that would allow looping in a JSP?

There is a package of custom tags that is known as the *Java Standard Template Library* (JSTL). To install the library, add the following jar files to the *lib* directory of the web application.

```
jstl.jar
standard.jar
```

Add JSTL to a JSP by adding the following tag. It is a directive that informs the JSP that additional HTML tags will be used and that they are defined at the given location. It also indicates that the new HTML tags will be preceded by a given prefix: core. Only include it once in each JSP that uses it, no matter how many JSTL tags are used in the page. Place the taglib statement before any of its tags are used.

```
<%@ taglib uri="http://java.sun.com/jsp/jstl/core"
      prefix="core" %>
```

JSTL adds HTML tags that can be used in JSPs. These tags allow for looping and conditional testing without having to expose Java code to the JSP.

One of these tags is a forEach tag. It has two parameters that are similar to a for statement in Java 1.5. The first parameter is named var and it represents the loop control variable. The second parameter is named items and is the collection that is being looped through. On each pass through the loop, the var becomes the next element in the items collection. The value of the control variable can be retrieved in the body of the tag using EL.

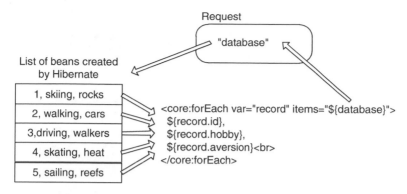

Fig. 5.12 Accessing each row from the database from a JSP

```
<core:forEach var="control" items="collection">
    do something with ${control}
</core:forEach>
```

Looping Through the Database
In the JSP, use a JSTL loop to access all the rows in the database and display the details. On each pass through the loop, the var will be another bean that was retrieved from the database (Fig. 5.12).

Every public accessor in the bean can be accessed from a JSP using EL. The bean has three public accessors: getId, getHobby and getAversion. If the name of the loop control variable is *row*, then these can be accessed using EL of ${row.id}, ${row.hobby} and ${row.aversion}.

```
<core:forEach var="row" items="${database}">
    ${row.id},
    ${row.hobby},
    ${row.aversion},
    ${row.daysPerWeek}<br>
</core:forEach>
```

The above statement will display all the data from the database. Each row will appear on its own line with its id, hobby and aversion displayed.

5.5.7   Data Persistence in Hibernate

There are several methods in Hibernate that can be used to save data to the database: save, update, saveOrUpdate. The save method will always write a new row to the database. The update method will only work if the bean was previously saved

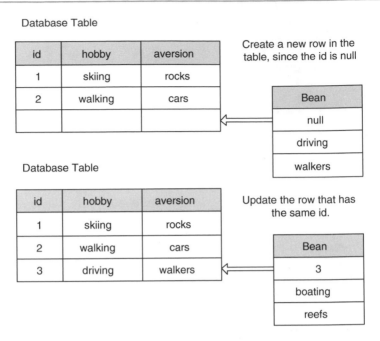

Fig. 5.13 Data persistence depends on the primary key

to the database, in which case, the data in the bean will replace the data in the database. The third method is a combination of these two. If the bean has not been saved previously, then it will be added to the database; otherwise, it will update the bean in the database.

The method that is used by the `updateDB` method in Hibernate helper is the `saveOrUpdate` method. If a bean has already been saved in the database, then any changes to this bean will update the row in the database, instead of adding a duplicate row.

By placing such a bean in the session, it means that all JSPs will be accessing and modifying the data that was retrieved from the database. When the `updateDB` method is called, the new data will replace the data that is in the database.

Reading Session Data

If the user accesses the application via a GET request, then the old data from the session will be discarded. The new data will not have its primary key set, since it has never been saved to the database. Even if the data that the user enters is identical to the data in the database, the bean will be added in a new row in the database (Fig. 5.13).

If the user accesses the application via a POST request, then the old data from the session will replace the data that is in the current helper. If the old data was saved to the database, then its primary key was set by Hibernate. This means that when the bean is saved to the database again, it will replace the data that is already in the database.

In the `Post Servlet` application, there is a distinction between GET and POST requests. GET requests do not read data from the session; POST requests do. An additional form can be added to a JSP that allows the user to initiate a GET request, thereby starting the application from the beginning.

```
<form method="GET" action="Controller">
  <p>
  <input type="submit" name="editButton"
                       value="New">
</form>
```

Contrast this form with the form that is already in the process page. This form uses POST and allows the user to edit the current data.

```
<form method="POST" action="Controller">
  <p>
  <input type="submit" name="editButton"
                       value="Edit">
</form>
```

Both buttons have the same name; they only have different words on the button. The big difference is the type of the request that the forms use. With the GET request, the session will not be read, so a new bean will be used to retrieve the user's data. With the POST request, the old bean will be copied into the current application. The effect of this is that when the bean is saved to the database, it will replace the data that was already saved in the database.

5.6   Application: Persistent Data

The post controller example can be extended to save data to the database. The following modifications need to be made:
1. Add the Hibernate JAR files to the *lib* directory of the web application.
2. Initialise Hibernate when the controller is loaded into memory.
3. Add the `WebappListener` class to the `shared` package.
4. Add the statements to the *web.xml* file for starting the listener class or annotate the listener class with *WebListener*.
5. Annotate the bean class as an entity.
6. Add an Id field to the bean, by extending it from `PersistentBase`.
7. If there are any properties in the bean that do not need to be saved, mark them as transient.
8. Add the statements to the *web.xml* file for the servlet definition and servlet mapping (do not use the `WebServlet` annotation); add the Hibernate initialisation parameter for creating the database tables to the servlet tag.

9. Add the initHibernate method to the controller helper.
10. In the process method of the controller helper, validate the data again, save the data and add the list of beans from the database to the request object.
11. In the process page, display the data from the database using EL.

5.6.1 Controller: Persistent Data

The details of the init method have already been covered. All that is left is to show the skeleton of the controller to see where this method belongs.

```
package ch5.persistentData;

import java.io.IOException;
import javax.servlet.ServletException;
import javax.servlet.http.HttpServlet;
import javax.servlet.http.HttpServletRequest;
import javax.servlet.http.HttpServletResponse;

public class Controller extends HttpServlet {

    @Override
    public void init() {
        ...
    }

    @Override
    protected void doGet(HttpServletRequest request,
            HttpServletResponse response)
            throws IOException, ServletException {
        ...
    }

    @Override
    protected void doPost(HttpServletRequest request,
            HttpServletResponse response)
            throws IOException, ServletException {
        ...
    }
}
```

Since the servlet has the create initialisation parameter, it will be configured using the *web.xml* file. The *web.xml* from Listing 5.1 contains the servlet definition, servlet mapping and initialisation parameter. To change whether the database table is created, edit the *web.xml* file, then restart the web application. The new value will be read when the web application is reloaded. If the value is true, then all the old data will be erased and the database table will be recreated.

5.6.2   ControllerHelper: Persistent Data

The other steps above have been covered in detail, except for modifying the controller helper so that it writes to the database. The data will be saved to the database when the user presses the process button. The data does not need to be written until this point, because the user has not confirmed that the data is correct.

Be sure to validate the data before it is written to the database. This may seem redundant, but the data is being saved in the session. Sessions expire after a period of inactivity. It is possible that the user entered all the data and then pressed the process button many hours later. In this case, the data would be lost and an empty bean would be added to the database. To avoid this, validate again; if the data is invalid, route the user to an expiration page.

The data retrieved from the database will be made available for JSPs, so it is added to the request object. It is essential that the database is added to the request object and not the session object.

Modify the method that is associated with the process button so that it validates the data, writes to the database and makes the list of data available to the JSPs.

```
@ButtonMethod(buttonName = "processButton")
public String processMethod() {
    if (!isValid(data)) {
        return jspLocation("Expired.jsp");
    }
    HibernateHelper.updateDB(data);
    java.util.List list =
            HibernateHelper.getListData(data.getClass());
    request.setAttribute("database", list);
    return jspLocation("Process.jsp");
}
```

The other changes to make to the controller helper are to rename all occurrences of the bean class to the name of the annotated bean and to modify the return value of jspLocation to point to the directory of the JSPs.

 Try It

http://bytesizebook.com/book/ch5/persistentData/Controller

Enter some data and navigate to the process page: all the data you entered will be displayed, along with data that is already in the database.

That is all there is to it! Honestly, it may seem a little complicated at first, but that is only because you might not be familiar with what would need to be done if this task were completed using SQL alone. Hibernate generates all the SQL statements that are needed to access the database. It will even create the tables in the database.

5.7   Hibernate Configuration Files

Some of the properties for Hibernate will be the same every time you call it. Instead
of placing these in the servlet, they can be placed in a configuration file named
hibernate.cfg.xml. This is an XML file and will take precedence over the
properties added in the initHibernate method of the controller helper.

5.7.1   XML File

The statements in the XML file are similar to the statements that were added as
properties in Java code. Be sure to update the connection URL, username and
password for your database server. If you are using a different type of database, you
will need to update the dialect and driver class.

```xml
<?xml version='1.0' encoding='utf-8'?>
<!DOCTYPE hibernate-configuration PUBLIC
"-//Hibernate/Hibernate Configuration DTD 3.0//EN">

<hibernate-configuration>
  <session-factory>
    <property name="dialect">
      org.hibernate.dialect.MySQLDialect
    </property>
    <property name="connection.driver_class">
      com.mysql.jdbc.Driver
    </property>
    <property name="connection.url">
      jdbc:mysql://your-server:your-port/your-database
    </property>
    <property name="connection.username">
      your-user-name
    </property>
    <property name="connection.password">
      your-password
    </property>
    <property name="c3p0.min_size">1</property>
    <property name="c3p0.max_size">5</property>
    <property name="c3p0.timeout">300</property>
    <property name="c3p0.max_statements">50</property>
    <property name="c3p0.idle_test_period">300</property>
  </session-factory>
</hibernate-configuration>
```

Warning: the config file will override the initHibernate method.

5.7.2   File Location

Place this file in the *classes* directory of the web application, since your web application will always have access to it. If you are using NetBeans, then place it in the *Source Packages* folder under the default package.

5.7.3   Simplified Controller Helper

This file simplifies the `initHibernate` method of the controller helper.

```
static public void initHibernate(boolean create) {
    if (create) {
        HibernateHelper.createTable(RequestDataPersistent.class);
    }
    HibernateHelper.initSessionFactory(RequestDataPersistent.class);
}
```

 Try It

http://bytesizebook.com/book/ch5/persistentData/configure/Controller

5.8   Summary

Required validation is used to verify that the user has entered valid data. Regular expressions are a powerful tool for performing complicated validations with simple code.

Hibernate can simplify the process of required validation. It is easy to specify the validation rules using annotations in Hibernate and to generate an array of error messages. Hibernate's array is not as convenient as is needed in a JSP, so a map was created that contains the error messages and can be accessed easily from a JSP. The methods `isValid` and `getErrors` were also added to facilitate generating and retrieving the error messages.

Two types of requests can be made to a servlet: post and get. POST requests can send an unlimited amount of data and the data cannot be viewed in the URL. GET requests are useful for bookmarking a page with the parameters that were needed to find the page. A servlet can handle the two types of requests differently.

Hibernate can be used to save data to a relational database. Once Hibernate has been configured, it is a simple matter to save a bean to a database. Retrieving the data from the database is also a simple task.

Once a bean has been retrieved from the database, any changes to that bean will replace the data that is already in the database instead of adding a new row. Hibernate determines if a bean has already been written to the database by looking at the primary key. If the primary key has not been set, then Hibernate will add the bean to the database; if the primary key is not null, then Hibernate will update the corresponding row in the database.

Hibernate can use annotations to indicate how the table in the database can be created from the bean. Through the use of annotations, the configuration statements can be placed in the bean instead of in a separate configuration file.

If rows from the database are sent to the JSP, then a loop is needed to display the data. It is better to use a custom HTML tag than to add Java code to the JSP. The JSTL has many useful predefined tags, including a tag that does looping.

Once a servlet has been configured, it is easy to place all of the configuration parameters into a configuration file that can be accessed by all the controllers.

5.9   Chapter Review

Terms
1. Required Validation
2. Regular Expressions
3. Character Class
4. Predefined Character Class
5. Repetition
6. Alternation
7. Grouping
8. Capturing
9. HTTP Request Types
    (a) GET
    (b) POST
10. Map
11. Error Map
12. Hibernate Validation Messages
13. Retrieving Error Messages
14. Hibernate Annotations
15. Servlet Context Listener
16. Primary Key
17. Transient Field

New Java
1. Annotations
    (a) @Pattern(regexp="...", message="...")
    (b) @NotNull
    (c) @Entity
    (d) @Id
    (e) @Transient
    (f) @GeneratedValue

2. Required Validation
   (a) errorMap
   (b) setErrors
   (c) isValid
   (d) getErrors
3. POST Request
4. GET Request
5. Hibernate Persistence
   (a) Transaction
   (b) Session
6. request.setAttribute
7. Servlet Methods
   (a) doPost
   (b) init
8. Hibernate Helper
   (a) updateDB
   (b) getListData
9. JSTL
10. Looping in a JSP

Tags
1. <form method="POST">
2. ${helper.errors.hobby}
3. taglib statement for JSTL
4. forEach in JSTL

Questions
1. If a bean is passed to a method only as an Object, what must be done in order to access the public methods in the bean?
2. How are the validation errors retrieved from a JSP?
3. Why does the method setErrors create a map of error messages in addition to the Hibernate validation messages?
4. Name two advantages of a POST request over a GET request.
5. Name an advantage of a GET request over a POST request.
6. How is a GET request generated from a browser?
7. How is a POST request generated from a browser?
8. Name an advantage for having two different methods for handling GET and POST requests.
9. What can be done in an application to ensure that whenever a user clicks a button in a form, then a POST request will be made to the controller?
10. What are the three Hibernate properties that must be changed in order to connect to a MySQL server?

Tasks

1. Create regular expressions for the following:
   (a) Match one of the following words ignoring case. Try to create one expression: ned, net, nod, not, ped, pet, pod, pot, red, ret, rod, rot, bed, bet, bod, bot.
   (b) A full name.
      There must be at least two words.
      Each of the two words must start with an uppercase letter.
   (c) A telephone number with the following formats:
      999-999-9999
      999.999.9999
      999 999 9999
      9999999999

2. Initialisation Parameters.
   (a) Define a servlet tag in *web.xml* for a servlet that will have an initialisation parameter named *interest* with a value of *4.23*.
   (b) Write the Java code that would read the value of the initialisation parameter and cast it to a double.
   (c) Add an initialisation parameter for the database username for a controller that uses Hibernate to save data. Read the initialisation parameter in the `init` method and use its value as the username when configuring Hibernate.

3. If a bean has properties named make, model and year, then write the code for a JSP that will display all the values for a collection of these beans. Assume that the collection was sent under the name 'database'.

4. Write an application that accepts city, state and zip. Validate that the zip code is 5 digits and that the state is FL, GA, NO, LA or MS. Write the data to a database.

5. Write an application that accepts first name, last name, age and email. Use the `@Range` annotation to validate that the age is between 15 and 115. Hibernate provides the `@Email` annotation for validating email. It only has an optional parameter for message. Use the `t` annotation to validate the email. Write the valid data to a database and display all the values that are in the database.

Advanced HTML and Form Elements

6

The first time I saw a web page, I was amazed at hypertext links, images, advanced layout, colours and fonts. Of these, hypertext links already existed in another protocol on the web: gopher. Gopher used a series of index pages to navigate a site; the links on one index would take you to another index page or to some text file. Libraries were the principal users of the gopher protocol. A lot of information could be retrieved using gopher; however, it never became popular like the web. It was the remaining features that made the web as popular as it is: images, advanced layout, colours and fonts.

It has been said that a picture is worth a thousand words. This is certainly true for the web. An HTML tag is used to include an image in the current page. This tag is different from all the other tags: it inserts a separate file into the current page at the location of the tag.

There are two aspects of every HTML page: the layout of the page and the style used to display the page. The layout indicates that some text should stand out from the rest of the text, regardless of the browser that is used to display it. The style controls the actual appearance of the text: how much larger than normal text will it be, how many lines precede and follow the text, the type of font that is used to display the text. Many other aspects, like the colour of the text, could also be controlled by the style.

HTML tags have a mix of layout and style. Some tags are very specific about the layout, while others are more specific about the style. Those that indicate a specific layout include tables, lists and rules. Those that indicate a specific style include italic, bold and underline. Many more tags are more generic about the layout and the style. These tags are intended to be used with a separate file that defines the style to be used for these tags.

A separate syntax is used to describe the style used in a page: *Cascading Style Sheets* (CSS). By using CSS, the style definition can be saved in one file that can be used by multiple HTML pages; such a file is known as a *style sheet*. By using a style sheet, only one file needs to be edited in order to change the appearance of all pages that use it.

T. Downey, *Guide to Web Development with Java: Understanding Website Creation*,   185
DOI 10.1007/978-1-4471-2443-6_6, © Springer-Verlag London Limited 2012

The recommended way to create HTML pages is to use HTML to define the layout of the page and to use a style sheet to control the appearance of the page.

There are other input elements besides the text box. There are elements for entering passwords and many lines of text. There are also elements for displaying checkbox and radio button groups, as well as elements for drop-down and multiple selection lists.

Checkbox groups and multiple selection lists are more difficult to initialise with data from the query string. A technique will be introduced to simplify the process. It is also more difficult to save the multiple values if they are to be saved in a readable format in the database.

6.1   Images

Images are different from other tags. They reference an external file, but the content of the file is displayed in the current file. The tag for embedding an image in a page is `<img>`, and it has one attribute named `src` for indicating the location of the image file and a second attribute named `alt` that is used by non-graphical browsers to indicate the content of the image.

<img src="happy.gif" alt="smiley face" >

When referencing graphics on the web, you must know the complete URL of the source in order to create a link to it. However, depending on where the resource is located, you may be able to speed up the loading of your page by using relative references. The `src` attribute uses relative and absolute references just like the `action` attribute in a form.

1. If the resource is not on the same server, then you must specify the entire URL.
   <img src="http://server.com/images/happy.gif" alt="smiley face">
2. If the resource is on the same server, but is not descended from the current directory, then include the full path from the document root, starting with a /.
   <img src="/not_my_images/happy.gif" alt="smiley face">
3. If the resource is in the same directory as the HTML page that references it, then only include the file name, not the server or the directory.
   <img src="happy.gif" alt="smiley face">
4. If the resource is in a subdirectory of the directory where the HTML page that references it is located, then include the name of the subdirectory and the file name.
   <img src="my_graphics/happy.gif" alt="smiley face">

6.2   HTML Design

HTML tags contain layout and style. The basic layout for a tag is whether it is an in-line tag or a block tag: in-line tags are embedded in the current line, whereas block tags start a new line. A default style has been defined for each HTML tag.

Table 6.1 Tags to avoid in HTML5

HTML4 tag	Suggested alternate
<b>	<strong>
<i>	<em>
<u>	<ins>
<strike> (obsolete)	<del>
<font> (obsolete)	Use CSS instead
<center> (obsolete)	Use CSS instead

For instance, HTML has a tag for emphasis, <em>. To the HTML designer, the use of this tag meant that the text should indicate emphasis, but did not define what emphasis meant. The only thing that the designer knew was that this was an in-line tag, so the text would be embedded in the current line, and that the text would look different from normal text when displayed in the browser. It was up to the browser to implement emphasis: it might underline the text; it might make the text bold; it might invert the colours of the foreground and background. The designer could not specify how the text should be emphasised. There were many such tags that could be used to specify general style, but not to specify the exact appearance.

Other tags were added to HTML that were more specific about the style used to display the text within them. For instance, the italic tag, <i>, indicated that text should be italicised. The special style associated with these tags has been removed in HTML5. It is recommended to use other tags instead, as listed in Table 6.1. Some of the tags are now obsolete and should not be used.

There are tags that are more specific about the layout. These include tags for organising data into lists and tables.

Designers liked the ability to specify the exact appearance of the page, so more ways to specify style were added to HTML. Attributes were added to individual tags to specify colour and alignment. However, these additional ways to add style made it difficult to update a website. These style attributes that were placed in the layout tags are now deprecated in HTML5 and should not be used; a style sheet should be used instead.

6.2.1   In-line and Block Tags

There are two ways that tags are inserted into pages: in-line and block. *In-line* tags can be embedded in a line of text. *Block* tags will start on a new line. The emphasis tag, *em*, is an in-line tag: it can be used repeatedly in the same sentence. The paragraph tag, *p*, is a block tag: every appearance of the tag will start a new line. If the emphasis tag is used several times in one sentence, there will still be only one sentence in the browser.

```
This <em>is</em> a <em>sentence</em> with several
points of <em>emphasis</em>.
```

If the paragraph tag is used several times in the same line, there will be many lines in the browser.

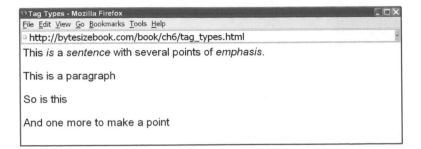

Fig. 6.1 In-line and block tags viewed in a browser

```
This is a paragraph</p><p>So is this</p><p>And one
more to make a point</p>
```

The above lines of HTML will appear, in most browsers, as in Fig. 6.1.

6.2.2 General Style Tags

There are many tags in HTML that can be used to add style to a document. These styles are named for the type of text that they represent in a document. There are tags for citations, variables, inserted text, deleted text, etc. There is no indication in the tag as to how it will be displayed in a browser; in fact, several of these tags might have the same appearance in a browser. Table 6.2 lists the in-line tags and Fig. 6.2 shows how they would appear in a browser.

Many of the in-line tags seem to do the same thing; for instance, kbd, sample and code all use a fixed space font to display the text. As will be covered soon, through the use of a style sheet, the web designer could define these tags differently. The style could also be changed easily in the future.

Additional tags are defined for blocks of code. There are six tags for headings, one for preformatted text and one for quoted text. Figure 6.3 lists the block tags and how they appear in a browser.

Two additional tags are declared that have no additional formatting. These tags are for setting layout and style that is not met by the other tags. The span tag is an in-line tag; the div tag is a block tag. Neither tag has additional formatting beyond being in-line or block. The style and layout for each is meant to be controlled by a style sheet.

6.2.3 Layout Tags

There are more ways to lay out a web page than using the paragraph and line break tags. Lists are a useful way to display a table of contents at the top of a page. Tables are used to display data from a spreadsheet or database.

Table 6.2 In-line tags and how they appear in a browser

Tag	Description
cite	Represents the title of a work
code	Text from a computer program
del	Text to be deleted
ins	Inserted text
dfn	Text that is a definition
em	Text with emphasis
kbd	Text that is to be entered from the keyboard
abbr	Represents an abbreviation
samp	Text that is taken from another source
strong	Text that is important
var	Text that represents a variable from a program

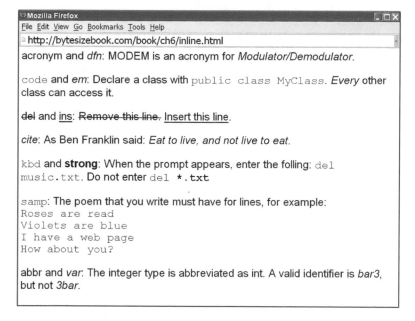

Fig. 6.2 In-line tags and how they appear in a browser

Consider the table of contents at the top of a page; such a layout cannot be achieved using paragraph and line breaks. There is no way to indent text or to insert automatic numbering using such simple tags. Think of a website that lists the transactions on a credit card; the data is displayed in columns on the page. There is no way to do this using paragraph and line break tags.

Lists

Lists are a good way to organise data in an HTML page. There are three types of lists: ordered, unordered and definition.

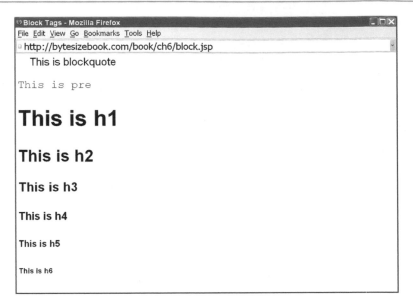

Fig. 6.3 Block tags and how they appear in a browser

Ordered and unordered lists have similar structures. They each use nested `<li>` tags to indicate an item in the list. All the items in the list are enclosed within the paired tags for the list. Ordered lists start with `<ol>` and end with `</ol>`. Unordered lists start with `<ul>` and end with `</ul>`. List items for ordered lists will have a number inserted automatically. List items for unordered lists will have a bullet inserted automatically.

```
<ol>
  <li>First
  <li>Second
  <li>Third
</ol>
<ul>
  <li>Red
  <li>Green
  <li>Blue
</ul>
```

Definition lists start with the `<dl>` tag and end with the `</dl>` tag. Two tags are needed to define each item in a definition list: the term and the definition. The idea of a definition list is that there will be a short term, and then a longer definition of this term. Use the `<dt>` tag to indicate the term, and use the `<dd>` tag to indicate the definition.

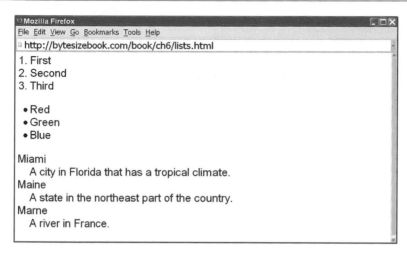

Fig. 6.4 The HTML code for lists and how they might appear in a browser

```
<dl>
  <dt>Miami
  <dd>
  A city in Florida that has a tropical climate.
  <dt>Maine
  <dd>
  A state in the northeast part of the country.
  <dt>Marne
  <dd>
  A river in France.
</dl>
```

Figure 6.4 shows how the different lists might appear in a browser.

Tables

Tables are useful for representing tabular data, like from a spreadsheet or database. Tables begin with the `<table>` tag and end with the `</table>` tag. Tables use nested `<tr>` tags to indicate rows in the table. Each row has nested `<td>` tags that indicate the data that is in each row. Each `<td>` tag represents one square in the table. The browser will adjust the table so that all rows will display the same number of squares, even if the rows are defined with different numbers of `<td>` tags. The row with the most `<td>` tags determines the number of squares for all the rows in the table.

The default for a `<td>` tag is that it is equivalent to one square in the table. This can be altered with the *rowspan* and *colspan* attributes in the `<td>` tag. The *rowspan* indicates that the `<td>` tag will cover successive squares in different rows, starting in the current row. The *colspan* indicates that the `<td>` will occupy successive squares in the same row. A `<td>` tag can have both a *rowspan* and *colspan* attributes.

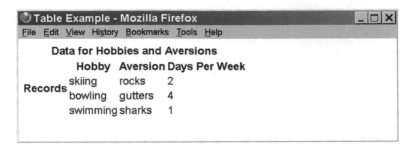

Fig. 6.5 Viewing a table from a browser

In addition to the <td> tag, there is also the <th> tag. The <th> tag behaves just like a <td> tag, except that the all text in it is centred and bold.

```
<table cols="112 112 112 112">
  <tr>
    <th colspan="4">Data for Hobbies and Aversions</th>
  </tr><tr>
    <th rowspan="4">Records</th>
    <th>Hobby</th><th>Aversion</th><th>Days Per Week</th>
  </tr><tr>
    <td>skiing</td><td>rocks</td><td>2</td>
  </tr><tr>
    <td>bowling</td><td>gutters</td><td>4</td>
  </tr><tr>
    <td>swimming</td><td>sharks</td><td>1</td>
  </tr>
</table>
```

Figure 6.5 shows how a table might appear in a browser. Note the effect of the *rowspan* and *colspan* attributes.
1. The only cell in the first row extends over four columns.
2. The first cell in the second row extends over four rows.
3. The remaining cells in the second row contain the property names for the columns.
4. The remaining rows are partially filled by the first cell from the second row.

6.3   Cascading Style Sheets

As HTML progressed, more tags were added to control style. However, this soon became unmanageable. Additional attributes were added to the body tag to control the background colour of the page and the text colour of the page. Additional attributes were added to each tag to control alignment; tables could specify borders and padding. Soon, style information was added throughout the layout. If a website wanted to change the style that was used on every page, there was a lot of tedious editing to do.

If code was embedded in every page that defined the colour of the text, it is quite reasonable to want to change the colour from time to time. This would require that the web designer edit each page and make a simple change. If there were 100 pages, it would be time consuming.

Style sheets allow the designer to place all the style in a separate file. Many HTML pages can use the same style sheet. The style for all the general styles, like kbd, sample and var, can be redefined using a style sheet. If all the web pages used the same style sheet, then all the pages could be updated by editing the single style sheet.

6.3.1   Adding Style

The simplest way to add style to an HTML page is to include a style sheet. The style sheet is a separate file that contains style definitions. The contents of the file will be covered in the next section. Use a <link> tag in the *head* section of the HTML file to include the style sheet. The <link> tag has three attributes.

Href
This contains the URL for the style sheet file. It has the same format as the HREF attribute in the anchor tag, <a>.

Rel
This will always have a value of *stylesheet.*

Type
This will have a value of *text/css.*

For example, if the style sheet is named *style.css* and is located in the same directory as the HTML file, then the basic tags for an HTML page might look like the following:

```
<!DOCTYPE HTML>
<html>
  <head>
    <link rel="stylesheet" type="text/css"
          href="style.css">
    <meta charset="utf-8">
    <title>Simple Page</title>
  </head>
  <body>
    <p>
      This is a <em>simple</em> web page.
    </p>
  </body>
</html>
```

Whatever styles are defined in the file, *style.css* would be applied to the web page. Any changes to the style sheet would affect the web page the next time it was loaded into a browser. If the style sheet was referenced from 100 different pages, then every change to the style sheet would immediately affect all 100 pages.

The style sheet topics covered in this chapter are intended as an introduction to style sheets. There are many other features of style sheets that are covered in detail on the W3C website.

6.3.2   Defining Style

CSSs have been defined by W3C. CSS is a recommendation that has been adopted by most web browsers. Each browser is different in its level of compliance with the W3C recommendation. Some features will work one way on one browser and another way on a different browser. The effects will be similar, but will have slight differences.

The best way to define a style sheet is to place it in a separate file from the HTML that it will control. The reason for this is so that the style sheet can be used by many different pages. If the style needs to be changed, then it can be modified in one place and all the pages that reference it will be updated as well.

A style sheet file contains one or more style blocks. A style block contains one or more of the styles that have been defined by W3C. A style block has an HTML tag and a set of curly braces that enclose the styles that will be applied to it.

```
HTML_tag {
    style-name:  style-value;
    style-name:  style-value;
    style-name:  style-value;
}
```

The name of the style block must match an HTML tag. The styles within the block will be applied to all tags that have that name.

Scales
Many of the styles deal with a measurement. Table 6.3 lists many different ways that length can be specified in a style sheet.

Common Styles
There are many styles defined for CSS. Only a few will be used in this book. The basic styles to be used are in the following list:

Background-color: green;
The colour can be a standard colour name or can be a three or six hex digit number (*#036* or *#003568*).

Background-image: url(fiu.gif);
Enclose the path to the image inside the parentheses. Do not have a space after *url*.

Color: #003399;
The colour can be a standard colour name or can be a three or six hex digit number (*#036* or *#003568*).

Table 6.3 CSS measurements

Abbreviation	Measurement
px	Pixels – dots on the screen. Usually there are 96 to the inch
pt	Points – a point is 1/72″ and is usually used to specify a font size
in	Inches
cm	Centimetres
em	The height of the letter M in the current font
ex	The height of the letter x in the current font
%	Percentage of the parent's property

Font-family: Bazooka, 'Comic Sans MS', sans-serif;
A number of fonts can be listed. Separate the names by a comma. Enclose multi-word fonts in quotes. The browser will use the first font that it finds. List your fonts from most specific to most general. The generic font family names *serif, mono-space, cursive, fantasy* and *sans-serif* can be used as the last option in the list. They act as defaults; if the browser can't find any other font specified, it will be guaranteed to have one of each of these font family categories.

Font-size: 30 pt;
Change the size of the font. The measurement is required. Do not have a space between the number and *pt*. Internet Explorer will default to *pt*, but other browsers will not. If you want your page to be readable in all browsers, then include the measurement.

Font-style: italic;
Choices are italic, normal, oblique.

Font-weight: bold;
Choices are bold, lighter, bolder, normal.

Text-align: left;
Choices are left, right, center, justify.

Text-decoration: underline;
Choices are underline, overline, none, line-through, blink, normal.

Text-transform: lowercase;
Choices are lowercase, uppercase, normal, capitalize.

Margin: 20%;
Indents the object from each edge of the enclosing element. It accepts all measurements. Each margin can be controlled separately with margin-right, margin-left, margin-top, margin-bottom.

Padding: 20%;
Adds additional space from the margin to the content of the element. It accepts all
measurements. The padding on each side can be controlled separately with padding-
right, padding-left, padding-top, padding-bottom.

Text-indent: 20%;
Indents the first line of text from the margin. You can use percentage or a number.
The value may also be negative.

List-style-type: lower-alpha;
Choices are decimal, lower-alpha, upper-alpha, lower-roman, upper-roman, disc,
circle, square.

Border: thin solid black;
Sets the border for an element. It contains the thickness of the border, the style of
the border and the colour of the border. The thickness can be thick, thin. The style
can be solid, dashed. Each edge of the element can be controlled separately with
border-right, border-left, border-top, border-bottom.

Default Styles

The above styles should be included within curly braces after the name of the HTML
tag to be affected. To affect the entire document, include the properties with the
style block for the body tag. The following will make the text colour red for the
document, everything will be aligned to the centre and there will be a left margin
that is 20% of the total width of the page.

```
body {
    color: red;
    text-align: center;
    margin-left: 20%;
}
```

It is also possible to define styles for just a paragraph, table or any other HTML tag.
The following will force all paragraphs to have blue text and to be aligned to the right:

```
p {
    color: blue;
    text-align: right;
}
```

Since the <p> tag is nested within the <body> tag in HTML pages, it will
inherit the left margin that was set in the body tag.

Multiple Definition

It is possible to have the same style apply to several tags. Use a comma to separate the names of tags that should use this style. The following style would apply to all `<h1>` and `<h2>` tags.

```
h1, h2 {
    text-align: center;
}
```

Nested Definition

It is possible to indicate that a style should be used only if it is nested inside other tags. Specify the order of nested tags that must appear in order to use this style. For example, to control a heading that appears inside a table element, use the following:

```
td h1 {
    font-size: 20pt;
}
```

The nested tag does not need to be a child of the first tag. The nested tag can be any descendent of the first tag.

Named Styles

It is also possible to define several styles for a specific tag. For instance, the `<td>` tag could have several styles like these.

```
td.money {
    color: green;
    text-align: left;
}

td.sky {
    color: lightblue;
    text-align: center;
}
```

Then, the particular *td* would be specified with the *class* attribute within the *td* tag in the HTML code.

```
<table>
  <tr>
    <td>Normal
    <td class="sky">TD with sky style
    <td class="money">TD with money style
</table>
```

Generic Styles

Styles that can be applied to all tags can be created by naming the tag, but omitting the name of an HTML tag. For instance, to create a style to set the colour to orange that can be used with any HTML tag, just give it a name that starts with a period.

```
.warning {
  color: orange;
}
```

Then, any tag could be specified with the class attribute within the tag in the HTML code.

```
<strong class="warning">This is a strong warning.</strong>
<em class="warning">This is an emphatic warning.</em>
```

Uniquely Named Styles

If the # is used instead of the dot notation in a generic style. Styles named this way should only appear once in a page. It indicates a unique identifier for one tag in the HTML page. It is commonly used on a *div* tag to control advanced layout. There will be an example for this in Chap. 7.

```
div#about {
    position: relative;
    float: right;
}
```

It is referenced from the HTML code with the *id* attribute instead of the *class* attribute.

```
<div id="about">
  This is a div that will have special layout controlled by a style sheet.
</div>
```

Pseudo Styles

In addition to the normal tags like *body*, *p* and *td*, there are some pseudo-tags that allow the hypertext links to be controlled.

a:link
Controls the appearance of an unvisited hypertext link

a:visited
Controls the appearance of a visited hypertext link

Style Examples

The following listing contains the code for a style sheet that includes the styles similar to those listed above:

```
body {
  text-align: center;
}

p {
  font-style: italic;
  text-align: right;
}

table, td {
  border: thin solid black;
}

td.under {
  text-decoration: underline;
  text-align: right;
}

td.center {
  font-weight: bold;
  text-align: center;
}

.warning {
  font-size: 150%;
}
```

Next is an example of a page that uses the above style sheet. Note how the specific *td* tag is specified by <td class="under"> or <td class="left">.

```
<!doctype html>
<html>
  <head>
    <title>Test page for CSS</title>
    <meta charset="utf-8">
    <link REL="stylesheet" TYPE="text/css"
          HREF="test.css">
  </head>
  <body>
      This is some text that is not included in
      a paragraph. It should be centered across the page.
    <p>
      This is the text for the paragraph. It should
      be italicised and aligned to the right side of the
      page.
    <table>
      <tr>
        <td>Normal Text</td>
```

```
            <td>is not centered. It is not centered because
                tables have a default alignment of left, so
                the center of the body does not cascade. It
                has a strong <strong class="warning">warning</strong>.
            </td>
        </tr>
        <tr>
            <td class="under">In a TD: under</td>
        <td class="under">is underlined and right aligned</td>
        </tr>
        <tr>
            <td class="center">In a TD: center</td>
            <td class="center">is bold and centered</td>
        </tr>
    </table>
    <p>
        This is in a paragraph, too. It has right alignment.
        It has an underlined <ins class="warning">warning</ins>.
    </p>
    This is not in a paragraph, it is centered.
    It has an emphatic <em class="warning">warning</em>.
  </body>
</html>
```

The above page will look like Fig. 6.6, when viewed in a browser.

6.3.3 Custom Layout with CSS

Each HTML page has a default way to display tags. An in-line tag is laid out next to the previous in-line tag, unless the tag is wrapped to the next line. A block tag is displayed below the previous block tag. CSS can be used to change the default layout of the page. Two tags that are important for custom layout are *position* and *float*. Additional tags control the height, width and top left corner of the tag.

The *position* tag controls how the tag will be displayed in the page. It has the following choices:

static
Static is the default. In this case, there is no custom layout. The tag will be displayed in its normal location in the flow of the document.

fixed
Fixed forces the element to stay in the same location relative to the window, even when the page is scrolled.

absolute
Absolute sets the location from the upper left corner of the parent element's position; the element is removed from the normal layout of the page, so it does not affect the position of other elements.

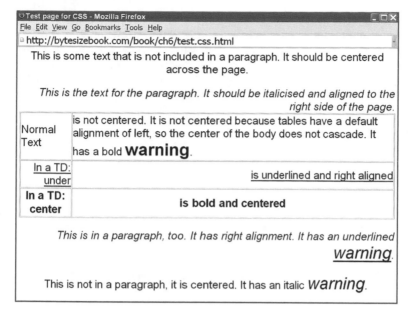

Fig. 6.6 A page that uses a style sheet, as seen in a browser

relative
Relative offsets the element from its normal position in the layout of the page. Its old space is still occupied in the flow of the document, so other elements will be positioned as if this element had not been moved. It is as if the entire page is laid out normally, then any relatively positioned elements are moved.

The *float* tag is for block tags. It controls if the tag will attempt to anchor itself to an edge of the previous block tag. It has the following choices:

none
The block tag will not anchor itself to the edge of a previous tag. It will display from the edge of its parent container.

left
If there is room for the current tag between the right edge of the previous block tag and the right edge of the parent container, then the left edge of the current tag will be anchored to the right edge of the previous block tag.

right
If there is room for the current tag between the left edge of the previous block tag and the left edge of the parent container, then the right edge of the current tag will be anchored to the right edge of the previous block tag.

inherit
The tag inherits the *float* style from its parent.

The *position* and *float* styles allow a tag to be positioned anywhere in the page. The remaining tags define the height, width and upper left corner of the tag. Once the *position* element is set to something other than *static*, the location and size of the tag can be changed.

Width: 100px;
Sets the width of the element. Any measurement can be used to define the width.

Height: 100px;
Sets the height of the element. Any measurement can be used to define the height.

Top: 5ex;
Sets the vertical offset of the element. Any measurement can be used to define top. Only valid for elements that have a position of fixed, relative, absolute.

Left: 5ex;
Sets the horizontal offset of the element. Any measurement can be used to define left. Only valid for elements that have a position of fixed, relative, absolute.

If the size of a tag is too small for the content in the tag, then there is a question about what should happen to the extra content. Should it be shown or ignored? Should the extra content extend beyond the dimensions of the tag or should scroll bars be added to the tag to allow the extra content to be scrolled into view? The tag that answers these questions is named *overflow*. It has the following choices:

visible
The content of the tag is allowed to extend beyond the edge of the element. The dimensions of the element do not change, but the extended content may overwrite the content of another tag.

hidden
The extra content is not displayed.

scroll
The extra content is available, but not all of it is in view. Scroll bars are added to the tag to allow the extra content to be scrolled into view. The scroll bars are visible, even if there is no extra content.

auto
Scroll bars are only added if there is extra content that does not fit within the size of the tag.

inherit
The tag inherits the value of the *overflow* style from its parent.

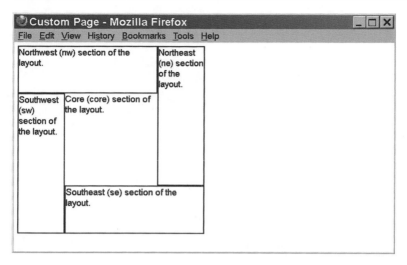

Fig. 6.7   A page that has a custom layout, defined in a style sheet

Custom Layout Example

As an example of a custom layout, a style sheet will be used to create the layout shown in Fig. 6.7, when viewed in a browser.

The HTML page that uses the layout will use *div* for five sections of the page: northwest, northeast, southeast, southwest and core. Each of these tags has a named style and a uniquely named style. The named style uses the *class* attribute and the uniquely named style uses the *id* attribute. A sixth section will be used as a container for all the other sections.

```
<!DOCTYPE HTML>
<html>
  <head>
    <link rel="stylesheet" type="text/css"
          href="custom.css">
    <meta charset="utf-8">
    <title>Custom Page</title>
  </head>
  <body>
  <div class="layout" id="outer">
        <div class="layout" id="nw">
             Northwest (nw) section of the layout.
        </div>
        <div class="layout" id="ne">
             Northeast (ne) section of the layout.
        </div>
```

```
      <div class="layout" id="sw">
            Southwest (sw) section of the layout.
      </div>
      <div class="layout" id="core">
            Core (core) section of the layout.
      </div>
      <div class="layout" id="se">
            Southeast (se) section of the layout.
      </div>
   </div>
   </body>
</html>
```

The style sheet has named and uniquely named tags. The named tag has the default layout for a custom tag. It sets the position, overflow and float styles. The uniquely named style defines the unique characteristics for the tag, such as width, height and background image.

All but one of the tags will use a *float* value of *left*. The other tag, the northwest section, will use a *float* value of *right*. Since all of the tags are using a relative position, each tag affects the layout of subsequent tags. The northwest section would force the remaining tags to start below it, and there would be a gap in the layout. It becomes a puzzle to find the values of the style tags that allow the default layout to be used without having to override a lot of values.

All of the elements have the overflow value set to auto, so that scroll bars will appear if there is additional content that cannot be displayed in the specified size. Most elements will have a border. The only exceptions will be the outer section and the core section. The core section does not need a border, since all the sections around it do have borders.

The *outer* uniquely named style defines the overall dimensions of the layout. The width and height need to be increased to account for the borders. A border is outside the area it surrounds. If the northwest and northeast sections both have borders, then they each have a left and a right border, so the width must be incremented by four widths of the border.

```
div.layout {
   position: relative;
   float: left;
   overflow: auto;
   border: 2px solid black;
   font-family: arial, sans-serif;
   font-size: 14pt;
}
```

```
div#outer {
  width: 408px;
  height: 408px;
  border: none;
}

div#nw {
  width: 300px;
  height: 100px;
}

div#ne {
  width: 100px;
  height: 300px;
  float: right;
}

div#sw {

  width: 100px;
  height: 300px;
}

div#core {
  width: 200px;
  height: 200px;
  border: none;
  padding: none;
}

div#se {
  width: 300px;
  height: 100px;
}
```

Try It

http://bytesizebook.com/book/ch6/custom.html

6.4   Form Elements

While being able to enter text in a form and to click a button is all that is needed for data entry, there are form element tags that allow more flexibility when entering data. These tags specify a layout to be used in the browser. There are tags for passwords, multiple lines of text, radio buttons, checkbox buttons and selection lists.

Although there are many ways for the user to enter data in a form, they all have one of three HTML syntaxes: those that look like the *input* tag, the *textarea* tag and the *select* tag.

The *input* tags already include the *text* tag and the *submit* tag for submitting data. In addition, there are variations for entering a password, displaying a radio button, displaying a checkbox button and resetting a form.

The *textarea* tag is used to enter multiple lines of text.

The *select* tag can display a drop-down list or a multiple selection list. The drop-down list only allows one option to be chosen and the available options can be viewed from a list that drops down from the element in the browser. The multiple selection list allows more than one option to be chosen and displays a scrollable window that displays the available options.

6.4.1   Input Elements

Up until this point, all HTML forms have used only three different form elements: text, hidden and submit. All three of these use the same tag: *input*.

```
<input type="text" name="hobby"
                   value="${helper.data.hobby}">
<input type="hidden" name="hobby"
                   value="${helper.data.hobby}">
<input type="submit" name="confirmButton"
                   value="Confirm">
```

There are additional elements that have this same format. The only difference is the content of the *type* attribute.

The *password* type behaves just like a text box, but the value in the browser appears as a row of asterisks. There is not really any security in this. If the form uses the GET method, then the value will appear as plain text in the query string.

```
<input type="password" name="pswd"
                   value="${helper.data.pswd}">
```

The *radio* type has the appearance of a radio button. The user cannot change the value: it is hidden. The button can have two states: checked and unchecked. If it is in the checked state when the form is submitted, then the value will be sent to the server.

There is an additional attribute for radio elements named *checked*. If this word appears in the tag, then the button will be checked whenever the page is loaded.

```
<input type="radio" name="happiness"
                   value="1" checked>
```

The *checkbox* type has the appearance of a checkbox button. The user cannot change the value: it is hidden. It can have two states: checked and unchecked. If it is in the checked state when the form is submitted, then the value will be sent to the server.

There is an additional attribute for checkbox elements named *checked*. If this word appears in the tag, then the button will be checked whenever the page is loaded.

```
<input type="checkbox" name="extra"
                        value="sprinkles" checked>
```

The *reset* type has the appearance of a submit button. It does not need a name. The default value is *Reset*. This input element is never sent to the server. The only purpose of the button is to reset the form to the initial state that was received from the server. All values that the user has entered since the page was loaded will be reset to the initial values defined in the form.

```
<input type="reset" value="Reset">
```

Radio Group

Radio buttons are most useful when they are placed in groups. A group of radio buttons all have the same name, with different values. Only one of the radio buttons with that name can be in the checked state at any time. Whichever is checked, that is the value that will be sent in the query string.

In the following listing, if *Ecstatic* is checked by the user, then the radio group will be included in the query string as happiness = 2. Even though *Elated* is checked when the page is loaded, the value that the user selects will override the initial value.

```
Level of Happiness:<br>
<input type="radio" name="happiness"
       value="1" checked>
       Elated
<input type="radio" name="happiness"
       value="2">
       Ecstatic
<input type="radio" name="happiness"
       value="3">
       Joyous<br>
```

It is not necessary that the values for a radio group be numeric. All values are actually strings, even if they appear to be numeric. Numbers were used in this example only to demonstrate that numbers can be used as values.

Checkbox Group

A group of checkboxes all have the same name, with different values. More than one element in a checkbox group can be in the checked state at any time. Checkbox groups are especially useful for the programmer. In a servlet, a checkbox group can be processed using a loop.

All the checked values will be sent in the query string as separate name = value pairs. For instance, if *Chocolate Sprinkles* and *Hot Fudge* are checked, then they would be included in the query string as extra = sprinkles&extra = fudge.

```
Preferred Extras:<br>
<input type="checkbox" name="extra"
       value="sprinkles">
       Chocolate Sprinkles
<input type="checkbox" name="extra"
       value="fudge" checked>
       Hot Fudge
<input type="checkbox" name="extra"
       value="cream">
       Whipped Cream<br>
```

6.4.2   Textarea Element

Text boxes can only include one line of text. To enter multiple lines of text, use a *textarea* element.

```
<textarea name="comments"></textarea>
```

This will display as a box in which text can be typed. All the text in the box will be sent to the server when the form is submitted. If you want an initial value to display when the page is loaded, place it between the opening and closing *textarea* tags.

6.4.3   Select Elements

There are two types of select lists: single selection lists and multiple selection lists. The single selection list is also known as a drop-down list. The multiple selection list is also known as a scrollable list.

Single Selection List

This appears in the browser as a drop-down list of values. Whichever value the user selects, that is the value that will be sent to the browser. The first value in the list is the default value that will be sent to the browser, if the user does not make a selection.

The selection list has nested tags for each of the options in the list. To have one of them selected as the default, include an attribute named *selected* in the option.

```
Grade
<select name="grade">
  <option value="4.0">A
  <option value="3.67">A-
  <option value="3.33" selected>B+
  <option value="3.00">B
  <option value="2.67">B-
  <option value="2.33">C+
  <option value="2.00">C
</select>
```

By default, only one option appears in the drop-down list. The optional attribute named *size* can be used to set how many options will be visible in the list. Even if more than one option is visible, only one option can be selected from the list.

It is not necessary that the values for a select list be numeric. All values are actually strings, even if they appear to be numeric. Numbers were used in this example only to demonstrate that numbers can be used as values.

Multiple Selection List

The only differences between the single selection list and the multiple selection list is the attribute *multiple*. The attribute *multiple* indicates that more than one option may be selected by using the shift or control key.

Just like the single selection list, the attribute *size* is used to set the number of options that are visible in the scrollable window. If the size is omitted, then the number of options that are displayed is browser-specific.

More than one option can have the optional attribute named *selected* to indicate that the option should be selected when the form is loaded or reset.

```
<select name="team" multiple size="2">
  <option value="heat">Heat
  <option value="marlins" selected>Marlins
  <option value="dolphins" selected>Dolphins
  <option value="panthers">Panthers
</select>
```

6.4.4   Bean Implementation

With the introduction of additional form elements, the bean must be modified to handle the new elements. Some of the new elements are handled the same way that text boxes are handled. Other elements require more work to store the multiple values in the bean and to display the values in a JSP.

Bean Properties

All the bean properties we have seen until now have been single-valued: the variable is a primitive type; the mutator has a primitive parameter; the accessor returns a primitive type (Listing 6.1).

```
protected String comments;

public void setComments(String comments) {
    this.comments = comments;
}

public String getComments() {
    return comments;
}
```

Listing 6.1 Template for a single-valued property

With the introduction of checkbox groups and multiple selection lists, there must be a way to store the multiple values in the bean. This requires the notion of a multiple-valued bean property. If a property in a bean is multiple-valued, then declare the variable as an array and change the signatures of the mutator and accessor to agree (Listing 6.2).

```
protected String[] extra;

public void setExtra(String[] extra) {
    this.extra = extra;
}

public String[] getExtra() {
    return extra;
}
```

Listing 6.2 Template for a multiple-valued property

Even though there are many different form elements, there are only two types of bean properties: single-valued and multiple-valued. In the bean, there is no way to determine if a single-valued property was set using a text box or a radio button; there is no way to determine if a multiple-valued property was set using a checkbox group or a multiple selection list. This makes it easier for the developer to implement a bean: there are only two possible choices for implementing a bean property.

Filling the Bean

For multiple-valued elements, there will be multiple `name = value` pairs in the query string. For instance, if a checkbox group named *team* has the teams *heat* and *marlins* checked, then the query string will appear as

```
?team=heat&team=marlins
```

For these elements, there is another method that is part of the request object that will retrieve all of these values: `getParameterValues`. This method returns an array of strings that contains all of the values that are in the query string. If there are no values, then the method returns *null*.

In order to copy all the values from the query string, it would be necessary to call the property's accessor with the values from the query string.

```
data.setTeam(request.getParameterValues("team"));
```

The good news is that the `fillBeanFromRequest` method that has been used to copy the values from the query string to the bean will also work for multiple-valued properties. The `fillBeanFromRequest` method that is in the bean base class does not need to be modified to work for multiple-valued properties.

In the bean for this example, the happiness property has been defined as an integer and the grade property has been defined as a double.

```
protected int happiness;
protected double grade;
...
public void setHappiness(int happiness) {
    this.happiness = happiness;
}

public int getHappiness() {
    return happiness;
}
...
public void setGrade(double grade) {
    this.grade = grade;
}

public double getGrade() {
    return grade;
}
```

This was done to demonstrate that the `fillBeanFromRequest` method could also process these types; it will convert the value from the string in the form into the correct numeric type. If there is an error, then a value of zero is returned.

Please do not think that all radio groups must use integers or that all single select lists must use doubles. These types were chosen for demonstration purposes, and a string could have been used for either of these properties.

Resetting Nullable Fields

As long as a form element that is a text box has a name, data for the text box will be sent in the query string. If no data is entered by the user, then the name of the text box will be in the query string, but the value will be the empty string.

```
hobby=&confirmButton=Confirm
```

This is also true for hidden elements, password elements, text areas and single selection lists.

Radio groups, checkbox groups and multiple selection lists are different. If the user does not make a choice in these elements, then the name of the element will not be in the query string. Clicking a reset button and then clicking a submit button will also cause these elements to be omitted from the query string, if no default values were set for them.

This causes a problem for the `fillBeanFromRequest` method. It calls the mutators for all the properties that are named in the query string. If the name of a property is not in the query string, then the mutator of that property will not be called.

Imagine that the user makes some choices in a checkbox group and hits the confirm button. The values that the user chose will be placed into the query string.

```
extras=fudge&extras=cream&confirmButton=Confirm
```

When the values from the query string are copied to the bean, the mutator for the property will be called, with an array containing *fudge* and *cream*. A bean with these values will be placed in the session.

Now imagine that the user clicks the edit button, returns to the edit page and unchecks all the values. When the user clicks the confirm button, the name of the checkbox group will not be in the query string, because all of the values were unchecked.

```
confirmButton=Confirm
```

In this case, the mutator for the checkbox group's property will not be called, since the `fillBeanFromRequest` method only calls the mutators for properties that are in the query string. The effect of this is that the old values from the session will not be erased. The only way to erase those values is to call the setter again with new values. Since the user did not specify any new values, then the old values will still be there.

The solution to this problem is to manually call the setters for those properties that might not be included in the query string. These types of elements are often called *nullable* elements. Create a method that will call the mutators for each of the nullable elements.

```
public void resetNullable() {
    data.setExtra(null);
    data.setTeam(null);
    data.setHappiness(0);
}
```

Use appropriate values to reset the properties. For multiple-valued elements, *null* is the correct value to send to clear the array of values. Radio groups need a little more thought. If the property for the radio group is a string, then *null* can be used; if the property is numeric, then choose a value that is not listed in the radio group.

Call this method before new values are copied from the request into the bean.

```
resetNullable();
fillBeanFromRequest(data);
```

Only call this method when there is new data in the query string that will be used to refill the nullable elements. For instance, if this method were called when moving from the process page to the confirm page, then data would be lost; the values in the bean would be reset, but there would be no new values in the query string to restore them.

Accessing Multiple-Valued Properties

Since the accessors for multiple-valued elements return arrays, the JSP can access the values using a loop like the one that was used for displaying the database in Chap. 5. In this case, the array contains strings, so it is easy to display each of the values.

Note that the *taglib* statement must appear in the confirm page once and before any references to its tags.

```
<%@ taglib uri="http://java.sun.com/jsp/jstl/core"
           prefix="core" %>
...
<li>Extras:
  <ul>
  <core:forEach var="extra"
                items="${helper.data.extra}">
    <li>${extra}
  </core:forEach>
  </ul>
...
<li>Teams:
  <ul>
  <core:forEach var="team"
                items="${helper.data.team}">
    <li>${team}
  </core:forEach>
  </ul>
```

In these two examples, the multiple values have been displayed using one of the advanced layout tags: unordered list. The opening and closing list tags are placed before and after the loop tag. In the loop, each element in the array is displayed with a list item tag.

6.5   Application: Complex Elements

An application will be developed that uses all of these new form elements. There will be a password field, a radio group, a checkbox group, a textarea for multiple lines of text, a single selection list (drop-down list) and a multiple selection list (scrollable list).

6.5.1   Controller: Complex Elements

In order to see what the query string looks like for each request, all forms will use the GET method. The controller will only need to be able to process GET requests.

6.5.2   ControllerHelper: Complex Elements

The controller helper will be the same as the controller helper from the *Enhanced* example in Chap. 4, except for the name of the bean, the helper base class and the location of the JSPs. The helper base will be the one from Chap. 5.

6.5.3   Edit.jsp: Complex Elements

The edit page is the page that defines the data for the application. The edit page is where the user will enter all the data, so this is the page that will be defined first. All the other pages depend on this page; the bean will depend on the names of the form elements that are added to this page.

Listing 6.3 shows the edit page. It has a password field, a radio group, a checkbox group, a textarea, a single selection list and a multiple selection list. Each of these elements in the form is identical to the examples that were just developed above.

```
<!DOCTYPE html>
<html>
<head>
  <meta charset="utf-8">
  <title>Complex Form - Edit Page</title>
  <link rel="stylesheet" href="/${request.contextPath}/complex.css"
        type="text/css">
</head>
<body>
  <form method="get" action="Controller">
    Secret Code
    <input type="password" name="secretCode"><br>
    Level of Happiness:<br>
    <input type="radio" name="happiness"
           value="1" checked>
           Elated
```

```
<input type="radio" name="happiness"
        value="2">
        Ecstatic
<input type="radio" name="happiness"
        value="3">
        Joyous<br>
Preferred Extras:<br>
<input type="checkbox" name="extra"
        value="sprinkles">
        Chocolate Sprinkles
<input type="checkbox" name="extra"
        value="fudge" checked>
        Hot Fudge
<input type="checkbox" name="extra"
        value="cream">
        Whipped Cream<br>
Comments<textarea name="comments"></textarea>
<br>
Grade
<select name="grade">
  <option value="4.0">A
  <option value="3.67">A-
  <option value="3.33" selected>B+
  <option value="3.00">B
  <option value="2.67">B-
  <option value="2.33">C+
  <option value="2.00">C
</select>
<br>
Team
<select name="team" multiple size="2">
  <option value="heat">Heat
  <option value="marlins" selected>Marlins
  <option value="dolphins" selected>Dolphins
  <option value="panthers">Panthers
</select>
    <br>
    <input type="submit" name="confirmButton"
                         value="Confirm">
  </form>
</body></html>
```

Listing 6.3 An edit page that uses complex form elements

6.5.4   Java Bean: Complex Elements

The edit page is the most important file in the application; it defines the data. Once the edit page has been created, it is a straightforward process to create the bean.

The names of the bean properties will correspond to the names of the form elements in the edit page. The type of form element that is used in the edit page

Table 6.4 Correlation between the form elements and the bean properties

Element		Property	
Name	Type	Accessor	Type
secretCode	password	getSecretCode	single-valued
happiness	radio	getHappiness	single-valued
extra	checkbox	getExtra	multiple-valued
comments	textarea	getComments	single-valued
grade	select	getGrade	single-valued
team	select	getTeam	multiple-valued

will determine whether the bean uses a single-valued property or a multiple-valued property.

The names and types of the form elements from the edit page are listed in Table 6.4 along with the corresponding name of the accessor for the property and the type of the property.

All of the single-valued properties will look like the property for the text area field, `comments`, from Listing 6.1.

All of the multiple-valued properties will look like the property for the checkbox group, `extra`, from Listing 6.2.

The only differences for the other elements will be the name of the property and, possibly, the type of the property.

6.5.5   Confirm.jsp, Process.jsp: Complex Elements

The data from the bean is displayed in the confirm page. A nested ordered list is used to display the data from the bean. A loop is used to display the data from the multiple-valued elements: extra and team (Listing 6.4).

```
. . .
<%@ taglib uri="http://java.sun.com/jsp/jstl/core"
           prefix="core" %>
  <p>
       This page displays the values from some
       complex form elements.
  </p>
  <ul>
    <li>Secret Code: ${helper.data.secretCode}
    <li>Level of Happiness: ${helper.data.happiness}
    <li>Extras:
      <ul>
      <core:forEach var="extra"
                    items="${helper.data.extra}">
        <li>${extra}
```

```
      </core:forEach>
      </ul>
    <li>Comments: ${helper.data.comments}
    <li>Grade: ${helper.data.grade}
    <li>Teams:
      <ul>
      <core:forEach var="team"
                    items="${helper.data.team}">
        <li>${team}
      </core:forEach>
      </ul>
  </ul>
. . .
```

Listing 6.4 A confirm page that loops through the values in complex form elements

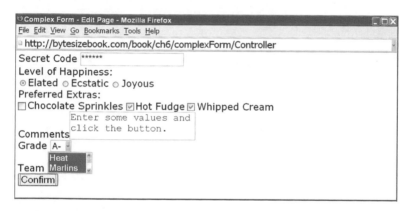

Fig. 6.8 Make some choices in the form elements

Except for having only one button, instead of two, the process page is identical to the confirm page.

 Try It

http://bytesizebook.com/book/ch6/complexForm/Controller

See how the elements look and interact with them. Submit the form to inspect the query string.

Choose some values in the form (Fig. 6.8).

Press the confirm button. The chosen values are displayed in the page and appear in the query string (Fig. 6.9).

The entire query string will not be visible in the location window of the browser. If it could all be seen at once, it would look like the following string. The multiple-valued properties each have more than one item selected, so each one has multiple entries in the query string.

Fig. 6.9 The confirm page with all the choices listed

```
?secretCode=secret+code&happiness=1&extra=fudge&extra=cream
&comments=Enter+some+values+and+click+the+button.
&grade=3.67&team=heat&team=marlins&confirmButton=Confirm
```

6.6   Using Advanced Form Elements

Using these new tags makes it easier for the user to enter data, but makes life a little more complicated for the developer. There is a new technique for initialising buttons in the checked state and for initialising the selection lists with selected options that are in the query string. For elements that allow the user to select multiple choices, a new technique is needed to save the data to the database.

6.6.1   Initialising Form Elements

Initialising password fields is identical to initialising text elements.

```
<input type="password" name="secretCode"
        value="${helper.data.secretCode}">
```

Textareas are a little different, because they are paired tags. Place the initial value between the opening and closing tags.

```
<textarea name="comments"
        >${helper.data.comments}</textarea>
```

The radio, checkbox and selection lists are a bit more complicated. The initial state of a radio button or checkbox button is controlled by an attribute named *checked*. If this attribute is present in the tag, then the button will be in the checked state; if the attribute is missing, then the button will be in the unchecked state.

In the following listing, the radio button for *Elated* will be in the checked state every time the page is loaded; the *Ecstatic* button will not be checked.

```
<input type="radio" name="happiness"
       value="1" checked>
       Elated
<input type="radio" name="happiness"
       value="2">
       Ecstatic
```

Somehow, the attribute *checked* must be set dynamically. If the value associated with the checkbox or radio button is in the query string, then the button should have the attribute *checked* inserted into the tag.

One way to solve this problem is to place each tag in an if block and test if the corresponding value is in the query string. The following code demonstrates how a JSTL *if* tag could be used to dynamically set the *checked* attribute:

```
<input type="radio" name="happiness" value="1"
       <core:if test="${param.happiness==1}">
          checked
       </core:if>
       >Elated
<input type="radio" name="happiness" value="2"
       <core:if test="${param.happiness==2}">
          checked
       </core:if>
       >Ecstatic
<input type="radio" name="happiness" value="3"
       <core:if test="${param.happiness==3}">
          checked
       </core:if>
       >Joyous
```

This is the code for one radio group. Similar code would need to be added for each checkbox group and selection list. The approach gets very messy, very quickly. It makes the JSP very difficult to read, because there are many if statements scattered amongst the HTML.

Try It

http://bytesizebook.com/book/ch6/checked_if.jsp

In the JSP, click one of the radio buttons and then submit the form. The radio button value will appear in the query string. The radio button will remain in the checked state.

A solution to the problem of initialising form buttons, that avoids using any `if` statements to determine if *checked* should be inserted into the tag, is to add a map to the helper base that will associate the string *checked* with those values that are in the query string.

The idea is to create a map that associates a form element with the word *checked*. Each radio button or checkbox button in the form will have an entry in the map if the button was checked by the user. If the user did not check the button, then that button will not have an entry in the map.

6.6.2   Map of Checked Values

The way this will be done is to create a map of maps. There will be a map for each radio group or checkbox group that has a button checked. Each of these maps will be placed in an all-encompassing map. This will allow the JSP to access the big map and be able to access the individual maps by the name of the radio group or checkbox group.

Each of the smaller maps will associate a string with a string, so the Map should be instantiated as such.

```
Map<String, String>
```

The all-encompassing map will associate a string with one of the smaller maps. This map will have a key that is a string, but the value will be a smaller map.

```
Map<String, Map<String, String>>
```

The map will store the word *checked* for all those buttons that have been checked by the user, so it will be called *checked*.

```
Map<String, Map<String, String>> checked
          = new HashMap<String, Map<String, String>>();
```

One way to envision this is to think of a map of the world. Each country will be represented on the world map, but to obtain specific information about a country, a more detailed map for just that country would be needed.

Fig. 6.10 The big map with two small maps

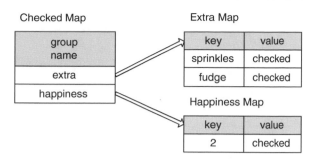

A Small Map

For each radio and checkbox group that has a button checked, there must be a small map added to the big map. Each group will have its own small map inside the larger map.

Consider a radio group named *happiness*.

```
<input type="radio" name="happiness" value="1">Elated
<input type="radio" name="happiness" value="2">Ecstatic
<input type="radio" name="happiness" value="3">Joyous
```

A small map must be created for the radio group in the *checked* map. The name of the group will be used as the key to retrieve the small map from the *checked* map.

```
checked.put("happiness",
            new HashMap<String, String>());
```

Each checked button in the group will be added to this small map.

Adding a Key

If the user has chosen *Ecstatic* in the radio group, then the value in the query string for the radio group will be 2. That is the string that will be used as the key for the radio group's map; the value will be the word *checked*.

```
checked.get("happiness").put("2", "checked");
```

The call to `checked.get("happiness")` returns the map for the radio group. In this map, the word *checked* is associated with the key 2 by using the put method of the small map.

Figure 6.10 shows the big map with a small map for a radio group and a small map for a checkbox group.

Retrieving Map Values

Later, to determine if the *Ecstatic* button should be checked, use the name of the group to retrieve the small map for the group, then retrieve the word stored in the map for the button, using the button's value as the key to the map.

```
if (checked.get("happiness") != null) {
  checked.get("happiness").get("2")
}
```

Assuming that the user clicked this button, this will return the word *checked*. To avoid a null pointer exception, always verify that the small map for the group is not null before attempting to access a value from the map.

Note that the parameter to the first get is the name of the group for the button and the parameter to the second get is the value of the button.

```
<input type="radio" name="happiness" value="2">Ecstatic
```

What will be returned if the map is accessed with the other values in the radio group?

```
checked.get("happiness").get("1")
checked.get("happiness").get("3")
```

In both cases, the map will return *null*. Since neither button was clicked, neither value was sent in the query string and neither value was placed into the map for the radio group.

Select lists use the word *selected* to select an option in the list. In addition to a map for the checked values, a similar map will be created for the selection lists. This map will associate the word *selected* with those values that have been chosen by the user.

Modifying the Helper Base

Both of these maps will be added to the helper base class.

```
protected Map<String, Map<String, String>> checked =
        new HashMap<String, Map<String, String>>();
protected Map<String, Map<String, String>> selected =
        new HashMap<String, Map<String, String>>();
```

Two accessors will be added to the helper base class so that the maps can be accessed from a JSP.

```
public Map getChecked() {
    return checked;
}

public Map getSelected() {
    return selected;
}
```

For each selected group or list, a new map must be created. If the map for a group or list does not exist when an item is added, then the map will be created for that group. This will be encapsulated in a method that accepts the name of the group or list and the value that the user has chosen. If there is no map for the group or list, then a new map will be created. Then, the appropriate word will be added to the map for the value.

```
public void addChecked(String group, String item) {
    if (checked.get(group) == null) {
        checked.put(group,

                new HashMap<String, String>());
    }
    checked.get(group).put(item, "checked");
}

public void addSelected(String list, String item) {
    if (selected.get(list) == null) {
        selected.put(list,
                new HashMap<String, String>());
    }
    selected.get(list).put(item, "selected");
}
```

A method will be added for clearing all values from the maps.

```
public void clearMaps() {
    checked.clear();
    selected.clear();
}
```

Figure 6.11 contains a diagram of the helper base class. The maps, accessors and helper methods have been added. An additional method has been added, which will be explained in the next section.

6.6.3 Automating the Process

The process of calling the addChecked and addSelected methods can be automated by annotating the properties in the bean that correspond to radio groups, checkbox groups and selection lists. A new annotation will be used to mark the accessors of those properties.

Since these properties are set by adding the *checked* or *selected* attribute to the element in the form, the annotation will be called SetByAttribute. The annotation will have an attribute that indicates whether this property is set by using the word *checked* or *selected*. To reduce errors, an enumeration has been created for the two possible values (Fig. 6.12).

The annotation uses a value from the enumeration to configure the property. For those properties that correspond to radio and checkbox groups, use the

Fig. 6.11 The helper base
class with the checked and
selected maps

HelperBase
HttpServletRequest request HttpServletResponse response Logger logger Map errorMap Map checked Map selected
abstract copyFromSession() addHelperToSession() executeButtonMethod() fillBeanFromRequest() setErrors() getErrors() isValid() addChecked() addSelected() getChecked() getSelected() clearMaps() setCheckedAndSelected()

Fig. 6.12 The enumeration
of `AttributeType`

enum AttributeType
CHECKED SELECTED

`AttributeType.CHECKED` value; for those that correspond to selection lists, use the `AttributeType.SELECTED` value.

```
import shared.SetByAttribute;
import shared.AttributeType;
...
@SetByAttribute(type=AttributeType.CHECKED)
public int getHappiness() {
    return happiness;

}

@SetByAttribute(type=AttributeType.SELECTED)
public double getGrade() {
    return grade;
}
```

Like the `ButtonMethod` annotation, a method has been added to the helper base that loops through all the methods in the bean and looks for those that have been marked with the `SetByAttribute` annotation. For those accessors that have been marked, the appropriate `addChecked` or `addSelected` method will be called. If the accessor returns an array, then all of the values will be added to the map. The name of this method is `setCheckedAndSelected`; it has been added to the helper base class.

```
protected void setCheckedAndSelected(Object data) {
    . . .
}
```

By calling `setCheckedAndSelected`, all the values in the bean for radio groups, checkbox groups and selection lists will be added to the corresponding checked or selected map. As long as the annotations have been added in the bean, this is the only method that needs to be called to add the values to the maps.

Setting the Maps
The maps should be filled every time the bean has new data added to it. This corresponds to the time when `fillBeanFromRequest` is called.

```
fillBeanFromRequest(data);
setCheckedAndSelected(data);
```

JSP Access
The big payoff for this technique can be seen from a JSP. Since accessors were added to the helper base that returns the all-encompassing maps for *checked* and *selected*, EL can access the maps from a JSP.

```
${helper.checked}
${helper.selected}
```

EL is especially useful when accessing a map; the `get` method of a map can be accessed using the dot notation. Therefore, the map for the radio group can also be retrieved.

```
${helper.checked.happiness}
```

Finally, the word associated with the value 2 in the radio group can be retrieved. For those values in a map that are numbers or have embedded spaces, the dot notation cannot be used to retrieve them. However, EL also allows array notation to be used to access the `get` method of a map. EL automatically avoids a null pointer exception by testing that the *happiness* map is not null before accessing a value from the map.

```
${helper.checked.happiness["2"]}
```

Consider the complete radio group that has the code added to it for retrieving the values from its map.

```
Level of Happiness:
<input type="radio" name="happiness" value="1"
       ${helper.checked.happiness["1"]}>Elated
<input type="radio" name="happiness" value="2"
       ${helper.checked.happiness["2"]}>Ecstatic
<input type="radio" name="happiness" value="3"
       ${helper.checked.happiness["3"]}>Joyous
```

Ask yourself what will happen if the user chooses the *Ecstatic* button.

In this case, `${helper.checked.happiness["2"]}` will return the value *checked*. Both `${helper.checked.happiness["1"]}` and `${data.checked.happiness["3"]}` will return *null*, which EL will render as the empty string.

The radio group will be returned to the browser with the button for *Ecstatic* checked and the other buttons unchecked.

```
Level of Happiness:
<input type="radio" name="happiness" value="1"
          >Elated
<input type="radio" name="happiness" value="2"
          checked>Ecstatic
<input type="radio" name="happiness" value="3"
          >Joyous
```

A similar process will occur if the user checks one of the other buttons. The trick is that the value that was sent in the query string to the controller has been used as a key in the map for the radio group, while the other values in the radio group have not been added to the map.

Data Flow

To take a closer look at how the data moves from the JSP to the controller and back again, modify the checkbox group in the JSP so that all the boxes whose values are in the query string are checked whe the page is loaded.

```
<input type="checkbox" name="extra" value="sprinkles"
       ${helper.checked.extra.sprinkles}>
       Chocolate Sprinkles
<input type="checkbox" name="extra" value="fudge"
       ${helper.checked.extra.fudge}>
       Hot Fudge
<input type="checkbox" name="extra" value="cream"
       ${helper.checked.extra.cream}>
       Whipped Cream
```

Assuming that the user selects *sprinkles* and *fudge*, this is the path that the data would follow.
1. There are three options in the checkbox group: *sprinkles*, *fudge* and *cream*.
2. The user selects *sprinkles* and *fudge*.
3. The query string would contain `extra` = `sprinkles&extra` = `fudge`.
4. These values would be placed into an array by the servlet engine: `{"sprinkles",` `"fudge"}`
5. This array would be returned by the `getExtra` method in the bean.
6. This `setCheckedAndSelected` method would loop through these values and call `addChecked` for each, adding *sprinkles* and *fudge* to the hash map for the checkbox group.
7. The map for the checkbox group would be created before the first value is added to it.
8. The map for the checkbox group would have the pairs
   (`"sprinkles"`, `"checked"`) and (`"fudge"`, `"checked"`) in it.
9. In the JSP
   (a) `${helper.checked.extra["sprinkles"]}` would return the value *checked*.
   (b) `${helper.checked.extra["fudge"]}` would return the value *checked*.
   (c) `${helper.checked.extra["cream"]}` would return `null` and would be displayed as the empty string.

Figure 6.13 demonstrates how the EL statement in a JSP accesses a small map for a checkbox group named *extra*.

6.7   Application: Initialised Complex Elements

The *Complex Form* example will be modified so that the form elements are initialised with data that is in the query string. This means that if the user enters data in the edit page, proceeds to the confirm page and returns to the edit page, then all of the user's choices will be initialised in the form.
1. The controller will handle GET and POST requests.
2. The JSP forms will be modified so that they use the POST method.
3. The maps for the checked and selected values will be added to the helper base.
4. The accessors and helper methods for the checked and selected maps will be added to the helper base.
5. The methods for automating the process of setting the values in the maps will be added to the helper base.
6. The bean will be annotated with the `SetByAttribute` annotation.
7. The edit page will have the EL added to it for retrieving the *checked* and *selected* attributes.

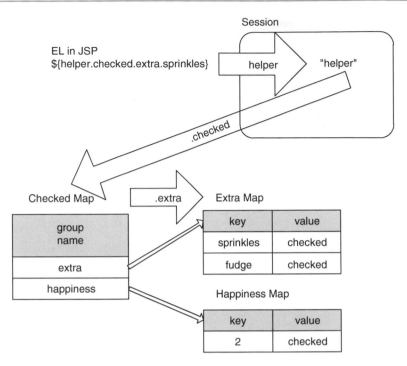

Fig. 6.13 Accessing the small map for a checkbox group

6.7.1   Java Bean: Initialised Complex Elements

Annotate all the accessors for radio groups, checkbox groups and select lists with the SetByAttribute annotation.

```
...
@SetByAttribute(type=AttributeType.CHECKED)
public int getHappiness() {
    return happiness;
}

@SetByAttribute(type=AttributeType.SELECTED)
public double getGrade() {
    return grade;
}

@SetByAttribute(type=AttributeType.CHECKED)
public String[] getExtra() {
    return extra;
}

@SetByAttribute(type=AttributeType.SELECTED)
    public String[] getTeam() {
    return team;
}
...
```

6.7.2   HelperBase: Initialised Complex Elements

The maps for *checked* and *selected* values will be added to the helper base class as member variables. The helper methods for setting values in the maps will be added. Accessors will be added for retrieving the maps from JSPs. The method for automating the process will be added.

```
protected Map<String, Map<String, String>> checked =
        new HashMap<String, Map<String, String>>();
protected Map<String, Map<String, String>> selected =
        new HashMap<String, Map<String, String>>();
...
public Map getChecked() {
    return checked;
}

public Map getSelected() {
    return selected;
}
...
protected void setCheckedAndSelected(Object data) {
    ...
}
```

Additional methods for using the maps have also been added to the helper base. See the Appendix for a complete listing of the Helper Base class for Chap. 6.

6.7.3   ControllerHelper: Initialised Complex Elements

Up until now, whenever data was copied from the session, only the bean was copied. Now, there is additional data to be copied from the session into the current helper: the maps for selected and checked values. The copy method needs to be updated so that the maps are copied from the data in the session into the current helper.

```
...
public void copyFromSession(Object sessionHelper) {
  if (sessionHelper.getClass() == this.getClass()) {
    ControllerHelper helper =
        (ControllerHelper) sessionHelper;
    data = helper.data;
    checked = helper.checked;
    selected = helper.selected;
  }
}
...
```

The radio groups, checkbox groups and multiple select lists might not have any choices chosen by the user. In order to delete all the old values from the session, call the mutator for each nullable property. A method named resetNullable will be added to the controller helper. In it, each of the mutators for the radio, checkbox and multiple selection list have been called with appropriate values.

```
. . .
public void resetNullable() {
   data.setExtra(null);
   data.setTeam(null);
   data.setHappiness(0);
}
. . .
```

Reset the nullable elements before new data is added to the bean. Add the values for the checked and selected maps after new data has been added to the bean. Perform these tasks in the method for the confirm button, since this is the only time when there is new data.

```
. . .
@ButtonMethod(buttonName="confirmButton")
public String confirmMethod() {
   resetNullable();
   fillBeanFromRequest(data);
   setCheckedAndSelected(data);
   String address;
   if (isValid(data)) {
      address = jspLocation("Confirm.jsp");
   } else {
      address = jspLocation("Edit.jsp");
   }
   return address;
}
. . .
```

It is not necessary to reset the maps for the selected and checked values, since these are reset every time setCheckedAndSelected is called.

6.7.4   Edit.jsp: Initialised Complex Elements

Initialise the checkbox buttons with the values from the query string by including the code that accesses the maps.

```
<input type="checkbox" name="extra" value="sprinkles"
        ${helper.checked.extra.sprinkles}>
        Chocolate Sprinkles
<input type="checkbox" name="extra" value="fudge"
        ${helper.checked.extra.fudge}>
        Hot Fudge
<input type="checkbox" name="extra" value="cream"
        ${helper.checked.extra.cream}>
        Whipped Cream
```

The radio group is initialised in a similar way.

Initialise each option in the multiple selection list with the values from the query string by including the code that accesses the maps.

```
<select name="team" multiple size="2">
  <option value="heat"
          ${helper.selected.team.heat}>
          Heat
  <option value="marlins"
          ${helper.selected.team.marlins}>
          Marlins
  <option value="dolphins"
          ${helper.selected.team.dolphins}>
          Dolphins
  <option value="panthers"
          ${helper.selected.team.panthers}>
          Panthers
</select>
```

The single selection list is initialised in a similar way.

 Try It

http://bytesizebook.com/book/ch6/complexInit/Controller

Enter some values into the form, then click the confirm button. From the confirm page, click the edit button and you will see the edit page initialised with all the values that were selected before.

6.8   Validating Multiple Choices

Two annotations are used to validate the number of elements that have been selected for a multiple-valued property. While it may seem that the Size annotation is all that is needed, it cannot test if the array is null.

Use the NotNull annotation to verify that at least one item has been selected in the group. Use the *message* attribute to provide a clear error message for the user.

```
@NotNull(message=": must select at least one extra.")
public String[] getExtra() {
```

Use the Size annotation to verify the number of elements in the array. The annotation has two required attributes named *min* and *max*. Use them to set the minimum and maximum number of elements that can be entered. Testing for a minimum size of one is not the same as testing if the array is null. Use the *message* attribute to provide a clear error message to the user.

```
@Size(min=0, max=3, message=": cannot select all teams.")
public String[] getTeam() {
```

6.9   Application: Complex Validation

The *Complex Initialised* example will be extended by validating the number of elements that were entered into the multiple-valued properties. The only changes that are needed are for the bean and for Edit.jsp.

6.9.1   Java Bean: Complex Validation

Annotate the accessor for the extra property so that at least one element must be selected. Use the NotNull annotation for this. Annotate the team property so that the user cannot select all of the elements in the list. Use the Size annotation for this.

Since this is a continuation of the *Complex Initialised* example, the SetByAttribute annotation is used although it is not needed to validate a property.

```java
import javax.validation.constraints.NotNull;
import javax.validation.constraints.Size;
. . .
@NotNull(message=": must select at least one extra.")
@SetByAttribute(type=AttributeType.CHECKED)
public String[] getExtra() {
    return extra;
}

@Size(min=0, max=3, message=": cannot select all teams.")
@SetByAttribute(type=AttributeType.SELECTED)
    public String[] getTeam() {
    return team;
}
. . .
```

6.9.2   Edit.jsp: Complex Validation

For the edit page, add the EL statements that display the error messages for the multiple-valued elements of extras and team.

```jsp
Preferred Extras ${helper.errors.extra}
<input type="checkbox" name="extra" value="sprinkles"
        ${helper.checked.extra.sprinkles}>
        Chocolate Sprinkles
<input type="checkbox" name="extra" value="fudge"
        ${helper.checked.extra.fudge}>
        Hot Fudge
```

```
<input type="checkbox" name="extra" value="cream"
       ${helper.checked.extra.cream}>
       Whipped Cream
...
Team ${helper.errors.team}
<select name="team" multiple size="2">
  <option value="heat"
           ${helper.selected.team.heat}>
           Heat
   <option value="marlins"
           ${helper.selected.team.marlins}>
           Marlins
   <option value="dolphins"
           ${helper.selected.team.dolphins}>
           Dolphins
   <option value="panthers"
           ${helper.selected.team.panthers}>
           Panthers
</select>
```

⟨⟨ Try It

http://bytesizebook.com/book/ch6/complexValid/Controller

Click the confirm button without entering any values in any of the fields. An error message will appear for the extra checkbox group, indicating that at least one element must be chosen.

Select at least one value for the extra checkbox group and select all the values from the team multiple select list. Click the confirm button. An error will appear for the team list, indicating that not all of the elements can be selected.

6.10   Saving Multiple Choices

It is not difficult to save a bean that uses the advanced form elements. The single-valued properties behave just like text boxes. For multiple-valued properties, the accessors need two additional Hibernate annotations.

```
@ElementCollection
@IndexColumn
```

The ElementCollection annotation means that Hibernate will create an additional table for the multiple-valued property. This is completely transparent at the Java class level. Figure 6.14 is an example of data that is in the main table for the bean that has been developed in this chapter. It does not include the data for the multiple-valued properties; that data is stored in separate tables.

```
mysql> select * from complexdatapersistent;
+----+------------+--------------+-----------+-------+
| id | secretCode | comments     | happiness | grade |
+----+------------+--------------+-----------+-------+
|  1 | rutabega   | Nothing much |         1 | 3.33  |
|  2 | blahblah   | No comment.  |         2 |     4 |
+----+------------+--------------+-----------+-------+
2 rows in set (0.00 sec)
```

Fig. 6.14 The data for the collection of elements is not in the main table

```
mysql> select * from complexdatapersistent_extra;
+-------------------------+-----------+-----------+
| ComplexDataPersistent_id | element  | extra_pos |
+-------------------------+-----------+-----------+
|                       1 | sprinkles |         0 |
|                       1 | fudge     |         1 |
|                       1 | cream     |         2 |
|                       2 | fudge     |         0 |
+-------------------------+-----------+-----------+
4 rows in set (0.00 sec)
```

Fig. 6.15 The data for each collection of elements is in a separate table

The data for each multiple-valued property is stored in a separate table. Each separate table is related to the main table for the bean. In order to build this relationship, each row in the separate table will contain the primary key of the related row in the main table. However, there can be multiple rows in the separate table for one row in the main table.

In order to identify each of the rows uniquely, there is a secondary key in the related table. The secondary key distinguishes amongst multiple values for the same row in the main table. This is an example of a table that has a composite primary key. It is made up of two columns: the primary key from the main table and the secondary key from the related table. The secondary key will be generated by the database and is referred to as an index column.

Figure 6.15 shows the values for the checkbox group, named *extra*. The first column in the table contains the primary key from the main table. The last column in the table contains the secondary key. The primary key and the secondary key together will uniquely identify each row in this table.

The `IndexColumn` annotation sets the name of the column for the secondary key in the separate related table. The `base` attribute is where to start indexing. The usual values are zero or one.

```java
import javax.persistence.ElementCollection;
import org.hibernate.annotations.IndexColumn;
...
@ElementCollection
@IndexColumn(name="extra_pos", base=0)
@SetByAttribute(type=AttributeType.CHECKED)
public String[] getExtra() {
    return extra;
}
```

Only annotate properties that return an array with these annotations. If single-valued properties are annotated with them, there will be a runtime error.

6.11 Application: Complex Persistent

The *Complex Initialised* example will be extended by saving data to the database. Review the steps from Chap. 5 for writing an application that saves data to a database.

The only additional step that is needed to write a multiple-valued property to the database is to annotate the accessor of the property.

Since this servlet will access the database, it will have an initialisation parameter for creating the database, just like the persistent example from Chap. 5. Any servlet that has an initialisation parameter should use the *web.xml* file to declare the servlet, servlet mapping and initialisation parameter.

6.11.1 ControllerHelper: Complex Persistent

In the controller helper, instead of using Java to configure Hibernate, use a `hibernate.cfg.xml` (see Chap. 5). Place this file in the *classes* directory of the web app. Be sure to update the file with your server, port, username, password and database.

```
. . .
<property name="connection.url">
  jdbc:mysql://your-server:your-port/your-database
</property>
<property name="connection.username">
  your-user-name
</property>
<property name="connection.password">
  your-password
</property>
. . .
```

With this change, the `initHibernate` method in the controller helper is simplified.

```
static public void initHibernate (boolean create)
{
  if (create) {
    HibernateHelper
        .createTable(ComplexDataPersistent.class);
  }
  HibernateHelper
      .initSessionFactory(ComplexDataPersistent.class);
}
```

6.11.2 Java Bean: Complex Persistent

Each of the multiple-valued properties from the *Initialised Complex Elements* application needs to be annotated with two annotations, ElementCollection and IndexColumn. Only place these annotations before the properties that return arrays.

Since this is a continuation of the *Complex Initialised* example, the SetByAttribute annotation is used although it is not needed to save a property to the database.

```
import org.hibernate.annotations.IndexColumn;
import javax.persistence.ElementCollection;
. . .
@ElementCollection
@IndexColumn(name="extra_pos", base=0)
@SetByAttribute(type=AttributeType.CHECKED)
public String[] getExtra() {
    return extra;
}

@ElementCollection
@IndexColumn(name="team_pos", base=0)
@SetByAttribute(type=AttributeType.SELECTED)
public String[] getTeam() {
    return team;
}
. . .
```

6.11.3 Process.jsp: Complex Persistent

The only JSP that needs to be changed is the process JSP. It will display the list of data that is in the database. This is not a normal feature in an application; it is done in this application to demonstrate that the data has been updated in the database.

A table is used to organise the data in the database. An outer loop is used to access each row in the database; each field from the row is displayed in its own cell in the table. For a cell that contains a multiple-valued property, there is an inner loop that displays all of the property's values. The *taglib* statement for the JSTL must be included in the JSP before the first reference to a *core* tag.

```
<%@ taglib uri="http://java.sun.com/jsp/jstl/core"
           prefix="core" %>
. . .
<table>
  <core:forEach var="record" items="${database}">
    <tr>
```

```
  <td>${record.secretCode}
  <td>${record.happiness}
  <td>
    <ul>
      <core:forEach var="extra"
                    items="${record.extra}">
        <li>${extra}
      </core:forEach>
    </ul>
  <td>${record.comments}
  <td>${record.grade}
  <td>
    <ul>
      <core:forEach var="team"
                    items="${record.team}">
        <li>${team}
      </core:forEach>
    </ul>
  </tr>
 </core:forEach>
</table>
...
```

View Source
≽ **Try It**

http://bytesizebook.com/book/ch6/complexPersistent/Controller
Enter some data in the form, confirm the data and view all the rows from the database.

6.12   Summary

The basic structure of a web application was developed in the first four chapters. This chapter introduced features that added more style to a web application, not more substance.

There are more advanced ways to arrange content in a web page than using paragraph tags and new line tags. These advanced layout tags give the developer more control over how the content is arranged in the page. List tags allow indexes and table of contents to be generated with ease. A table tag can be used to display tabular data from a spreadsheet or database.

There are also additional tags that add style to the page. These tags are of a generic sort; they allow the developer to arrange content according to what the content represents and not the actual style of the content. It is up to the browser to decide how to display these elements.

Web designers wanted more ways to set the style of a page. Developing more tags like italic was one possibility, but it was not a good possibility. Instead, it was recommended that style be separated from the HTML as much as possible. The way to do this was with cascading style sheets. This allowed the developer to define the style for a website in one file and let all the HTML files use the same style sheet. This is now the preferred way to add style to a website.

There are also additional tags for specifying input in an HTML form. While text boxes and submit buttons are all that are needed for user input, there are additional input elements that use radio buttons, checkbox groups, drop-down lists, scrollable lists, password fields and multiline text boxes. These elements make it easier for a user to enter data in a form.

While these new tags make it easier for the user, they add some complexity to the web application for the developer. It is more difficult to initialise some of these elements with data in the query string, and it is more difficult to save some of them to a database.

6.13   Chapter Review

Terms
1. In-line Tag
2. Block Tag
3. Ordered List
4. Unordered List
5. Definition List
6. Table
    (a) Table Row
    (b) Table Data
    (c) Table Heading
7. Embedded Image
8. Cascading Style Sheet (CSS)
    (a) Scales
    (b) Default Styles
    (c) Multiple Definitions
    (d) Nested Styles
    (e) Named Styles
    (f) Unique Styles
    (g) Generic Styles
    (h) Pseudo Styles
    (i) Class
    (j) Id
    (k) Font Family
    (l) Generic Font Family
9. External Style Sheet
10. Radio Group
11. Checkbox Group
12. Selection Lists

13. Single-Valued Properties
14. Multiple-Valued Properties
15. Nullable Fields
16. Map of Checked Values
17. Map of Selected Values

New Java
1. Annotations
   (a) @ElementCollection
   (b) @IndexColumn(name="…", base = 0)
   (c) @SetByAttribute(type="AttributeType….")
   (d) @Size(min="…", max="…")
2. Enumerations
   (a) AttributeType {CHECKED, SELECTED}

Tags
1. JSP
   (a) ${helper.checked}
   (b) ${helper.selected}
   (c) ${helper.checked.extra}
   (d) ${helper.selected.team}
   (e) ${helper.checked.extra.fudge}
   (f) ${helper.selected.team.heat}
   (g) ${helper.checked.extra["whipped cream"]}
   (h) ${helper.selected.team["2"]}
2. In-line tags: cite, code, del, ins, dfn, em.kbd, abbr, samp, strong, var, span
3. Block tags: p, blockquote, pre, h1 .. h6, div
4. ol
   (a) li
5. ul
   (a) li
6. dl
   (a) dt
   (b) dt
7. Table
   (a) tr
   (b) td
       rowspan attribute
       colspan attribute
   (c) th
       rowspan attribute
       colspan attribute
8. img
   (a) *src* attribute
   (b) *alt* attribute

9. Link
  (a) *href* attribute
  (b) *rel* attribute
  (c) *type* attribute
10. Form elements
  (a) Input
  (b) Password
  (c) Radio
        checked attribute
  (d) Checkbox
        checked attribute
11. Textarea
12. Select
  (a) *multiple* attribute
  (b) *size* attribute
13. Option
  (a) *selected* attribute

Style
  1. background-color
  2. background-image
  3. border
  4. color
  5. float
  6. font-family
  7. font-size
  8. font-weight
  9. font-style
  10. list-style-type
  11. margin-left
  12. margin-right
  13. text-decoration
  14. text-transform
  15. text-align
  16. text-indent
  17. padding
  18. position
  19. width

Questions
  1. What is the difference between an in-line tag and a block tag?
  2. How many predefined headings are there?
  3. How is the `<ol>` tag different from the `<ul>` tag?
  4. How is the `<th>` tag different from the `<td>` tag?
  5. What does the rowspan attribute control?

6. What does the colspan attribute control?
7. List the fixed scales in a style sheet.
8. List the relative scales in a style sheet.
9. What is a font family?
10. What is a generic font family?
11. How can strong tags inside paragraphs be given a different appearance from strong tags inside tables?
12. How can two paragraphs have different styles defined for them?
13. If *special* is a named style for paragraphs, how can a paragraph in an HTML page be given this named style?
14. List all the different types of input elements in a form (not just the new ones from this chapter).
15. Explain how a radio button can be placed into the checked state.
16. What would the query string look like if a password field named *secret* had the value *top secret code* typed into it?
17. What would the query string look like if a textarea named *comments* had the value *I love Java* typed into it?
18. What would the query string look like if a radio group named *team* had the value *marlins* checked?
19. What would the query string look like if a single selection list named *team* had the value *panthers* selected?
20. What would the query string look like if a checkbox group named *team* had the two values *heat* and *dolphins* checked?
21. What would the query string look like if a multiple selection list named *team* had the two values *hurricanes* and *dolphins* selected?
22. What is the difference between the mutator for a single-valued property and the mutator for a multiple-valued property in a bean?
23. Write the JSP code that will display all the values for a checkbox group named *team*.
24. Write the JSP code that will display all the values for a multiple selection list named *team*.
25. What is the purpose of the resetNullable method?
26. Explain how a hash map is used to simplify the initialisation of a checkbox group in a JSP.
27. What annotations are needed to save a checkbox group to a database?
28. What annotations are needed to save a multiple selection list to a database?
29. Explain how nested loops are used to display all the values in a collection of beans if there are multiple-valued properties in the bean.

Tasks

1. Create an HTML page that has six paragraphs. Give each paragraph a different heading from the predefined headings. Include some content in each paragraph. Be sure that each heading is separate from each paragraph.
2. Create an HTML page that has three paragraphs. Make one paragraph bold, one italic and one underlined. Do not use the bold, italic and underline tags.

3. Create an HTML page that has a table with four rows and three columns. Include text or graphics in each cell in the table.
   (a) Make one of the cells in the table span two rows.
   (b) Make one of the cells in the table span two columns.
   (c) Make one of the cells span two columns and two rows.
4. Create an HTML page that has four divisions: top, left, right, center. The top division will fill the top third of the page. The right and left will fill the left and right area of the bottom two-thirds of the page. The center section will fill the space between the left and right divisions. Use a style sheet to control the layout, not a table.
5. Create a style sheet that will set the colours, margins and font for a page. Give a list of preferred fonts, with a final choice that is one of the generic font families.
6. Create an HTML page that has an outline. There should be three levels in the outline. Create a style sheet for the page that will set the numbering for the outline as uppercase Roman letters, then uppercase English letters, then decimal numbers.
7. Create a style sheet that forces all predefined headings to be displayed in uppercase letters. Create an HTML page that uses this style sheet and demonstrates the styles.
8. Create a style sheet that sets the margin for all paragraphs to five widths of the letter 'x'. In this style sheet, also create a named style for paragraphs that creates a hanging indent. A hanging indent indents the entire paragraph, except for the first line. Create an HTML page that uses this style sheet and demonstrates the styles.
9. Create an HTML page that has three paragraphs. Make one paragraph bold, one italic and one underlined. Do not use the bold, italic and underline tags. Create a style sheet for the page that defines three named styles for paragraphs.
10. Create a style sheet that will set the width of ordered lists to three-fourths the width of the page. Also set the width of horizontal rulers to three-fourths the width of the page. Create an HTML page that uses this style sheet and demonstrates the styles.
11. Create an application with a JSP that has a form with a textarea and a password.
    (a) Create a bean to encapsulate the data.
    (b) Create a controller.
    (c) Validate that the password has at least six characters.
    (d) Validate that the textarea has at least six words.
    (e) If the data is invalid, display the form again with the textarea and password initialised with any values that the user had supplied.
    (f) If the data is valid, display the data and allow the user to confirm it or edit it.
    (g) If the user confirms the data, save it to a database and display a page with the user's data.

12. Create an application with a JSP that has a form with a radio group and a single selection list.
  (a) Create a bean to encapsulate the data.
  (b) Create a controller.
  (c) Validate that at least one of the radio buttons has been checked.
  (d) Validate that at least one of the options in the list has been selected.
  (e) If the data is invalid, display the form again with the radio group and list initialised with any values that the user had supplied.
  (f) If the data is valid, display the data and allow the user to confirm it or edit it.
  (g) If the user confirms the data, save it to a database and display a page with the user's data.
13. Create an application with a JSP that has a form with a checkbox group and a multiple selection list.
  (a) Create a bean to encapsulate the data.
  (b) Create a controller.
  (c) Validate that at least two of the checkboxes are checked.
  (d) Validate that not all of the items in the selection list are selected.
  (e) If the data is invalid, display the form again with the checkbox group and list initialised with any values that the user had supplied.
  (f) If the data is valid, display the data and allow the user to confirm it or edit it.
  (g) If the user confirms the data, save it to a database and display a page with the user's data.

Accounts, Cookies and Carts

7

An application will be developed that requires a user to log into the site. Once the user has logged in, the user's previous data will be retrieved from the database.

Finding a row in the database using the primary key is a simple matter. However, the primary key that we have been using has been generated by the database, and its value is unknown to the user. In order to find a row in the database, there must be a way for the user to uniquely specify the desired row. In the simple case, there will be a field that uniquely identifies each row in the database, like social security number, phone number, e-mail address or account number. In other cases, several fields might need to be combined to identify a row. We shall only consider the simple case where one field can identify a row. Once a bean has been retrieved from the database, it will be placed in the session and used to store all the information that the user enters. When this bean is written to the database, the values will be used to update the row that is already in the database.

Web applications are stateless: the developer must add code so that the application will remember what the user has done recently. Because of this, it is difficult to identify users until they log into a database. For this reason, cookies were developed. Cookies allow information to be stored on a user's computer. When the user visits a site, the stored information is sent to the site. The application can use this information to identify the user.

Cookies can be created for specific URLs and specific times. More than one cookie can be set by an application and more than one cookie can be received by an application. An application can delete a cookie by setting its time to zero. A user can delete a cookie through the browser's menus.

Most e-commerce sites allow the user to enter data into a shopping cart. This allows the user to browse the site, adding items to the cart for later purchase. A shopping cart is easy to implement using Java 1.5 generics. A complete application will be developed that uses a shopping cart.

T. Downey, *Guide to Web Development with Java: Understanding Website Creation*,
DOI 10.1007/978-1-4471-2443-6_7, © Springer-Verlag London Limited 2012

7.1   Retrieving Rows from the Database

For all the applications that have been developed in this book, a primary key has been assigned by the database to each row that is added to a table. This primary key is used internally by the database and has no relationship with the data that is being stored. By allowing the database to assign the primary key, we are relieved of the responsibility of ensuring that each row in the database has a unique primary key value. However, there is a drawback; the user does not know the value of this primary key so cannot use it to retrieve the row from the database.

In order to retrieve a row from the database, it is necessary to be able to identify a row based upon the values that are stored in the row. In many applications, there will be a field in the data that can be used to identify the row uniquely: social security number, phone number, username, e-mail address or account number. In other applications, it may be more difficult. It may be necessary to look at several fields in order to identify a row. For instance, a person's address could be used to identify a row, but this would require looking at several fields: street, apartment, city, postal code.

When retrieving a row from the database, it is common to validate the fields that are used to identify a row before validating any new data that the user will enter. The isValid method developed in Chap. 5 is an all-or-nothing approach. A new method will be introduced that can validate a few fields at a time.

Once a row has been retrieved and placed into the session, it is only necessary to use the bean that has been added to the session. As long as all changes are made to that bean, then when the bean is written to the database, it will update the information that is in the database.

7.1.1   Finding a Row

Hibernate has the ability to retrieve a row from the database using one or more fields. There are several methods that can be used: SQL, Hibernate SQL, Criteria. The Criteria technique will be used in this book; it uses Java and requires no knowledge of SQL. The Hibernate Criteria class is a robust class. Only a simple example will be used here. Refer to the references for more information.

The Hibernate helper class has a method that will retrieve all rows that match a given field. The class that contains the property, the name of the property and the value to match are passed to the method. The method then creates search criteria that Hibernate will use to find all rows that match the criteria.

```
static public java.util.List getListData(
        Class classBean, String strKey, Object value) {
    java.util.List result = new java.util.ArrayList();

    Session session = null;
    try {
        session = sessionFactory.openSession();
        Transaction tx = session.beginTransaction();

        Criteria criteria =
                session.createCriteria(classBean);
        if (strKey != null) {
            criteria.add(Restrictions.like(strKey, value));
        }
        result = criteria.list();

        tx.commit();

    } finally {
        if (session != null) {
            session.close();
        }
    }
    return result;
}
```

The like expression is used to test strings. If the special character % is in the string, then it will be treated as a wild card and will match any additional sequence of characters. This is the same syntax that is used in SQL queries. If the special character is not in the string, then the expression will test for equality.

Additional methods could have been added to the Hibernate helper class for testing two, three, four or more properties. For instance, to test for two properties, add another restriction to the criteria.

```
Criteria criteria = session.createCriteria(classBean);
if (strKey1 != null) {
  criteria.add(Restrictions.like(strKey1, value1));
}
if (strKey2 != null) {
  criteria.add(Restrictions.like(strKey2, value2));
}
```

Each restriction that is added in this manner is treated as an *and* condition. The query will only find a record from the database that matches both of these conditions.

It is left as exercises to write the complete method for the above code fragment and to write a method that can accept any number of property names and values.

The criteria class is robust. It is possible to add *or* conditions and test for numeric comparisons. The following code fragment would test that *age* is greater than 13 and less than 18 or the *withParent* property is true.

```
criteria.add(
  Restrictions.or(
    Restrictions.and(
      Restrictions.gt("age", 13),
      Restrictions.lt("age", 18)),
    Restrictions.eq("withParent", true)
  )
);
```

Advanced features of criteria queries are not needed in this book. For more information on criteria queries, please refer to *Hibernate in Action* (Bauer and King 2005).

The getListData method always returns a list of objects. For unique records in the database, it will be helpful to have a method that returns a single object. The getFirstMatch will limit the results of the query to one record and will return that record.

```
static public Object getFirstMatch(
        Class classBean, String strKey, Object value) {

    Object result = null;
    Session session = null;
    try {
        session = sessionFactory.openSession();
        Transaction tx = session.beginTransaction();
        Criteria criteria =
                session.createCriteria(classBean);
        if (strKey != null) {
            criteria.add(Restrictions.like(strKey, value));
        }
        criteria.setMaxResults(1);
        result = criteria.uniqueResult();

        tx.commit();

    } finally {
        if (session != null) {
            session.close();
        }
    }
    return result;
}
```

The method `getFirstMatch` will be used to retrieve the bean for a persistent row and set it as the bean in the session. If there is a bean returned from this method, it will be set as the bean in the session.

```
...
Object dataPersistent =
  HibernateHelper.getFirstMatch(data,
    "accountNumber", data.getAccountNumber());
if (dataPersistent != null) {
  data = (RequestDataAccount)dataPersistent;
}
...
```

7.1.2   Validating a Single Property

The account number will be used to find a row in the database. It should be validated before it is used to access the database. At the least, it should be tested that it is not null or empty. New methods have been added to the helper base class that allow for one field in a bean to be tested instead of testing all the fields in the bean at once.

```
...
public boolean isValidProperty(String name) {
    String msg = errorMap.get(name);
    return msg == null || msg.equals("");
}
...
```

This method uses the `errorMap`, but does not call `setErrors`. To validate one field, the validation messages must be set first. In order to do this, call the `setErrors` method. Previously, this method was called by the `isValid` method, but, now, it will be more efficient if it is called directly. It should only be called once, since it will create the validation errors for all the properties in the bean.

After calling `setErrors`, the `isValidProperty` method can be called for as many properties as need to be validated. Only call `setErrors` once, no matter how many times `isValidProperty` is called.

```
...
setErrors(data);
if (isValidProperty("accountNumber")) {
...
```

It is left as an exercise to add another method that calls `setErrors` and validates any number of properties.

7.2   Application: Account Login

An application will be developed that is based upon the *Persistent Data* example from Chap. 5.

1. The bean will be modified so that it has an account number.
2. The account number will be validated as being two letters followed by three digits.
3. Each user will be required to log onto the site by specifying an account number.
4. If the user has saved data before, then the data from the database will be used to initialise the data in the edit page.
5. The bean that is retrieved from the database will be placed in the session and will be accessible from all of the JSPs.
6. When the data is written to the database, the new data will overwrite the previous data in the database.

The simplicity of this application is that once the user has logged onto the site, the code is exactly the same as it was in Chap. 5. By adding a front end of a login page, the user is able to retrieve and edit the data in the database.

Since this servlet will access the database, it will have an initialisation parameter for creating the database, just like the persistent example from Chap. 5. Any servlet that has an initialisation parameter should use the *web.xml* file to declare the servlet, servlet mapping and initialisation parameter.

7.2.1   Java Bean: Account Login

The only change to the bean is the addition of the account number property. It is important to realise that this field is not the primary key for the bean; the primary key is still needed. The primary key is used internally by the database; the account number is used by the user to identify each row in the database.

```
...
@Pattern(regexp="[a-zA-Z]{2}\\d{3}",
         message="must be in the format AA999.")
@NotNull
public String getAccountNumber() {
    return accountNumber;
}

public void setAccountNumber(String accountNumber) {
    this.accountNumber = accountNumber;
}
...
```

7.2.2   Login.jsp: Account Login

There is a new JSP added to this application. It contains the account number element and a button for gaining access to the site.

```html
<!DOCTYPE HTML>
<html>
  <head>
    <meta charset="utf-8">
    <title>Login Page</title>
  </head>
  <body>
    <p>Please enter your account number
       to access your data.
    <form method="POST" action="Controller">
      <p>
        Account Number ${helper.errors.accountNumber}
        <input type="text" name="accountNumber"
               value="${helper.data.accountNumber}">
        <input type="submit" name="loginButton"
               value="Login">
      </p>
    </form>
  </body>
</html>
```

7.2.3   ControllerHelper: Account Login

When the user selects the login button from the login page, the controller will validate that the account number has the correct format and will search the database for a row that has that account number. If it finds one, then the bean that is returned from Hibernate will replace the one that is in the session.

For the rest of the session, all changes that are entered by the user will be stored in this bean. When the bean is written to the database, Hibernate will realise that it is a bean that came from the database and will update the values for that row in the database instead of adding a new row.

The method for the login page is similar to the method for the confirm page, except it is only validating that the account number has the right format. The other properties in the bean will still be validated when the user selects the confirm button.

```
@ButtonMethod(buttonName="loginButton")
public String loginMethod() {
  String address;
  fillBeanFromRequest(data);
  setErrors(data);
  if (isValidProperty("accountNumber")) {
    Object dataPersistent =
      HibernateHelper.getFirstMatch(data,
        "accountNumber", data.getAccountNumber());
    if (dataPersistent != null) {
      data = (RequestDataAccount)dataPersistent;
    }
    clearErrors();
    address = "Edit.jsp";
  } else {
    address = "Login.jsp";
  }
  return jspLocation(address);
}
```

⟩⟨ Try It

http://bytesizebook.com/book/ch7/accountLogin/Controller

Log into the site. Use an account that is two letters followed by three digits. Enter some data into the database.

Move the cursor into the location bar of the browser and hit the enter key. This will start the application from the beginning. Log into the site with the same account number. The data that was entered into the site will still be displayed in the edit page.

Close the browser and reopen it. This will close the session. Log into the application again with the same account number. The data is still there. Change the data and save it to the database. Log into the site again. The new data will be retrieved.

7.3   Removing Rows from the Database

Building on the last application, it is an easy matter to remove rows from the database. The method removeDB, in the Hibernate helper class, allows a row to be removed from the database.

```
static public void removeDB(Object obj) {
    Session session = null;
    try {
        session = sessionFactory.openSession();
        Transaction tx = session.beginTransaction();
        session.delete(obj);

        tx.commit();
    } finally {
        if (session != null) {
            session.close();
        }
    }
}
```

Once the bean has been saved to the database, it can be removed by calling this method.

7.4   Application: Account Removal

This application only has a few changes from the last one, so inheritance can be used to implement the controller helper. The process page has a new button for removing the account that was just added. There is a new method in the controller helper to process the new button.

Like the last example, this should use the *web.xml* file to declare the servlet, servlet mapping and initialisation parameter.

7.4.1   Process.jsp: Account Removal

The process page has a new button for removing the current bean from the database. This could have been done from any page in the application once the user has logged in.

```
. . .
<form method="POST" action="Controller">
  <p>
    Edit the current record.
    <input type="submit" name="editButton"
                         value="Edit">
    Remove the current record.
    <input type="submit" name="removeButton"
                         value="Remove">
  </p>
</form>
. . .
```

7.4.2   ControllerHelper: Account Removal

Since this application is identical to the previous application, except for the addition of a new button for removing rows, the controller helper can be extended from the *Account Login* controller helper. The bean from that application can also be reused.

The method to process the removal button calls the `removeDB` method with the bean that was just saved to the database. If the `removeDB` method is called with a row that was never saved, then Hibernate will ignore the request. After removing the row, it is necessary to erase all the data from the bean. The simplest way to do this is to create a new bean.

```java
package ch7.accountRemove;

import javax.servlet.ServletException;
import javax.servlet.http.HttpServlet;
import javax.servlet.http.HttpServletRequest;
import javax.servlet.http.HttpServletResponse;
import shared.ButtonMethod;
import shared.HibernateHelper;

public class ControllerHelper
    extends ch7.accountLogin.ControllerHelper {

  public ControllerHelper(
          HttpServlet servlet,
          HttpServletRequest request,
          HttpServletResponse response) {
      super(servlet, request, response);
  }

  @Override
  public String jspLocation(String page) {
    return "/WEB-INF/classes/ch7/accountRemove/" + page;
  }

  @ButtonMethod(buttonName="removeButton")
  public String removeMethod() {
    HibernateHelper.removeDB(data);
    data = new ch7.accountLogin.RequestDataAccount();
    return jspLocation("Login.jsp");
  }

}
```

In this example that uses inheritance, it is necessary that the doGet and doPost methods have public access. In other examples, it did not matter, since the controller and helper were in the same class. In Java, protected access also includes package access.

It is also necessary that jspLocation be implemented as a method and not as a string. In most examples in the book, the new JSP address could be calculated as jspLocationString + "page.jsp"; however, strings are not polymorphic. The jspLocationString would always refer to the string in the current class, even if the extended class defined jspLocation-String too.

 Try It

http://bytesizebook.com/book/ch7/accountRemove/Controller

Fig. 7.1 Yahoo! offers to
remember data on the current
computer

To see that a record has been removed from the database, follow these steps:
1. Log into the site with an account number that is already in the database.
2. Proceed to the process page.
3. Click the remove button to delete the current bean from the database.
4. Click in the location window of the browser and hit the enter key. This will delete
   the data from the session and display the login page.
5. Enter a different account number, enter some data and view the database.
6. The database will appear on the process page, but there will be no row for the
   account number that was just deleted.

7.5   Cookie

A server has the ability to ask a browser to store information. The next time the
browser requests data from that server, the browser will send the stored data back
to the server. A piece of information that is being stored is known as a *cookie*.

Many sites use cookies to identify users. Sites will ask if you would like your
information remembered on the current computer so that the next time you access
the same site from that computer, you will not need to enter your data again. It is
important to understand that the information is only being stored on the current
computer; if you log into the site from a different computer, you will need to enter
your data again.

Table 7.1 Information stored in a cookie

Property	Purpose
name	The *name* is used as the index into the browser's store of cookies
value	The *value* is the data associated with the cookie
expiration	The *expiration* is the date and time when the browser should remove the cookie from its store
domain	The *domain* is the Internet domain that can receive the cookie from the browser
path	The *path* is the prefix for all URLs in the domain that can receive the cookie
secure	*Secure* indicates if the cookie should only be sent over secure connections

Many sites offer to remember a user on the current computer. Such sites typically have a check box to indicate that the user's information should be stored on the local computer (Fig. 7.1).

If this is checked, then the user's data will be stored as a cookie on the current computer. Whenever you see such a request, the site is asking to store information on your computer in a cookie.

7.5.1   Definition

Cookies are stored in a cookie jar. In computer terms, a cookie is a row in a database and the cookie jar is the database. The primary key to the database is the URL of the site that the user is requesting.

On every request that is made by the user, the browser searches through the database, looking for any cookies that were created for the current URL. All the cookies that are found are sent to the server as part of the request headers.

Table 7.1 lists the information that is stored in a cookie.

The cookie is stored in the browser under the name with the given value. Every time a request is made, the browser looks through all the cookies and sends all cookies to the request that match the domain and path of the request. Periodically, the browser will inspect the expiration date of all its cookies and delete those that have expired.

7.5.2   Cookie Class

The Java package `javax.servlet.http.cookie` encapsulates this information and is defined in the `Cookie` class. There are accessors and mutators for all of the above properties.

Cookie
The constructor takes the name and value as parameters.
```
Cookie team = new Cookie("team", "marlins");
```

setName/getName
It is not necessary to call setName since the name is included in the constructor.

setValue/getValue
It is not necessary to call setValue since the value is included in the constructor.

setMaxAge/getMaxAge
The default age is −1 seconds, which means that the cookie will be deleted when the browser closes. Set the age to 0 seconds to have the browser delete the cookie immediately. Use a positive number of seconds to indicate how long the browser will keep the cookie. The number of seconds will be translated into a date by the Cookie class.

setDomain/getDomain
The default domain is the server that set the cookie. This can be changed to the subdomain of the computer. If the domain starts with a dot, then the cookie can be sent back to all servers on the sub-domain. The domain must always be to an actual domain or sub-domain, and it must be the domain or sub-domain of the server that sets the cookie.

setPath/getPath
The default path is the path to the directory of the servlet that set the cookie.

setSecure/getSecure
The default security level is that the cookie can be sent over any type of connection.

7.6 Application: Cookie Test

A controller application will now be developed to explain and test the different actions for creating, deleting and finding cookies. The application will not receive any data from the user so there is no need for a bean. This simplifies the doGet method in the controller helper, since there is no need to update the session.

```
. . .
protected void doGet()
   throws ServletException, IOException
{
   String address = executeButtonMethod();

   request.getRequestDispatcher(address)
       .forward(request, response);
}
. . .
```

The controller is the same as the controller for the *Enhanced* application from Chap. 4. This controller may use the `WebServlet` annotation to define the servlet mapping, since it does not need an initialisation parameter.

7.6.1 JSPs: Cookie Test

There is only one JSP for this application. The primary function of the page is to list the cookies that were sent to it from the browser. The page loops through the cookies that were sent to it.

A map of the cookies can be retrieved from a JSP using the EL statement of `${cookie}`. A loop can be placed into the JSP to access the elements in the map. Each element in the map has public accessors to retrieve the key and the value. The key is the name of the cookie and the value is the cookie.

If there is a loop control variable named `element`, then each cookie can be retrieved from the map with `${element.value}`. Since the value in the map is a cookie, its name and value can be retrieved from the cookie's public accessors. The EL statements to access the name and value of the cookie from the value in the map are `${element.value.name}` and `${element.value.value}`. The name and value of the cookie are displayed in a table.

```
. . .
<table border>
  <tr><th>Name<th>Value
  <core:forEach var="element" items="${cookie}">
    <tr><td>${element.value.name}<td>${element.value.value}
  </core:forEach>
</table>
. . .
```

This application will also create a cookie that can only be read by one URL. Two servlet mappings will be created so that this servlet can be called by two different URLs. In this way, the servlet will have access to different cookies based upon the URL that is used to access it.

If the servlet mapping is defined in the *web.xml* file, then add a second URL pattern to it.

```
<servlet-mapping>
  <servlet-name>CookieController</servlet-name>
  <url-pattern>
    /ch7/cookie/Controller
  </url-pattern>
  <url-pattern>
    /ch7/cookie/specific/Controller
  </url-pattern>
</servlet-mapping>
```

If the mapping is defined with the `WebServlet` annotation, then add a second string to the array of mappings in the *urlPatterns* attribute.

```
@WebServlet(urlPatterns={
    "/ch7/cookie/Controller",
    "/ch7/cookie/specific/Controller"})
public class Controller extends HttpServlet {
```

There are two forms in the JSP. Each form has a different URL in the *action* attribute. However, each URL is mapped to the same servlet in the *web.xml* file. The buttons in the second form create and access a cookie that can only be accessed from the URL used in that form. The buttons in the first form create cookies that can be accessed by both URLs.

```
...
<form action="/book/ch7/cookie/Controller">
  <input type="submit" name="showCookieButton"
         value="Show Cookies">
  <input type="submit" name="setCookieButton"
         value="Set Cookies">
  <input type="submit" name="deleteCookieButton"
         value="Delete Cookie">
  <input type="submit" name="findCookieButton"
         value="Find Cookie">
</form>
<form action="/book/ch7/cookie/specific/Controller">
  <input type="submit" name="showCookieButton"
         value="Show Specific Cookies">
  <input type="submit" name="setSpecificCookieButton"
         value="Set Specific Cookie">
</form>
...
```

Figure 7.2 shows how the page will appear in a browser.

7.6.2 Showing Cookies

All the work for showing cookies is done in the JSP. The default button in the controller helper only needs to return the address of the JSP.

```
...
buttonName="showCookieButton", isDefault=true)
  public String showMethod() {
    return jspLocation("ShowCookies.jsp");
  }
...
```

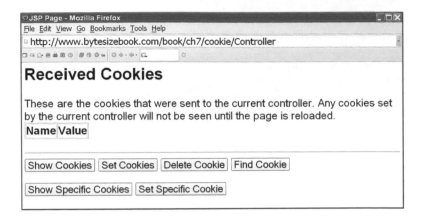

Fig. 7.2 The JSP for testing cookies

7.6.3   Setting Cookies

Setting a cookie is a two-step process: create the cookie and then attach it to the response with the `addCookie` method.

The action for the *Set Cookie* button will construct two cookie objects, change some default values and attach the cookies to the response. One of the cookies will have the default age, so it will be deleted when the browser is closed. The other cookie will have its age set to 15 seconds. After setting the cookie, the browser will delete it after 15 seconds.

```
...
@ButtonMethod(buttonName="setCookieButton")
public String setMethod() {
   Cookie dolphins
      = new Cookie("dolphins",
                   "The Dolphins are here to stay");
   dolphins.setPath("/");
   response.addCookie(dolphins);

   Cookie marlins
      = new Cookie("marlins",
                   "The Marlins will be gone soon");
   marlins.setMaxAge(15);
   marlins.setPath("/");
   response.addCookie(marlins);

   return jspLocation("ShowCookies.jsp");
}
...
```

Be sure to change any default values before attaching the cookie to the response. The `addCookie` method generates a string that contains all the information about the cookie. This string is created during the call to `addCookie` and is added to the response headers at that time. Subsequent changes to the cookie will not alter the string that is already in the response headers.

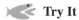 **Try It**

http://bytesizebook.com/book/ch7/cookie/Controller

An additional cookie might be displayed, named *JSESSIONID*, which was not created by the application. This is the cookie that is used to maintain the session for the servlet engine.

Since web applications are stateless, information must be stored on the browser in order to identify the current session. There are several places where the identifying data could be stored: in a hidden field, in the URL or in a cookie. The simplest solution is to use a cookie. The servlet engine can also be configured so that it will use the URL to store the identifying information.

Click the *Set Cookies* button, followed by the *Show Cookies* button. Cookies are only set in the response. In order to see the state of the cookies after the previous response, it is necessary to make a new request.

7.6.4 Deleting Cookies

The path and domain of a cookie must be known in order to delete the cookie. The cookies that are retrieved from the browser only have a name and value: the domain and path information are null. There is no way to know the path and domain of the original cookie by reading the cookie from the browser. If the domain was set to something other than the default when the cookie was created, then that domain will need to be set again in order to delete that cookie.

The action for the *Delete Cookie* button will delete one of the cookies that was created when the *Set Cookies* button was clicked. It will delete the cookie that expires in 15 seconds. So, if too much time has elapsed, there won't be a cookie to delete. By setting the age to zero and adding the cookie to the response, the browser will delete the cookie that it has in its store.

```
. . .
@ButtonMethod(buttonName="deleteCookieButton")
public String deleteMethod() {
  Cookie marlins = new Cookie("marlins", "bye-bye");
  marlins.setMaxAge(0);
  marlins.setPath("/");
  response.addCookie(marlins);
  return jspLocation("ShowCookies.jsp");
}
. . .
```

 Try It

http://bytesizebook.com/book/ch7/cookie/DeleteCookies

Run the application and click the *Set Cookies* button. Click the *Show Cookies* button to see the current state of the cookies. Remember that cookies are sent in the response, so an additional request is needed to see what happened to the cookies after the last response.

To delete a cookie, click the *Delete Cookies* button. This will delete one of the cookies. To see that it has been deleted, click the *Show Cookies* button once again.

7.6.5 Finding Cookies

There can be more than one cookie that is sent to the servlet, even if the servlet only sets one cookie. This can happen when other servlets on the same sub-domain set a cookie that can be accessed from the entire sub-domain.

It is necessary to do a linear search through the array of cookies in order to find the desired one in a controller. If there are no cookies, then the array will be null, so it is important to test for this before accessing the array.

The action for the *Find Cookie* button will look for one of the cookies that was created when the *Set Cookies* button was clicked. It will look for the cookie that expires in 15 seconds. So, if too much time has elapsed, there won't be a cookie to find.

Whether or not the cookie is found, a value is set and made available to the JSP. The value is added to the request object. Since the cookie is sent from the browser on each request, it does not make any sense to save this value in the session object.

```
. . .
@ButtonMethod(buttonName="findCookieButton")
public String findMethod() {
   Cookie[] cookieArray = request.getCookies();
   Cookie marlins = null;
   if (cookieArray != null) {
       for (Cookie cookie : cookieArray) {
           if (cookie.getName().equals("marlins")) {
               marlins = cookie;
           }
       }
   }
   String result = "The Marlins have left town";
   if (marlins != null) {
       result = marlins.getValue();
   }
   request.setAttribute("marlins",result);

   return jspLocation("ShowCookies.jsp");
}
. . .
```

In a JSP, it is possible to locate a cookie without doing a linear search, if you know the name of the cookie: ${cookie.marlins.value}.

Try It

http://bytesizebook.com/book/ch7/cookie/FindCookie

To see a search in action, follow the buttons in this order.
1. Set Cookies
2. Find Cookie
3. Delete Cookie
4. Find Cookie

Each time that *Find Cookie* is called, a linear search is performed on the cookies that are received by the application.

7.6.6   Cookie Utilities

A class has been added to the `shared` package that has two static methods for retrieving cookies. Each method performs a linear search through the cookies that are sent from the browser. Each look for a cookie with a given name: one returns the cookie, the other returns the value in the cookie. The name of the class is *CookieUtil*.

```
public class CookieUtil {

    static
    public Cookie findCookie(HttpServletRequest request,
                             String name)
    {
        ...
    }

    static
    public String findCookieValue(HttpServletRequest request,
                                  String name)
    {
        ...
    }

}
```

The complete listing of the *CookieUtil* class can be found in the Appendix.

7.6.7   Path Specific Cookies

The cookies that were created above changed the path to / , meaning that all servlets on the server will receive the cookie. If the path is not set, then it will default to the path of the directory of the servlet that set the cookie.

The action for the *Set Specific Cookie* button will create a cookie without setting its path. This means that only the current URL will receive the cookie. The button is located in the second form in the JSP. This form accesses the controller through a different URL. Only the buttons for setting and showing the specific button will have access to this cookie.

All of the cookies from the previous examples can be viewed from this URL, since the path was set so that those cookies are sent to all URLs on the server.

```
...
@ButtonMethod(buttonName="setSpecificCookieButton")
public String setSpecificMethod() {
  Cookie specific
      = new Cookie("specific",
                   "Not all pages can see this cookie");
  specific.setMaxAge(15);
  response.addCookie(specific);
  return jspLocation("ShowCookies.jsp");
}
...
```

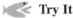 **Try It**

http://bytesizebook.com/book/ch7/cookie/specific/SetCookie

To experiment with the cookie that is only seen from one URL, click the following buttons in the following order:
1. Set Specific Cookie.
2. Show Specific Cookie.
3. Show Cookie – the specific cookie will not be seen, since the URL does not match the one that set the cookie.
4. Show Specific Cookie – the specific cookie will be seen. The cookie will expire after 15 seconds.

7.7   Application: Account Cookie

The *Account Login* application can be extended to implement cookies. Whenever a bean is written to the database, its account number will be stored as a cookie. The next time a GET request is made, the account number can be retrieved from the cookie and used to retrieve the user's data. By using a cookie, the user will not have to see the login page. A new button will be added to the edit and process pages in case a different user wants to log in.

Like previous examples, this should use the *web.xml* file to declare the servlet, servlet mapping and initialisation parameter.

7.7.1 Edit.jsp: Account Cookie

A new button is added to the edit page, to allow a different user to log in.

```
. . .
<input type="submit" name="confirmButton"
                     value="Confirm">
<input type="submit" name="newUserButton"
                     value="New User">
. . .
```

7.7.2 Process.jsp: Account Cookie

A new button is added to the process page to allow a new user to log in.

```
. . .
<input type="submit" name="editButton"
                     value="Edit">
<input type="submit" name="newUserButton"
                     value="New User">
. . .
```

7.7.3 ControllerHelper: Account Cookie

When using a cookie, two questions need to be answered:
1. When will it be created?
2. When will it be read?

   In this application, the cookie will be written whenever the data is saved to the database. This makes the most sense, since the idea of having a cookie is so that data that has already been stored in the database can be retrieved automatically. Note that only the account number is being saved in the cookie.

```
@ButtonMethod(buttonName = "processButton")
public String processMethod() {
    if (!isValid(data)) {
        return jspLocation("Expired.jsp");
    }
    response.addCookie(
            new Cookie("account", data.getAccountNumber()));
    HibernateHelper.updateDB(data);
    List list = HibernateHelper.getListData(RequestDataAccount.class);
    request.setAttribute("database", list);
    return jspLocation("Process.jsp");
}
```

The cookie will be retrieved whenever there is a GET request to the application. A GET request signifies that a new user is trying to access the application. At that time, the cookies will be searched for an account number. If there is an account number, then the database will be searched. If a bean is returned from the database, it will replace the bean that is stored in the session, and the next page will be the edit page instead of the login page.

```java
@ButtonMethod(isDefault = true)
public String getMethod() {
    String address = "Login.jsp";
    Cookie accountCookie =
            CookieUtil.findCookie(request, "account");
    if (accountCookie != null) {
        Object dataPersistent = HibernateHelper.getFirstMatch(data,
                "accountNumber",
                accountCookie.getValue());
        if (dataPersistent != null) {
            data = (RequestDataAccount) dataPersistent;
        }
        address = "Edit.jsp";
    }
    return jspLocation(address);
}
```

When the *New User* button is clicked from the edit or process pages, it signifies that the cookie does not have the correct account number for the current user. As a result, the data that is stored in the bean should be cleared by creating a new bean.

```java
@ButtonMethod(buttonName = "newUserButton")
public String newUserMethod() {
    data = new RequestDataAccount();
    return jspLocation("Login.jsp");
}
```

In previous examples, a *New User* button was implemented using a GET request. This works as long as a cookie is not being used, since the old data will be ignored and the edit page will be shown. When a cookie is being used to store the account number for the database, then a GET request does not start with an empty bean; it starts with the bean from the database for the last user. When a cookie is being used, the old data must be removed by creating a new bean.

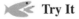 Try It

http://bytesizebook.com/book/ch7/accountCookie/Controller

Enter an account number and save some data to the database. When the process page is displayed, the cookie is sent to the browser.

Click in the URL location in the browser and hit the enter key. This will create a new request that will not read data from the session. The cookie will be sent from the browser. The value of the cookie will be used to retrieve data from the database. The login page will be skipped and the edit page will be displayed with the data from the database.

Click the *New User* button and a new request will be made that does not read the cookie.

7.8   Shopping Cart

A shopping cart is designed to access a database of items and to keep track of which items the user wants. A simple shopping cart application will be developed in this section. The application will be for a bookstore. The first page will display all the books that are available (Fig. 7.3).

The user can click on any of the buttons to view the details for that item: name, description, cost and item Id (Fig. 7.4).

After the user has selected some items, the *View Cart* button can be pressed to see a summary of the items that have been selected (Fig. 7.5).

After reviewing the items, the user can process the cart, which calculates the total cost and the number of items (Fig. 7.6).

The most important aspect of a shopping cart is the item that will be placed in the cart. The item is the data that will be entered by the user. The data will be specific to the application.

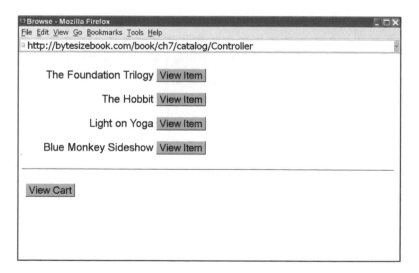

Fig. 7.3 All items are listed when the user visits the site

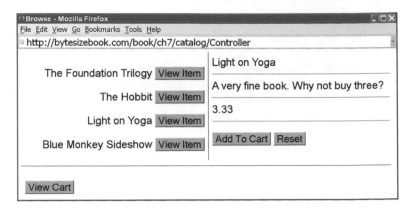

Fig. 7.4 Details of a selected item are displayed

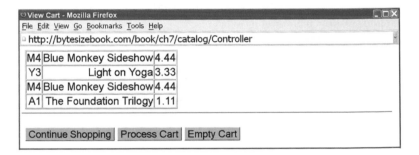

Fig. 7.5 The cart contains all the items that were selected

Fig. 7.6 The total cost is calculated when the cart is processed

There will be a database of items that are available from the store. It is the developer's responsibility to keep this database up to date.

Keeping the item information in a separate table makes it easier to keep the information on the website up to date. The only information that is hard-coded into the JSP is the item Id, which should never change. The rest of the information about an item is generated from the database whenever a page is reloaded.

The shopping cart itself is very simple. It needs a collection of objects and methods for adding and deleting items from the collection. Shopping carts are all very similar. Generics from Java 1.5 can be used to develop the shopping cart class.

7.8.1 Catalogue Item

The first thing that is needed for a shopping cart is a database that defines all the items that can go into the cart. An item in the database should have the following:
1. A name
2. A description
3. A price
4. An item Id

These would be implemented as standard properties in the bean. Only two of them will need annotations, as described below.

Catalogue Item Class

A separate table for the items will be created in the database, so the bean should be marked as an entity. Even though the item Id could be used as the primary key in the database, this application will still let the database manage an internal column that will be used as the primary key. The item class will extend the *PersistentBase* class, which contains an identifier for a primary key.

```
@Entity
public class CatalogueItem
    extends shared.PersistentBase implements Serializable {
```

Catalogue Item Constructors

Besides the default constructor, there will be a constructor that will set the values of all the properties. This will make it easy to create a complete item that can be added to the database of items. The default constructor will choose some default values for the properties. The default item Id will be null. An item with an Id of null should never be added to the database.

```
mysql> describe catalogitemdefault;
+-------------+--------------+------+-----+---------+----------------+
| Field       | Type         | Null | Key | Default | Extra          |
+-------------+--------------+------+-----+---------+----------------+
| id          | bigint(20)   | NO   | PRI | NULL    | auto_increment |
| itemId      | varchar(255) | YES  |     | NULL    |                |
| price       | double       | NO   |     |         |                |
| name        | varchar(255) | YES  |     | NULL    |                |
| description | varchar(255) | YES  |     | NULL    |                |
+-------------+--------------+------+-----+---------+----------------+
5 rows in set (0.03 sec)
```

Fig. 7.7 Strings have a default width of 255 characters

```java
public CatalogueItem() {
   this(null, "", "", 0.00);
}

public CatalogueItem(String itemId, String name,
                     String description, double price)
{
   this.itemId = itemId;
   this.name = name;
   this.description = description;
   this.price = price;
}
```

Catalogue Item Text Fields

When a column for a string property is added to a database table, the maximum length of the string must be set. The default length of a string column is database-specific, but might be 255 characters. If a field represents a phone number of an identification number, then 255 characters would be too many. If a field represents a catalogue description, then 255 characters might not be enough. Figure 7.7 shows the default implementation of three text fields from the CatalogueItem class in the MySQL database server.

Hibernate has annotations that will give the database server a hint for setting the width of a column in a table.

The Hibernate annotation @Length validates the minimum and maximum length of a string. This annotation also tells the database server what the width of the column in the database should be. For example, by adding validation that tests that the length of a text field in the database does not exceed 50, Hibernate will give the column a width of 50 in the table.

```java
import org.hibernate.validator.constraints.Length;
...
@Length(min=1,max=50)
public String getName() {
   return name;
}
```

```
mysql> describe catalogitem;
+-------------+-------------+------+-----+---------+----------------+
| Field       | Type        | Null | Key | Default | Extra          |
+-------------+-------------+------+-----+---------+----------------+
| id          | bigint(20)  | NO   | PRI | NULL    | auto_increment |
| itemId      | varchar(10) | NO   |     |         |                |
| price       | double      | NO   |     |         |                |
| name        | varchar(50) | YES  |     | NULL    |                |
| description | text        | YES  |     | NULL    |                |
+-------------+-------------+------+-----+---------+----------------+
5 rows in set (0.00 sec)
```

Fig. 7.8 Text fields whose length has been specified

The description of a catalogue item could be very long. The default length of a string column in a table is database-specific, but might only be 255 characters. When large amounts of text need to be entered, the field should be declared as a *large object*. The annotation that defines a property as a large object is @Lob. As the name implies, a large object property can contain a lot of information.

```java
import javax.persistence.Lob;
...
@Lob
public String getDescription() {
   return description;
}
```

The @NotNull annotation is very useful for a database. By marking a field with it, then the field must always have a value before data is entered into the database. This is particularly helpful when the session is being used to store user data.

If the user does not interact with the server for an extended period, then the session will be closed and the user data will be lost. If the user subsequently attempts to save that data, a check should be made by the database that the user data is still valid. The simplest way to accomplish this is to mark at least one field as not null. If there is an attempt to write a null field to that column in the database, an exception will be thrown. This is considered a last chance test. Hopefully, the controller will test that the data is valid before attempting to write to the database.

```java
import javax.validation.constraints.NotNull;
...
@NotNull
@Length(min=1,max=10)
public String getItemId() {
   return itemId;
}
```

Figure 7.8 shows the CatalogueItem class that has used annotations to set the length of two of the text fields and has marked the third as a large object.

The itemId field has also been marked as not null, since every item in the database should have an item identification code.

7.8.2   Create Catalogue Database

The next step is to define some items and create a database for them. This will only be done once by the site administrator. This database will not be modified by the cart: it is just a list of items that are available. Additional controllers could be defined to add items to the current database of items.

The controller will need access to Hibernate, but will not need any JSPs. The user interface is very simple in this administrator application, so the controller will send the response directly to the browser without using a JSP.

Controller with No JSPs

This controller is only supposed to be run by the site administrator to create the catalogue database. It does not need a sophisticated user interface; just a simple message, indicating that the database was created successfully, is enough. In such a situation, it is possible for the controller to write text directly to the browser.

As part of the response object, there is a method that returns a *PrintWriter* that has direct access to the browser. Whatever is written to the writer will be sent to the browser. It is possible to create an entire HTML page to send, but it is easier to just send a simple text message.

```
response.getWriter().print("Catalogue Created");
```

Catalogue Controller

The complete controller to create the catalogue must initialise Hibernate in the *init* method. It is assumed that the properties for initialising Hibernate are in a configuration file.

This controller may use the WebServlet annotation to define the servlet mapping, since it does not need an initialisation parameter.

The doGet method is very simple; it only calls updateDb to write the catalogue items to the database and uses the writer from the response object to send a simple message to the browser. The updateDb method in the Hibernate helper has been overloaded to accept a list of items.

```java
package ch7.catalogue;

import java.io.IOException;
import java.util.ArrayList;
import java.util.List;
import javax.servlet.ServletException;
import javax.servlet.annotation.WebServlet;
import javax.servlet.http.HttpServlet;
import javax.servlet.http.HttpServletRequest;
import javax.servlet.http.HttpServletResponse;
import shared.HibernateHelper;

@WebServlet(urlPatterns={"/ch7/catalogue/CreateCatalogue"})
public class CreateCatalogue extends HttpServlet {

    @Override
  public void init() {
    HibernateHelper.createTable(CatalogueItem.class);
    HibernateHelper.initSessionFactory(CatalogueItem.class);
  }

  static final List<CatalogueItem> itemList =
      new ArrayList<CatalogueItem>();

  static {
    itemList.add(new CatalogueItem(
        "A1", "The Foundation Trilogy",
        "A very fine book. Why not buy one?", 1.11));
    itemList.add(new CatalogueItem(
        "T2", "The Hobbit",
        "A very fine book. Why not buy two?", 2.22));
    itemList.add(new CatalogueItem(
        "Y3", "Light on Yoga",
        "A very fine book. Why not buy three?", 3.33));
    itemList.add(new CatalogueItem(
        "M4", "Blue Monkey Sideshow",
        "A very fine book. Why not buy four?", 4.44));
  };

    @Override
  protected void doGet(HttpServletRequest request,
                       HttpServletResponse response)
  throws ServletException, IOException {

    HibernateHelper.updateDB(itemList);
    response.getWriter().print("Catalogue Created");
    destroy();

  }
}
```

7.8.3 Shopping Cart Bean

Now that the catalogue of items exists, the shopping cart can be defined. The shopping cart should be able to store all the items that a user has selected. The details of the item are not important for the shopping cart; the cart only needs to be able to add an item, retrieve all items and clear all items. Additional properties will be added to the cart for storing the total cost and number of items that are in the cart.

Other features could be added to the cart, like the ability to delete an individual item or to maintain a count for each item in the cart. The implementation of these additional features will be left as exercises.

Since the details of the item that is being placed into the cart are unimportant to the cart, generics from Java 1.5 will be used to define the cart. By using generics, the objects returned from the cart will not need to be cast to the correct type, and syntax checking can be performed on objects returned from the cart.

```
public class ShoppingCart<Item> {
    ...
}
```

When the cart is created, the type of item that will be placed into the cart is included in the definition. For example, in the shopping cart application in this chapter, a shopping cart for the *CatalogueItem* will be created.

```
protected ShoppingCart<CatalogueItem> cart =
    new ShoppingCart<CatalogueItem>();
```

This will allow the shopping cart to return a specific type from a method instead of returning an *Object*.

Cart Data Structure
The cart will have a list of items from the database. Since the cart was declared with a generic type named *Item*, this generic type can be used to define the type of object that is placed into the list.

```
private List<Item> items;
```

The cart will be recreated whenever all the items should be removed from it. When creating the cart, the type of element that is in the cart is included in the call to the constructor. An *ArrayList* will be used to store the items. The method `resetItems` will be used to clear all the items from the cart.

```
public final void resetItems() {
    items = new ArrayList<Item>();
    ...
```

When the shopping cart is created, it will also create the list that stores the items by calling the `resetItems` method.

```
public ShoppingCart() {
    resetItems();
...
```

Accessing Items

There are only two additional features that are essential for a shopping cart: adding items and retrieving items.

When retrieving the items, the entire list of items will be returned. Individual access to the items can be handled in the controller helper, where the details of the items will be known. The `getItems` method will return a generic list of items, so that the objects retrieved from it will not need to be cast to the correct type.

```
public List<Item> getItems() {
    return items;
}

public void addItem(Item item) {
    items.add(item);
}
```

Total and Count

Additional properties will be added to the shopping cart for storing the total cost of the items and the count of all the items. There will be normal accessors and mutators for the total and count. These properties are not essential to a cart; they could always be generated when needed; however, they demonstrate that additional features could be added to the cart to make it more robust.

```
private double total;
private int count;

public void setTotal(double total) {
    this.total = total;
}

public double getTotal() {
    return total;
}

public void setCount(int count) {
    this.count = count;
}

public int getCount() {
    return count;
}
```

Additionally, there will be an accessor that returns the total as currency, a method for adding to the total and a method for incrementing the count. To format the total as currency, create a number format for the currency that is defined for the current region.

```
private static NumberFormat currency =
    NumberFormat.getCurrencyInstance();

public void addTotal(double amount) {
    total += amount;
}

public String getTotalAsCurrency() {
    return currency.format(total);
}

public void incrCount() {
    count++;
}
```

Complete Shopping Cart

The complete cart is simple and generic. It could be used for any application with any item. Any application that needs a shopping cart would only need to define the item class and use it to construct the shopping cart, as will be done in the shopping cart application in this chapter.

```
package ch7.catalogue;

import java.util.List;
import java.util.ArrayList;
import java.text.NumberFormat;

public class ShoppingCart<Item> {

    private static NumberFormat currency =
        NumberFormat.getCurrencyInstance();
    private List<Item> items;
    private double total;
    private int count;

    public ShoppingCart() {
        resetItems();
    }
```

```java
public final void resetItems() {
    items = new ArrayList<Item>();
    total = 0.0;
    count = 0;
}

public void setItems(List<Item> items) {
    this.items = items;
}

public List<Item> getItems() {
    return items;
}

public void addItem(Item item) {

    items.add(item);
}

public void setTotal(double total) {
    this.total = total;
}

public double getTotal() {
    return total;
}

public void setCount(int count) {
    this.count = count;
}

public int getCount() {
    return count;
}

public void addTotal(double amount) {
    total += amount;
}

public String getTotalAsCurrency() {
    return currency.format(total);
}

public void incrCount() {
    count++;
}
}
```

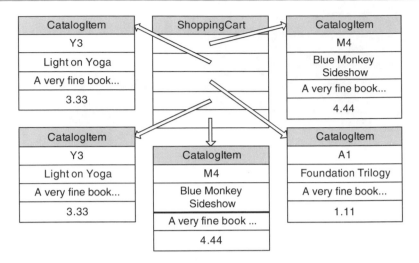

Fig. 7.9 Multiple beans with the same values might be in the cart

7.9   Application: Shopping Cart

Now that the items, the item database and the shopping cart bean have been defined,
it is possible to define the shopping cart application. The controller for this application is identical to previous controllers that save data to a database; all the work is
done in the controller helper.

This is a simple cart. If more than one item is added to the cart, then two identical
beans will be added to the cart. Figure 7.9 shows how the cart would appear if two
of the same items were added to the cart. It is left as an exercise to modify the cart
so that there is only one bean for each item that is ordered.

This controller may use the `WebServlet` annotation to define the servlet
mapping, since it does not need an initialisation parameter.

7.9.1   ControllerHelper: Shopping Cart

If the user is viewing a catalogue item, then the item Id should be sent to the controller
when a button is clicked. When the application receives the item Id, the item information will be read from the database. The bean that is returned from Hibernate will
be set as the bean in the controller helper. When the bean is returned in the next
response, the details of the item can be viewed in the JSP.

In addition to the current item bean, the shopping cart bean is also kept in the
helper. This is the first application that has two beans: the current catalogue item and
the shopping cart (Fig. 7.10).

Fig. 7.10 The controller
helper for the shopping cart
has two beans

ControllerHelper
CatalogItem item ShoppingCart cart
doGet() doPost() getItem() getCart() copyFromSession() jspLocation()

The controller helper will have member variables for both of these beans.

```
protected CatalogueItem item = new CatalogueItem();
protected ShoppingCart<CatalogueItem> cart =
    new ShoppingCart<CatalogueItem>();
```

Both of these beans should be accessible from the JSPs, so accessors for each will be added to the controller helper.

```
public Object getItem() {
    return item;
}

public Object getCart() {
    return cart;
}
```

The `copyFromSession` method should copy both beans from the session data. It is necessary to copy all the member variables that hold user data or the data will be lost.

```
public void copyFromSession(Object sessionHelper) {
    if (sessionHelper.getClass() == this.getClass()) {
        item = ((ControllerHelper)sessionHelper).item;
        cart = ((ControllerHelper)sessionHelper).cart;
    }
}
```

There are many buttons in this application, so there will be many methods to perform the tasks for the buttons. The default method should make the list of catalogue items available to the first page, *BrowseLoop.jsp*. As before, the items from the database are not added to the session; they are only added to the request attributes.

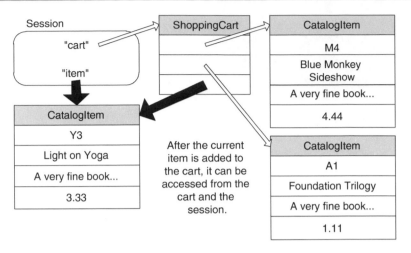

Fig. 7.11 The item is in the session and in the shopping cart

If they were added directly to the session, then the web application would crash whenever it was reloaded.

```
@ButtonMethod(isDefault=true)
public String methodDefault() {
   java.util.List list = HibernateHelper
      .getListData(CatalogueItem.class);
   request.setAttribute("allItems", list);
   return jspLocation("BrowseLoop.jsp");
}
```

The remaining buttons perform specific actions based on the button that the user clicked. Two of these methods encapsulate calls to methods in the shopping cart. When the user selects *Add Cart* or *Empty Cart*, the controller helper only has to call the corresponding method from the cart. After doing the specific tasks, the methods call the default method.

Using the session always complicates matters, especially when an item that is in the session has also been placed into a separate collection (Fig. 7.11). In this case, after an item has been added to the cart, the item will still be in the session. Upon the next request, the item in the session could be populated with new data. If this happens, then the data in the collection will be changed too.

This problem can be avoided by creating a new bean after the current item is added to the cart. This will create a new, empty bean that will be accessed from the session. The item that was just added will no longer be accessible from the session.

```
@ButtonMethod(buttonName="addCart")
public String methodAddCart() {
   cart.addItem(item);
   item = new CatalogueItem();
   return methodDefault();
}

@ButtonMethod(buttonName="emptyCart")
public String methodEmptyCart() {
   cart.resetItems();
   return methodDefault();
}
```

The button for viewing an item is more complicated. When the user chooses an item to view, the item Id is sent to the controller. The helper needs to look in the database of items and check that a valid Id was sent. If it is a valid Id, then the bean from the database is set as the bean in the helper. This is similar to the technique used in the *Account Login* application, when testing if the account was already in the database.

```
@ButtonMethod(buttonName="viewItem")
public String methodViewItem() {
   fillBeanFromRequest(item);
   if (item.getItemId() != null) {
      Object dbObj = HibernateHelper.
          getFirstMatch(item, "itemId",
                           item.getItemId());
      if (dbObj != null) {
         item = (CatalogueItem)dbObj;
      }
   }
   return methodDefault();
}
```

The *View Cart* method only has to redirect the application to the JSP that displays the contents of the cart. All the details of displaying the cart are encapsulated in the Cart page.

```
@ButtonMethod(buttonName="viewCart")
public String methodViewCart() {
   return jspLocation("Cart.jsp");
}
```

The final button is the one to process the cart. The corresponding method will loop through all the items, counting them and adding the price to the total in the cart. The method redirects to the final JSP in the application, Process.jsp.

```
@ButtonMethod(buttonName="processCart")
public String methodProcess() {
  cart.setTotal(0);
  cart.setCount(0);
  for(CatalogueItem anItem : cart.getItems()) {
    cart.addTotal(anItem.getPrice());
    cart.incrCount();
  }
  return jspLocation("Process.jsp");
}
```

The JSPs will be located in the same directory as the Controller.

```
public String jspLocation(String page) {
  return "/WEB-INF/classes/ch7/catalogue/" + page;
}
```

7.9.2   BrowseLoop.jsp: Shopping Cart

The main page of the application is the page that displays all the catalogue items that are in the catalogue item database. These are the items that can be placed in the shopping cart. If the user selects an item from the catalogue, its details will be displayed in the page.

When the page is first loaded, no item has been selected from the catalogue. In this case, the bean that has been sent to the JSP contains default information, including a null item Id. A bean with a null item Id should not be displayed in the page. There needs to be a way to hide the details of the bean when the item Id is null.

There are several ways to resolve the problem of conditionally showing an item from the catalogue. The simplest solution is to use a valid, default item Id when the page is first loaded, so that an item will always be displayed. A second solution is to conditionally generate the HTML for the item information in the controller and send it to the JSP. A third solution is to put an `if` statement into the JSP. The third solution will be used in this page using another custom tag from JSTL.

Another problem in this page is to identify which item the user selected. A common technique for doing this is to have a separate button for each item in the catalogue, but then how is each button made unique?

A complicated solution would be to name each button with the item Id, but this would require many button methods in the controller. A simpler solution is to place each button in a separate form and to place a hidden field in each form containing the item Id. Each button will have the same name, so there will only be one button method for all the items. The item Id can be retrieved from the hidden field.

Display Catalogue

The catalogue of items was added to the request attributes in the controller helper. This is the same way that the database was sent to the JSP in previous examples.

```
@ButtonMethod(isDefault=true)
public String methodDefault() {
    java.util.List list = HibernateHelper
        .getListData(CatalogueItem.class);
    request.setAttribute("allItems", list);
    return jspLocation("BrowseLoop.jsp");
}
```

The catalogue database can be retrieved using EL as ${allItems}. The individual items can be accessed just like any other collection: using a *forEach* tag.

```
<core:forEach var="oneItem" items="${allItems}">
accesss ${oneItem} here
</core:forEach>
```

Each item will have its own form, button and hidden field. The hidden field will contain the item Id and can be used by the controller to access the database of catalogue items. When the user clicks a button, the data for that item will appear in the page.

```
...
<core:forEach var="oneItem" items="${allItems}">
    <form method="post" action="Controller">
        <p>
        ${oneItem.name}
        <input type="hidden" name="itemId"
                              value="${oneItem.itemId}">
        <input type="submit" name="viewItem"
                              value="View Item">
    </form>
</core:forEach>
...
```

This is an example where a hidden field is needed; this technique could not be implemented using the session. There must be some information in the form that identifies the item Id.

Each button has the same name, which will correspond to one method in the controller helper. The controller helper will retrieve the value from the hidden field and use it to read the item information from the catalogue database.

Conditional Tag

The JSP will always receive a bean, but sometimes it will only have default data and not data from the database. In this case, the page should not display the bean. This means that a decision needs to be made in the JSP. As before, there are two ways to do this: use a custom HTML tag that performs an if statement or use Java code in the JSP.

It is better to use a custom HTML tag to solve the problem. It is better if the code in a JSP contains as much HTML as possible, so that an HTML designer could maintain the page more easily. Using a custom HTML tag also eliminates the possibility of unfriendly stack traces.

There is a tag from JSTL that defines an if statement.

```
<core:if test="boolean condition">
    conditional processing
</core:if>
```

With this tag, it is possible to conditionally include details about an item. The condition will be that the item Id is not null. If it isn't, then the additional HTML code between the tags will be displayed.

```
<core:if test="${helper.item.itemId != null}">
    HTML for item details
</core:if>
```

BrowseLoop

The BrowseLoop JSP will use a CSS custom layout to display the catalogue data. There will be three sections in the page: left, right, bottom. Each section will have a named style and a uniquely named style to control its appearance. All three sections will use a relative position, will have automatic scroll bars for extra content and will float to the left. Each section will define its width and any other special styles.

The remaining style is for the tables that display the shopping cart. The tables use borders to separate the rows and columns.

```
div.layout {
  position: relative;
  float: left;
  overflow: auto;
}

div#outer {
  width: 600px;
}

div#right {
  width: 275px;
  padding: 1%;
```

```
  border-left:thin solid black;
}

div#left {
  width: 275px;
  padding: 1%;
  text-align: right;
}

div#bottom {
  border-top: thin solid black;
  width: 95%;
  padding: 1%;
}

table, td {
    border: thin solid black;
}
```

In the JSP, the left section contains the list of catalogue items with their forms, hidden fields and buttons. It contains the loop that generates the form for each button.

The right section contains the conditional code for displaying the item details. The Boolean condition for the core:if statement tests if the item Id is not null. If the item Id is null, then the bean is a default bean, so the bean will not be displayed. If the user has selected an item, then the details will appear here.

The bottom section contains the button for viewing the cart.

The other JSPs in the application will have a similar layout.

```
. . .
<div class="layout" id="outer">
   <div class="layout" id="left">
      <core:forEach var="oneItem" items="${allItems}">
        <form method="post" action="Controller">
          <p>
          ${oneItem.name}
          <input type="hidden" name="itemId"
                               value="${oneItem.itemId}">
          <input type="submit" name="viewItem"
                               value="View Item">
        </form>
      </core:forEach>
   </div>
      <core:if test="${helper.item.itemId != null}">
        <div class="layout" id="right">
          ${helper.item.name}<hr>
          ${helper.item.description}<hr>
          ${helper.item.price}<hr>
          <form action="Controller" method="post">
            <p>
            <input type="hidden" name="itemId"
                    value="${helper.item.itemId}">
```

```
            <input type="submit" name="addCart"
                value="Add To Cart">
            <input type="reset">
          </form>
        </div>
      </core:if>
    <div class="layout" id="bottom">
      <form action="Controller" method="post">
        <p>
        <input type="submit" name="viewCart"
                              value="View Cart">
      </form>
    </div>
  </div>
. . .
```

The style sheet for the application is located in the root folder of the web application. Hard-coding the name of the web application in the reference to the style sheet makes the application less portable. Even using a relative reference with several ../.. makes the application less portable.

The name of the web application can be retrieved using EL. The *page context* contains information about the web application. It can be accessed from EL with pageContext and contains the request object. The request object has an accessor method named getContextPath for retrieving the name of the web application. All accessor methods can be called using EL. The following EL statement dynamically retrieves the base path for the web application. The other JSPs in the application will use a similar technique.

```
. . .
<link href="${pageContext.request.contextPath}/catalogue.css"
      rel="stylesheet" type="text/css" >
. . .
```

7.9.3   Cart.jsp: Shopping Cart

The cart page is simple: it only displays the items that are in the cart (Fig. 7.5). The cart has been added to the session, so it can be retrieved in the JSP. Once again, a loop will be used to display all the items from a collection. A table will be used to organise the items from the catalogue into a grid.

```
<!DOCTYPE HTML>
<%@ taglib uri="http://java.sun.com/jsp/jstl/core" prefix="core" %>
<html>
  <head>
    <meta charset="utf-8">
    <link href="${pageContext.request.contextPath}/catalogue.css"
          rel="stylesheet" type="text/css" >
    <title>View Cart</title>
  </head>
  <body>
    <div class="layout" id="outer">
```

```
        <div class="layout" id="left">
    <table>
      <core:forEach var="oneItem"
                    items="${helper.cart.items}">
        <tr>
          <td>${oneItem.itemId}
          <td>${oneItem.name}
          <td>${oneItem.price}
      </core:forEach>
    </table>
    </div>
        <div class="layout" id="bottom">
    <form method="post" action="Controller">
      <p>
      <input type="submit" name="shop"
                           value="Continue Shopping">
      <input type="submit" name="processCart"
                           value="Process Cart">
      <input type="submit" name="emptyCart"
                           value="Empty Cart">
    </form>
        </div>
    </div>
  </body>
</html>
```

7.9.4   Process.jsp: Shopping Cart

The process page is essentially the same as the cart page. In addition to showing the items in the cart, it also displays the total number and total cost of items (Fig. 7.6).

```
. . .
You ordered ${helper.cart.count} items for a total bill
of ${helper.cart.totalAsCurrency}.
. . .
```

 Try It

http://bytesizebook.com/book/ch7/catalogue/Controller
    View some items, add them to the shopping cart and process the cart.

7.9.5   Shopping Cart: Enhancement

The shopping cart is only part of a complete web application. After obtaining the cart of items from the user, a typical website would then obtain the user's billing information. This could be accomplished from the process page by adding a button that would send the user to an edit page, in which the user would enter the billing information. The edit page would be like the edit pages from the other examples in this book. There would then be a confirm page and a process page. The user's data would be entered into a database of user data.

```
protected RequestDataAddress data =
    new RequestDataAddress();
private CatalogItem item = new CatalogItem();
private ShoppingCart<CatalogItem> cart =
    new ShoppingCart<CatalogItem>();
...
public Object getData() {
  return data;
}

public Object getItem() {
  return item;
}

public Object getCart() {
  return cart;
}
...
public void copyFromSession(Object sessionHelper) {
  if (sessionHelper.getClass() == this.getClass()) {
    data = ((ControllerHelper)sessionHelper).data;
    item = ((ControllerHelper)sessionHelper).item;
    cart = ((ControllerHelper)sessionHelper).cart;
  }
}
```

Such an application would be using two tables from the database: one for the catalogue items and one for the user's data. There would also be three beans in the application: catalogue item, shopping cart, user information. Each of these beans would need an accessor in the controller helper and would need to be copied from the session data.

The details of implementing such an application are left to the reader. The only difference between this application and previous applications is that two tables are used in the database. When Hibernate is configured, all the tables that are marked as entities must be included in the call to `initSessionFactory`.

```
HibernateHelper
    .initSessionFactory(RequestDataAddress.class,
                        CatalogItem.class);
```

The catalogue item table should not be created by this application. It is created with a separate controller. For this reason, the call to `createTable` will only have one table, while the call to `initSessionFactory` will have both tables.

```
static public void initHibernate(boolean create) {

  if (create) {
    HibernateHelper
        .createTable(RequestDataAddress.class);
  }

  HibernateHelper
      .initSessionFactory(RequestDataAddress.class,
                          CatalogItem.class);
}
```

7.10 Persistent Shopping Cart

It is possible to save the shopping cart in a similar manner to saving a bean, but there is a complication. Up until this point, all properties in a bean have been a standard type or a collection of a standard type. The shopping cart has a collection of a bean.

The items in a shopping cart are from the catalogue database. One item could be in several different shopping carts for different uses. The items are in their own table, so it does not make sense for the shopping cart to keep a second copy of the items. Even though the items are in a list in the shopping cart, the items will not be stored in a Java list; they will be stored in a related table that is managed by Hibernate.

A shopping cart contains many items and each item could be in several shopping carts. In database theory, this is known as a *many-to-many* relationship. Hibernate has an annotation named @ManyToMany to represent such a relationship. The annotation belongs in the accessor for the property.

```
@ManyToMany
public List<CatalogueItemPersist> getItems() {
    return items;
}
```

Hibernate treats collections of beans differently than collections of standard types. Since the bean collection is stored in a separate table, Hibernate typically does not retrieve all the items from the related table when the shopping cart is retrieved. This is done to save memory. Imagine a database for a university. There could be related tables for home address, financial information, class schedule, class history, etc. It does not make sense to retrieve all the data for the student when only the home phone number is needed.

While this is a good default behaviour, it can cause problems when the database is accessed in the controller but referenced in a JSP. By the time the data is needed in the JSP, the database session has already closed, so the related table cannot be accessed.

Two solutions exist for this problem: keep the session open for the JSP or retrieve the related table when the shopping cart is retrieved. Since the shopping cart will not consume a lot of memory, this application will retrieve the items every time the cart is retrieved. While this is not a good solution for a large database, it will be sufficient for a small application.

Hibernate uses the term *lazy* to represent the default behaviour of only retrieving related data when it is needed. The behaviour of retrieving the items every time the shopping cart is retrieved is called *eager*.

The annotation named @LazyCollection controls how the collection is retrieved. If the annotation is not included, the default implementation is to be lazy. To change the collection so that it is *eager*, instead of lazy, use the *LazyCollection* attribute with the option LazyCollectionOption.FALSE. Include this annotation along with @ManyToMany on the accessor of the property.

```
import org.hibernate.annotations.LazyCollection;
import org.hibernate.annotations.LazyCollectionOption;
import javax.persistence.ManyToMany;
...
@LazyCollection(LazyCollectionOption.FALSE)
@ManyToMany
public List<CatalogueItemPersist> getItems() {
    return items;
}
...
```

The other option of leaving the database session open longer is covered in detail in the book *Hibernate in Action* (Bauer and King 2005). The book covers database theory and how to implement advanced database concepts using Hibernate.

7.11   Application: Persistent Shopping Cart

The application for the persistent shopping cart is similar to the previous applications for the shopping cart and account login. The bean has an additional property for an account number and the persistent annotations are added to the collection property. Additional pages are added for logging in and for saving the cart to a database. The controller helper has an additional method for saving the cart.

The controller is the same as the controller for the catalogue application. Since this servlet will access the database, it should define the servlet, servlet mapping and initialisation parameter in the *web.xml* file.

7.11.1 Bean: Persistent Shopping Cart

The bean for this application is the shopping cart. An account number property is added to allow the cart to be retrieved from the database, and the items collection has been annotated with the persistent annotations.

The items collection is marked as `ManyToMany` because a shopping cart can contain many items and an item can be saved in many shopping carts. The collection is marked as not *lazy*, making it *eager*. This forces the items to be retrieved from the database every time the shopping cart is retrieved.

```
. . .
protected String accountNumber;

@Pattern(regexp="[a-zA-Z]{2}\\d{3}",
        message="must be in the format AA999.")
@NotNull
public String getAccountNumber() {
    return accountNumber;
}

public void setAccountNumber(String accountNumber) {
    this.accountNumber = accountNumber;
}
. . .
protected List<CatalogueItemPersist> items;

@LazyCollection(LazyCollectionOption.FALSE)
@ManyToMany
public List<CatalogueItemPersist> getItems() {
    return items;
}

public void setItems(List<CatalogueItemPersist> items) {
    this.items = items;
}
. . .
```

7.11.2 JSPs: Persistent Shopping Cart

The JSPs for this application have slight modifications from the last application.
The Cart.jsp has an additional button to access a new page for saving the cart.

```
<form method="post" action="Controller">
  <p>
  <input type="submit" name="shop"
                       value="Continue Shopping">
  <input type="submit" name="processCart"
                       value="Process Cart">
  <input type="submit" name="emptyCart"
                       value="Empty Cart">
  <input type="submit" name="saveCart"
                       value="Save Cart">
  <p>
  <input type="submit" name="newUser"
                       value="New User">
</form>
```

The new page for saving the cart displays the contents of the cart, just like the
process page.

```
<body>
  <div class="layout" id="outer">
    <div class="layout" id="left">
      <table border>
        <core:forEach var="oneItem"
                      items="${helper.cart.items}">
            <tr>
        <td>${oneItem.itemId}
        <td>${oneItem.name}
        <td>${oneItem.price}
    </core:forEach>
  </table>
</div>
<div class="layout" id="right">
  <p>
  Thank you for your interest. Your cart has been
  saved for future use. When you return, your cart
  will be waiting for you.
</div>
<div class="layout" id="bottom">
  <p>
  Currently, there are ${helper.cart.count} items for a total bill
  of ${helper.cart.totalAsCurrency}.

  <form method="post" action="Controller">
    <p>
    <input type="submit" name="shop"
                         value="Continue Shopping">
```

```
         <input type="submit" name="processCart"
                               value="Process Cart">
         <input type="submit" name="emptyCart"
                               value="Empty Cart">
         <p>
         <input type="submit" name="newUser"
                               value="New User">
      </form>
   </div>
 </div>
</body>
</html>
```

7.11.3 ControllerHelper: Persistent Shopping Cart

An additional button method is added to the controller helper to save the cart to the database. The method calls the method for processing the cart for the original shopping cart application and then saves the cart to the database.

```
@ButtonMethod(buttonName="saveCart")
public String saveCartMethod() {
    methodProcess();
    HibernateHelper.updateDB(cart);
    return jspLocation("SaveCart.jsp");
}
```

A method to control gaining access to the application is added to the controller helper. This method is similar to the login method from the account login application. This method is the default method for the application. There should only be one default method per application, so the default attribute should be removed from the methodBrowseLoop method that was the default for the previous application.

```
@ButtonMethod(buttonName="loginButton", isDefault=true)
public String loginMethod() {
  String address;
  fillBeanFromRequest(cart);
  setErrors(cart);
  if (isValidProperty("accountNumber")) {
    Object dataPersistent =
      HibernateHelper.getFirstMatch(cart,
        "accountNumber", cart.getAccountNumber());
    if (dataPersistent != null) {
      cart = (ShoppingCartPersist<CatalogueItemPersist>)dataPersistent;
    }
    clearErrors();
    address = methodBrowseLoop();
  } else {
    address = jspLocation("Login.jsp");
  }
  return address;
}
```

The doGet method will ignore the session data and will always go to the default method.

```
public void doGet()
   throws IOException, ServletException
{
    addHelperToSession("helper", SessionData.IGNORE);
    String address = loginMethod();
    request.getRequestDispatcher(address)
        .forward(request, response);
}
```

7.12   Summary

It is better to let Hibernate manage the primary key, since it is used to indicate data persistence. There is often a separate key in the user's data that can also be used to identify a row. Other times, several fields will need to be combined to uniquely identify each row.

Finding a value in the database can be accomplished by using the Criteria class in Hibernate. Once an object has been retrieved from the database, Hibernate will remember that it came from the database and will update the row instead of adding a new one.

An application was developed that forced the user to log into the site. By doing this, the user's data can be retrieved from the database and stored in the session. When the bean in the session is written to the database, it will replace the old data in the database.

Cookies can be used to remember information about a user, so that personal information can be displayed every time the user visits a site. Cookies are stored in the browser and are sent back to the site that created it, whenever that site is visited. The user has control over cookies and can delete them at any time.

Cookies have a name and a value. Cookies can be created that will exist for a specific time and be sent to a specific server or page. Cookies can be configured so that they are only sent over a secure connection. Cookies are sent to the browser as part of the response headers.

Cookies can be used to save a user Id, so that the next time a site is accessed, the user does not have to log in. The browser will send the Id to the controller and the controller will use it to access the database.

Many sites have shopping cart applications that allow users to select and add items. Shopping carts are fairly simple in that they only need to be able to store the items, clear the items and add an item. The item that is stored in the shopping cart is not important when implementing a shopping cart. A shopping cart can be developed using Java 1.5 generics.

An application that uses a shopping cart was developed. A database of items was created. The same bean that was used to create the database was also used in the application. It is a natural choice, since the user will be selecting items from the catalogue to be added to the shopping cart. The cart was later saved to a database using an eager, many-to-many relationship.

The database will set the maximum length for a text field when a column is added to the table for the field. It is better to set the maximum value than to use the default length. Hibernate has annotations that will indicate the preferred length of the column in the table.

A new tag that implements an `if` statement was introduced from the JSTL. By using this tag, conditional content can be added to a JSP. This is a better approach than using Java, since Java can generate stack traces and Java can be difficult to change, for an HTML developer.

7.13   Chapter Review

Terms
1. Criteria Class
2. Restrictions Class
3. Cookie
    (a) Name
    (b) Value
    (c) Expiration
    (d) Domain
    (e) Path
    (f) Secure
4. Cookie Operations
    (a) Sending
    (b) Accessing
    (c) Deleting
    (d) Finding
5. Path Specific Cookies
6. Catalogue Item and Catalogue
7. Shopping Cart Bean
    (a) add
    (b) reset
    (c) set total
    (d) set count
8. Many-to-many Relationship
9. Eager Fetching
10. Lazy Fetching

New Java
1. Cookie Class
    (a) Constructors
    (b) getName, setName

    (c) getValue, setValue
    (d) getMaxAge, setMaxAge
    (e) getDomain, setDomain
    (f) getPath, setPath
    (g) getSecure, setSecure
    (h) Default Values
2. isValidProperty
3. response.addCookie
4. response.getCookies
5. HibernateHelper
    (a) getListData(bean, string, value)
    (b) getFirstMatch(bean, string, value)
6. LazyCollection
7. ManyToMany
8. LazyCollectionOption

Tags
1. core:if

Questions
1. Why was a new bean created after a row was removed from the database?
2. Explain the steps that are followed to retrieve a bean from the database and copy it into the current controller helper.
3. Explain the steps that are followed to read a cookie from the browser and then test if there is a corresponding row in the database.
4. Why does the new user method create a new bean?
5. What are the default values for all the properties in a cookie?
6. In a cookie, what does a maximum age of 0 mean? What does a maximum age of −1 mean?
7. What does it mean when the value of the domain property in a cookie starts with a period?
8. What does it mean when the value of the path property in a cookie is '/accounting:'?

Tasks
1. Create the following cookie and add it to the response.
    (a) Name it *fruit* and give it a value of *orange*.
    (b) Have it expire when the browser closes.
    (c) Have it returned only to the domain and path that created it.
    (d) It may be sent over a nonsecure connection.
2. Create the following cookie and add it to the response.
    (a) Name it *vegetable* and give it a value of *broccoli*.
    (b) Have it expire in 1 year.
    (c) Have it returned to all sub-domains of fiu.edu and to all paths.
    (d) It may be sent over a secure connection only.

3. For the create catalogue servlet, add a web interface so that items can be added to and deleted from the database.

4. Write the code that belongs in a JSP that will loop through all the cookies that it received.

5. Write the code that belongs in a controller that will delete a cookie named *pen* that can be read by all paths beginning with */bic* in the *www.pensforsale.com* domain. Don't just create the cookie; be sure that the cookie is sent to the browser.

6. Write the code that belongs in a servlet that will find a cookie named *auto*.

7. Modify the getListData method so that two different properties and values can be sent to it. Add an additional criterion to the search.

8. Modify the getListData method so that a variable number of properties and values can be sent to it. Add an additional criterion to the search for each new property. Hint: The initSessionFactory method has a parameter that can accept a variable number of arguments.

9. Modify the isValidProperty method in the HelperBaseCh5 file so that it calls setErrors and a variable number of property names can be sent to it. The method should return true only if all the properties are valid. Hint: The initSessionFactory method has a parameter that can accept a variable number of arguments.

10. For the shopping cart application, only allow one instance of an item in the cart and keep a total of the number of copies that are wanted.

    (a) On the confirm page, add a text box for changing the current item count and a button to recalculate the total for each item.

11. For the shopping cart application, after the cart has been processed, allow the user to proceed to additional pages named edit, confirm and process in which the user's billing information is added. Save the billing address and the purchased items in a new table in the database.

Web Services and Legacy Databases

8

In addition to developing a stand-alone web application, it is possible to connect to other web applications to simplify processing the user's data. Such a web application is known as a web service. For instance, there are services for calculating shipping costs, for accepting online payments and for finding maps. These services are not designed to interface with a user, but rather to interact with other web applications.

There are many different types of web services. The difficult part of any web service is discovering how to interact with it. Each web service can have its own methods and data types. SOAP and RESTful services are two standard ways to define a web service. SOAP services declare all the methods for connecting to the service, while RESTful services reuse HTTP request methods in an attempt to simplify connecting to services.

Today's IDEs have wizards that allow the developer to ascertain the methods and data types that are used by the service. Even with this information, it is often necessary to read about the web service on a company website in order to communicate with the service. Other services do not follow a common standard. In such cases, it is necessary to read about the service on a company website. Without proper documentation, it can be difficult to connect to a web service.

NetBeans has an excellent tool for accessing web services that are defined with SOAP or REST. SOAP services define a WSDL file that describes all the methods and data types that the service uses. REST services follow the RESTful design. The RESTful design standardises the methods that can be used to communicate with the service by limiting the methods to the HTTP request methods. While it is not required, many RESTful services define a WADL file that describes how to communicate with the service. Any service that has a WSDL or WADL file can be added to NetBeans.

While it is straightforward to generate a web application from scratch, it can be more complicated to generate a web application that accesses a database that already exists. There is a tool for Hibernate that will generate the annotated beans necessary to access a database. A developer would use the tool to connect to the database and Hibernate would reverse-engineer the definition of the beans that can access it.

T. Downey, *Guide to Web Development with Java: Understanding Website Creation*,
DOI 10.1007/978-1-4471-2443-6_8, © Springer-Verlag London Limited 2012

For all the applications in previous chapters, there are working examples on the book's website. While the source code for the applications in this chapter is available on the website, there are no working examples. The agreement for using the test sites for the web services stipulates that it is for personal use. It would not be within the bounds of the agreement to place an application on the web that anyone can use that would access these services.

8.1   Application: Google Maps

An application will be developed for showing how to call the Google Maps web service and incorporate the results of a call to a remote application into the current web application.

The application will start with a structure similar to the post controller from Chap. 5. The only differences will be the bean and the references to the bean in the JSPs.

8.1.1   Bean: Google Maps

The bean will have only one property for an address. The validation will be that the address is not empty. In a robust application, the interface would be more user-friendly, allowing the user to enter street, city, postal code, country in different text boxes. Such an interface would require a bean with more properties. To keep this application simple and focus on the web service, only the address will be entered by the user.

```
package ch8.services.google;

import javax.validation.constraints.NotNull;
import javax.validation.constraints.Pattern;

public class RequestDataServices {

    protected String address;

    @NotNull
    @Pattern(regexp=".*\\S.*", message="cannot be empty")
    public String getAddress() {
        return address;
    }

    public void setAddress(String address) {
        this.address = address;
    }
}
```

Fig. 8.1 Web services
in NetBeans

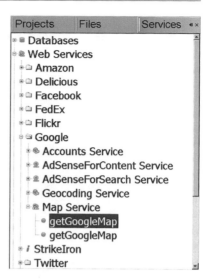

8.1.2   Service Method: Google Maps

Google Maps is a RESTful service and has a WADL file defined for it. This service comes registered in NetBeans in the `Services - > Web Services` tab (Fig. 8.1). Additional services can be added to NetBeans – all that is needed is the location of a WSDL or WADL file.

8.1.3   Process Method: Google Maps

The work will be done in the process method in the controller helper. This is where the code to access the web service will be added. The first step is to open the controller helper in NetBeans and find the process method. Next open the `Services - > Web Service` tab and navigate to the `Google - > Map Service` tab. Drag the `getGoogleMap` method name from the Map Service to the process method. Drop it on the blank line above the return statement.

An initialisation window for an address will appear. Accept the default address for now, it can be changed in code later.

The method for the service has three parameters: the address, the zoom factor for the map and the method that the map will be displayed in the HTML page. Pass the bean address to the method. A zoom factor of 15 is a good starting point.

The map can be retrieved in two ways. The first way will generate an entire HTML page that contains the map. The second way is to generate HTML code that can be inserted into another page. The second way is more useful and is specified by passing the string 'true' as the third parameter to the method.

The return value from the `getGoogleMap` method is a `RestResponse` object. The `RestResponse` contains methods for converting the response to a usable format. For this application, the map is returned as HTML code, so the getDataAsString method is most useful. Depending on the data that is returned, the other methods might be useful. For instance, if the data is returned as an XML file, then the getDataAsObject method can be used to cast the XML file to a bean.

```
...
@ButtonMethod(buttonName = "processButton")
public String processMethod() {

    try {
        String address = data.getAddress();
        java.lang.Integer zoom = 15;
        String iframe = "true";

        RestResponse result =
                GoogleMapService.getGoogleMap(address, zoom, iframe);
        request.setAttribute("googleMap", result.getDataAsString());
    } catch (Exception ex) {
        ex.printStackTrace();
    }

    return jspLocation("Process.jsp");
}
...
```

The result will be added to the request object so it can be accessed in the JSP. This technique was used in Chap. 5 to send the database to the process page.

8.1.4   Process.jsp: Google Maps

The process page will show the result from the Google Maps web service. The process page can access the map with ${googleMap}, because that is the name the process method will use to place it in the request.

```
<!DOCTYPE HTML>
<html>
  <head>
      <meta charset="utf-8">
      <title>Process Page</title>
  </head>
  <body>
    <p>
      Thank you for your information.
      Here is the map for the address.

    <p>
    ${googleMap}
    <form action="Controller">
      <input type="submit" name="editButton"
                          value="New">
    </form>
    <form method="POST" action="Controller">
      <input type="submit" name="editButton"
                          value="Edit">
    </form>
  </body>
</html>
```

Fig. 8.2 Error for Google Maps

Fig. 8.3 Packages created
for Google Maps

8.1.5 Properties File: Google Maps

If this application is run, then an error is displayed (Fig. 8.2).

This is where some creative investigation is needed. While it is now much easier to access a web service, it is still not easy. Even in this simple web service, there can be problems. As the services get more complex, so do the implementation problems.

The error message mentions a `googlemapservice.properties` file and a missing property. If you look back at the source files in the project, you will note that two packages were added to the application (Fig. 8.3). These packages contain all the information for accessing the web service. All web services will add code to the project. The WSDL and WADL files indicate what code needs to be generated in order to connect to the service.

For most web services, it is necessary to identify yourself with the company before you are allowed to access the service. In today's world of hacking and

```
 googlemapservice.properties
1 # To change this template, choose Tools | Templates
2 # and open the template in the editor.
3 api_key=
4
5
```

Fig. 8.4 The API key is missing

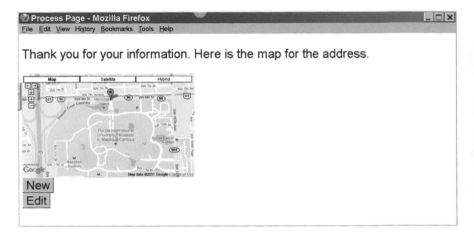

Fig. 8.5 The map for FIU

security threats, this is a reasonable practice. All of the services that are covered in this chapter will require some kind of authorisation.

For Google Maps, you will need a Google account and then you must register for the API and obtain credentials for accessing the service. The current URL for obtaining the API key is `http://code.google.com/apis/maps/signup.html`. Once you have the code, copy it to the `googlemapservice.properties` file and the application will run.

Open the `googlemapservice.properties` file. There is the missing property (Fig. 8.4).

Sign up with Google and place your API key in this file. Then the application will run. Figure 8.5 shows the output of the application for the address of Florida International University in Miami, FL.

8.2   FedEx: Rate Service

A common feature for a website is to calculate shipping charges. FedEx provides a web service for this. The WSDL file is not available on the web, but it can be downloaded from the samples page for FedEx. There are many services for FedEx; this section will only cover the Rate service. Other services would be implemented in a similar manner.

As with other services, it is necessary to register with FedEx before using the service. The developer site for FedEx is `http://fedex.com/us/developer/index.html`. Follow the instructions for obtaining credentials for using the service.

One way to implement the service is to download the sample and read the README file for the service. The instructions are good, but care must be taken that the same versions of all the packages are used. At this time, the samples are using Axis2 1.4, but Axis2 1.6 is now available. The sample code for connecting to the service does not work under Axis2 1.6.

This section will approach the implementation differently. The FedEx web service can be added to the NetBeans web services list. This will allow service methods to be dragged and dropped into an application. While this makes it easy to access the service, a lot of details are hidden. It will be necessary to explore a little bit in order to get the application working.

8.2.1   FedEx: Overview

After obtaining credentials from FedEx, use them to connect to each service. The credentials will be placed in a properties file and read when the service is initialised. Download the Rate Service sample from the FedEx developers' site too. It is a good reference for setting up the request and displaying the results.

The sample code uses a different implementation of web services than NetBeans. The sample code is using Axis2, while NetBeans uses JAX-WS. Both implementations do the same thing but use different syntax. The steps are

1. Create a request object.
2. Add credentials to the request object.
3. Set the version.
4. Create a shipment object.
5. Set the data of the shipment.
6. Set the *from* address of the shipment.
7. Set the *to* address of the shipment.

Fig. 8.6 FedEx rate service
in NetBeans

8. Set the payment method for the shipment.
9. Set the package details: height, width, length, weight, insurance.
10. Add the package to the shipment.
11. Connect to the service and display the results.

The automated code that is generated in NetBeans for the service does not contain the calls for all of these steps. The code contains the methods and data structures for communicating with the service, but it is up to the developer to initialise the request and process the response.

The biggest challenge for any web service is to determine how to communicate with it. Usually, the company will provide information for accessing the service. In the case of FedEx, there are many sample examples. The samples are good, but they require that the developer install older versions of packages. It is good to use the samples as a reference, but try to write the application code using the most recent versions of the required packages.

8.2.2   Application: FedEx

An application will be developed that is like the post controller from Chap. 5. Copy the example from Chap. 5 into a new package for Chap. 8. Modify the jspLocation method. Add a servlet definition and mapping to the *web.xml* file. Open the controller helper and go to the process method.

Next, open the Services tab in NetBeans and select the Web Services folder. Right-click the web services folder and select Add Group. Name the group *FedEx*. Right-click the *FedEx* group and select Add Web Service. On the next screen, select the local radio button and browse to the location of the rate WSDL file that you have just downloaded (Fig. 8.6).

Fig. 8.7 FedEx generated
code

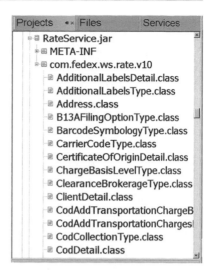

Drag and drop the `getRates` method from the *FedEx* web services into the
process method. The following code will be generated:

```
...
public void processMethodFedex() {
    try {
        RateRequest rateRequest = null;
        RateService service = new RateService();
        RatePortType port = service.getRateServicePort();
        RateReply result = port.getRates(rateRequest);
        System.out.println("Result = " + result);
    } catch (Exception ex) {
        ex.printStackTrace();
    }
}
...
```

There is only one minor problem with the code: it doesn't work. The generated
code shows the steps needed to connect to the service port, but does not provide the
details for setting up the request. The most important code in the block is

```
RateRequest rateRequest = null;
```

All of the details of the rate request must be filled in before the request can be
made. The following sections explain how to create the request.

Each web service will generate code in your application. Some services will add
libraries, some will add packages. The FedEx rate service adds a JAR file to the
application library. Open the libraries folder of your application and find the
`RateService.jar` file. Expand the folders in the JAR to see the list of classes
that have been generated. There are a lot of them (Fig. 8.7).

8.2.3   Bean: FedEx

The code that was generated by NetBeans contains all the code that is needed to communicate with the FedEx rate service. Included in the code are many beans that can be used to gather data from the user. After the data has been gathered, it can be added to the rate request. As an example, the *Address* and *Dimensions* beans will be used to gather information from the user. The *Address* will be used to obtain the shipper and recipient address. The *Dimensions* will be used to gather the dimensions of the package being shipped.

Most of the applications up to this point have only used one bean. This application will have one bean that is exposed directly to the JSPs, just like previous applications; however, the bean will not have any simple properties. All of the properties in the bean will refer to additional classes that extend the classes provided by the FedEx service.

```
public class RequestDataFedex {

    FedexAddress addressShipper;
    FedexAddress addressRecipient;
    FedexDimensions dimensions;

    public FedexAddress getAddressRecipient() {
        return addressRecipient;
    }

    public void setAddressRecipient(FedexAddress addressRecipient) {
        this.addressRecipient = addressRecipient;
    }

    public FedexAddress getAddressShipper() {
        return addressShipper;
    }

    public void setAddressShipper(FedexAddress addressShipper) {
        this.addressShipper = addressShipper;
    }

    public Dimensions getDimensions() {
        return dimensions;
    }

    public void setDimensions(FedexDimensions dimensions) {
        this.dimensions = dimensions;
    }
}
```

Address Bean: FedEx

The beans that are provided by the service are in a JAR file in the library of the application, so they are read-only. In order to add required validation to a bean, a new bean will be created that extends the bean from the Fedex package. Initially, all that needs to be added to the extended class is the accessors for the properties that are to be validated. Appropriate validations have been added to each field.

```
import com.fedex.ws.rate.v10.Address;
...
public class FedexAddress extends Address {

    @Override
    @NotNull
    @Pattern(regexp=".*\\S.*", message="cannot be empty")
    public String getCity() {
        return super.getCity();
    }

    @Override
    @NotNull
    @Pattern(regexp="\\d{5}(-\\d{4})?",
    message="must be 5 digits or ZIP+4")
    public String getPostalCode() {
        return super.getPostalCode();
    }

    @Override
    @NotNull
    @Pattern(regexp=".*\\S.*", message="cannot be empty")
    public String getStateOrProvinceCode() {
        return super.getStateOrProvinceCode();
...
```

At times, there will be a mismatch between how data is represented in the service and how data is gathered from the web. An example of this kind of property is the street address. The service allows many lines for a street address. It uses a list of strings to store the street address, so as many lines as are needed can be added. The easiest way to implement the gathering of any number of lines from the user is to use a text area element. This will require that the string that is returned from the browser is changed into a list of strings.

The property in the base class is named streetLines. A new property will be added to the Address bean that accepts a string but writes a list of strings to the base class. Similarly, the accessor for the new property will read the list of strings from the base class and concatenate them into one string.

```
. . .
public void setStreetAddress(String street) {
    if (street == null) return;
    BufferedReader reader =
            new BufferedReader(new StringReader(street));
    String line;
    try {
        if (super.streetLines == null) {
            super.streetLines = new ArrayList<String>();
        }
        super.streetLines.clear();
        while ((line = reader.readLine()) != null) {
            if (!line.trim().isEmpty())
                super.streetLines.add(line);
        }
    } catch (IOException ex) {
        Logger.getLogger(FedexAddress.class.getName())
                .log(Level.SEVERE, null, ex);
    }
}


@NotNull
@Pattern(regexp="(.*\\S.*\\r\\n)+", message="cannot be empty")
public String getStreetAddress() {
    StringBuilder result = new StringBuilder();
    for (String line : super.getStreetLines()) {
        result.append(String.format("%s%n", line));
    }
    return result.toString();
}
. . .
```

A buffered reader is used to read a line at a time from the string. Only nontrivial lines are added to the address. A string builder is used to combine all of the strings into one string separated by the new line character. The `format` method of the String class is used to format the output. The `%n` symbol generates a new line character, which is represented in Java as the two control characters `\r` and `\n`. This is why the pattern validation contains the pattern `(.*\\S.*\\r\\n)+`. The pattern matches one or more lines that contain at least one non-space character. The order of `\\r\\n` is important.

Dimensions Bean: FedEx

The properties in the *Dimensions* class are *BigInteger* and *BigDecimal* numbers. This is not a problem, since the validator can handle these types. The bean utilities package can also handle these types, so copying the values to the bean from the query string can be automated. The bean can be annotated in the same way that simple integer properties were entered.

An additional property was added to the class to store the weight of the package. This is another example where the way that data is entered is not the same as the way that data is stored. The weight is stored as a single property in the FedEx classes but is not stored in the *Dimensions* class. When gathering data, it is easier to collect the weight along with the dimensions, so it was added to this bean. Care must be taken later to remember that the weight needs its own statement when being added to the request.

```java
import com.fedex.ws.rate.v10.Address;
...
public class FedexDimensions extends Dimensions {

    @Override
    @Min(1)
    @Max(200)
    public BigInteger getHeight() {
        return super.getHeight();
    }

    @Override
    @Min(1)
    @Max(200)
    public BigInteger getLength() {
        return super.getLength();
    }

    @Override
    @Min(1)
    @Max(200)
    public BigInteger getWidth() {
        return super.getWidth();
    }

    protected BigDecimal weight;

    @Min(1)
    @Max(200)
    public BigDecimal getWeight() {
        return weight;
    }

    public void setWeight(BigDecimal weight) {
        this.weight = weight;
    }

}
```

8.2.4   JSPs: FedEx

A JSP is created for obtaining the data from the user. The validation technique from Chap. 5 can be used to display the error messages for failed validations. A table is used to organise the data.

```
...
<table>
    <tr><td>Street Lines ${helper.errors.streetAddress}<br>
            (enter multiple lines for street address)
        <td><textarea name="streetAddress"
                >${helper.data.addressShipper.streetAddress}</textarea>
    <tr><td>City ${helper.errors.city}
        <td><input type="text" name="city"
                value="${helper.data.addressShipper.city}">
    <tr><td>State ${helper.errors.stateOrProvinceCode}
        <td><input type="text" name="stateOrProvinceCode"
                value="${helper.data.addressShipper.stateOrProvinceCode}">
    <tr><td>Zip ${helper.errors.postalCode}
        <td><input type="text" name="postalCode"
                value="${helper.data.addressShipper.postalCode}">
</table>
  <p>
...
```

A similar page has been generated for the recipient's address. The code is the same as the above, except addressShipper is replaced with addressRecipient. The EL code is accessing the bean first and then accessing the reference to the next bean.

A JSP has been added that reads the dimensions and weight from the user.

```
...
<table>
    <tr><td>Width (inches) ${helper.errors.width}
        <td><input type="text" name="width"
                    value="${helper.data.dimensions.width}">
    <tr><td>Height (inches) ${helper.errors.height}
        <td><input type="text" name="height"
                    value="${helper.data.dimensions.height}">
    <tr><td>Length (inches) ${helper.errors.length}
        <td><input type="text" name="length"
                    value="${helper.data.dimensions.length}">
    <tr><td>Weight (lbs) ${helper.errors.weight}
        <td><input type="text" name="weight"
                    value="${helper.data.dimensions.weight}">
</table>
...
```

The flow of the pages is to gather the shipper information, then to gather the recipient information and then to gather the package information. Validation should be performed at each step. Once all the information has been gathered, the request can be created.

Process.jsp: Fedex

The process page displays the results of the service request. The return value from the request will be a bean. The bean contains a bean property for the details of the request. The details will be placed in the request in the process method so that the process page can retrieve information; it will be retrieved from the request with the EL statement ${fedexResult}.

The response contains a lot of information. Only a few of the properties will be displayed in the process page.

```
...
<core:forEach var="detail" items="${fedexResult}">
    Service Type = ${detail.serviceType}<br>
    Packaging Type = ${detail.packagingType}<br>
    Rate Type = ${detail.actualRateType}
    <ol>
    <core:forEach var="shipment" items="${detail.ratedShipmentDetails}">
        <hr>
        Total Weight =
            ${shipment.shipmentRateDetail.totalBillingWeight.value}<br>
        Total Surcharges =
            ${shipment.shipmentRateDetail.totalSurcharges.amount}<br>
        Total Net Charge =
            ${shipment.shipmentRateDetail.totalNetCharge.amount}
    </core:forEach>
    </ol>
</core:forEach>
...
```

8.2.5 ControllerHelper: FedEx

The controller helper for the application is like previous controller helpers, but now there are the equivalent of three confirm pages. The data has been separated into three different beans, so each bean can be validated separately.

Some helper methods will be added to the controller helper to create the credentials for connecting to FedEx and for creating the request.

Validated Methods: FedEx

After the user enters the shipper information, control should pass to the recipient page only if the shipper data is correct. This is exactly the logic of all other confirm pages: validate the data before proceeding to the next page. The fillBeanFrom-Request and isValid methods can be used as they were in previous examples. The code for the recipientButton should look familiar. The only significant difference is the use of data.addressShipper instead of data. By using a bean inside a bean, the data can be validated one step at a time.

```
...
@ButtonMethod(buttonName = "recipientButton")
public String recipientMethod() {
    fillBeanFromRequest(data.addressShipper);
    String address;
    if (isValid(data.addressShipper)) {
        address = jspLocation("RecipientAddress.jsp");
    } else {
        address = jspLocation("ShipperAddress.jsp");
    }
    return address;
...
```

There are similar methods for moving from the recipient page to the package info page and for moving from the package info page to the process page.

Credentials: FedEx

Add a properties file to your application. Place the file into the *Default Package* under the *Source Packages* folder. If the *Default Package* does not exist, place the file in the *Source Packages* folder. Fill in the missing details with your credentials for accessing FedEx. Obtain these credentials from the FedEx developers' site.

```
#Obtain credentials from the FedEx developer site.
accountNumber=
meternumber=
key=
password=
```

A static variable will be added to the helper that will store the credentials for FedEx. A static block will initialise the variable from the properties file. The class loader for the current class is being used to load the properties file. The class loader will look for the file in the same way that it looks for other classes. One of the places it will look is the *Default Package*.

```
...
private static final Properties credentials = new Properties();

static {
    try {
        credentials.load(
            ControllerHelper.class.getClassLoader().
                getResourceAsStream("fedex.properties"));
    } catch (IOException ex) {
        System.out.format("Could not open fedex properties: %s%n%s%n",
            ex.getMessage(), ex.getStackTrace());
    }
}
...
```

Table 8.1 Visible contents in a Web App

Property	Value
Group Package Count	1
Weight Units	pounds
Linear Units	inches
Timestamp	today
Country Code	US
Package Count	1
Service Type	FEDEX_GROUND

Create Request: FedEx

A helper method can now be added to the controller helper that will create the request. It will set the addresses for the shipper and the recipient. It will set the dimensions and weight of the package. There are many more properties that can be set for a shipment. Table 8.1 contains properties that are being set to constant values. In a complete application, these properties would also be set by the user.

There are many steps to setting up the request for the FedEx service. The following statements are all within the `getFedexRequest` method, but will be broken into logical code fragments.

The first steps are to create a request object, set the credentials and set the version. The credentials will be read from the properties file. The version is difficult to track down but can be found within the sample code from Fedex. The major number for the version is listed in the package name for the FedEx examples.

```
import com.fedex.ws.rate.v10.RateRequest;
...
protected RateRequest getFedexRequest() {
    RateRequest info = new RateRequest();

    info.setClientDetail(new ClientDetail());
    info.getClientDetail().
        setAccountNumber(credentials.getProperty("accountNumber"));
    info.getClientDetail().
        setMeterNumber(credentials.getProperty("meterNumber"));

    info.setWebAuthenticationDetail(new WebAuthenticationDetail());
    info.getWebAuthenticationDetail().
        setUserCredential(new WebAuthenticationCredential());
    info.getWebAuthenticationDetail().getUserCredential().
        setKey(credentials.getProperty("key"));
    info.getWebAuthenticationDetail().getUserCredential().
        setPassword(credentials.getProperty("password"));

    info.setVersion(new VersionId());
    info.getVersion().setServiceId("crs");
    info.getVersion().setMajor(10);
    info.getVersion().setIntermediate(0);
    info.getVersion().setMinor(0);
...
```

Next is the package information. There could be many packages in the same shipment. Each package is referred to as a line item. The user sets the weight and dimensions of the package.

```
...
RequestedPackageLineItem lineItem = new RequestedPackageLineItem();
lineItem.setGroupPackageCount(new BigInteger("1"));
lineItem.setWeight(new Weight());
lineItem.getWeight().setUnits(WeightUnits.LB);
lineItem.getWeight().setValue(data.dimensions.getWeight());

lineItem.setDimensions(data.getDimensions());
lineItem.getDimensions().setUnits(LinearUnits.IN);
...
```

Finally, the shipment information is added. This section will use the addresses that were gathered via the web forms.

```
...
RequestedShipment shipment = new RequestedShipment();

XMLGregorianCalendar today = null;
try {
    today = DatatypeFactory.newInstance().newXMLGregorianCalendar(
            new GregorianCalendar());
} catch (DatatypeConfigurationException e) {
    System.out.println(e.getStackTrace());
}
shipment.setShipTimestamp(today);

shipment.setShipper(new Party());
shipment.getShipper().
        setAddress((Address) data.addressShipper);
shipment.getShipper().getAddress().setCountryCode("US");
shipment.setRecipient(new Party());
shipment.getRecipient().
        setAddress((Address) data.addressRecipient);
shipment.getRecipient().getAddress().setCountryCode("US");

shipment.getRequestedPackageLineItems().add(lineItem);
shipment.setPackageCount(new BigInteger("1"));
shipment.setServiceType(ServiceType.FEDEX_GROUND);

info.setRequestedShipment(shipment);

return info;
...
```

Process Method: Fedex

The process method contains the code that was generated from the NetBeans wizard, but now it calls the getFedexRequest method to fill in the details of the request. The response from the service request is also a FedEx bean. This bean is placed in the HTTP request so that the results can be displayed in the JSP.

```
...
@ButtonMethod(buttonName = "processButton")
public String processMethod() {
    fillBeanFromRequest(data.dimensions);
    String address;

    if (isValid(data.dimensions)) {
        try {
            RateRequest rateRequest = getFedexRequest();
            RateService service = new RateService();
            RatePortType port = service.getRateServicePort();
            RateReply result = port.getRates(rateRequest);
            request.setAttribute(
                    "fedexResult", result.getRateReplyDetails());
        } catch (Exception ex) {
            ex.printStackTrace();
        }
        address = jspLocation("Process.jsp");
    } else {
        address = jspLocation("PackageInfo.jsp");
    }
    return address;
}
...
```

8.3   PayPal Web Service

The final web service example will be for PayPal. PayPal has different ways to connect to their services. One way is to use SOAP and a WSDL file, like the FedEx service that was just covered. PayPal also offers a service that uses *name/value pairs* (NVP) in the query string to send parameters to the service. There is a developers' site at PayPal that provides documentation and downloads, https://developer.paypal. com/. Once again, you will need to request credentials from PayPal in order to access the service.

The PayPal service uses the query string to send name/value pairs of information. While it is possible to do this by hand using Java, PayPal provides a *Software Development Kit* (SDK) that contains helpful methods for connecting to the service. The SDK can be downloaded from the PayPal developers' site.

PayPal offers sample code for connecting to the service using the SDK. These examples demonstrate how to send credentials and parameters in the query string. Only the *Express Checkout* example is used in this application.

PayPal has a separate server to handle requests for developers that are creating an application that uses the service. The separate service is known as the *sandbox*. In the sandbox, it is possible to create dummy accounts to test how the application is working. Once the developer is satisfied that the application is working, it can be moved to the production site.

The PayPal sandbox allows you to create fictitious accounts that can be used to test the PayPal services. Only two accounts are needed: a business account and a user account. More accounts can be created of many different types to test all the features that PayPal offers.

8.3.1   Application: PayPal

This example will use the PayPal Express Checkout service. With Express Checkout, the user clicks a PayPal button from a website. The user is then redirected to the PayPal site. When the user approves the payment at PayPal, the user is returned to the original site where the order can be processed.

When the PayPal button is clicked in the application, a normal HTTP request is made. This request will be handled like other requests in this book: a button name is translated to a button method. The button method that is executed when the PayPal button is clicked makes a call to the PayPal service. The service request initiates a conversation with PayPal. To continue the conversation with PayPal, the current HTTP request must be redirected to PayPal. If a separate request is made to PayPal, it will not be part of the same conversation.

Once the request has been redirected to PayPal, the user logs into PayPal and approves the payment. After the payment is approved, PayPal makes a return request to your application. The request will be a GET request. The return request can contain a query string, so the return request can be handled by a button method in the controller helper. This button method can then obtain information about the use, like the user's address. The method then finalises the transaction by making another call to the PayPal service that will deduct the money from the user's account.

The application for this service will start with the catalog example from Chap. 7. The application makes changes to the process page and adds a new page for processing the return from PayPal.

8.3.2   ControllerHelper: PayPal

The controller helper will extend the catalogue example from Chap. 7. It will also be placed in a sub-package for that controller. Since the sub-package is a sub-folder of the original, additional pages can be added to the application by using a relative path in the location of the page. References to pages in the original application do not need to be changed. For modified and new pages in the PayPal service application, the path `paypal/` will be added before the page that is sent to the `jspLocation` method.

```
...
return jspLocation("paypal/Process.jsp");
...
```

GET and POST: PayPal

A few modifications need to be made to the `doGet` and `doPost` methods. Both methods must test if the address is not the empty string. When accessing the PayPal service, the request must be redirected to PayPal. This means that the normal behaviour of forwarding to a JSP in the application must be suppressed. When the request needs to be redirected, the corresponding button method will return the empty string, indicating that the forward should be avoided.

When PayPal returns to the application, it will send a GET request. The doGet method must be modified so that it processes the query string, including the button name and the data. Instead of ignoring the data and always forwarding to the edit page, it will process the session data and execute the appropriate button method.

```java
...
public void doGet()
        throws IOException, ServletException {
    addHelperToSession("helper", SessionData.READ);

    String address = executeButtonMethod();

    if (address != null && !address.isEmpty())
        request.getRequestDispatcher(address).forward(request, response);
}

@Override
public void doPost()
        throws ServletException, IOException {
    addHelperToSession("helper", SessionData.READ);

    String address = executeButtonMethod();

    if (address != null && !address.isEmpty())
        request.getRequestDispatcher(address).forward(request, response);
}
...
```

Credentials: PayPal

As with most web services, each developer must register with the service. PayPal has a special server known as the sandbox. This is the development server. It is possible to create fictitious accounts that can be charged for purchases. Request credentials for the sandbox from the PayPal developers' site.

The credentials must be sent in every request to a PayPal service. To facilitate this, the credentials will be stored in a properties file and loaded in the controller helper, as was done in the FedEx example. Store the credentials file in the *Source Packages* folder. It will appear in the *Default Package*.

```java
static final Properties credentials = new Properties();

static {
    try {
        credentials.load(ControllerHelper.class.getClassLoader().
                getResourceAsStream("paypal.properties"));
    } catch (IOException ex) {
        Logger.getLogger(ControllerHelper.class.getName()).
                log(Level.SEVERE, null, ex);
    }
}
```

The properties file should have three fields for username, password and signature. These three values must be obtained from the PayPal developers' site.

```
APIUsername=
APIPassword=
Signature=
```

A helper method will be added for copying the credentials for each request to the PayPal services. The credentials are placed into a PayPal class named APIProfile.

```
APIProfile getAPIProfile() {
    try {
        APIProfile profile = ProfileFactory.createSignatureAPIProfile();
        profile.setAPIUsername(credentials.getProperty("APIUsername"));
        profile.setAPIPassword(credentials.getProperty("APIPassword"));
        profile.setSignature(credentials.getProperty("Signature"));
        profile.setEnvironment("sandbox");
        profile.setSubject("");
        return profile;
    } catch (PayPalException ex) {
        Logger.getLogger(ControllerHelper.class.getName()).
                log(Level.SEVERE, null, ex);
    }
    return null;
}
```

Each service method will call the helper method to set the credentials before the request to the service is sent.

Service Method: PayPal
The main classes in the NVP SDK are *NVPEncoder*, *NVPDecoder* and *NVPCallerServices*. These three classes are used in every service request to PayPal.

The caller services class has the method that makes the call to the service. The calling method sends a string containing name/value pairs in the format of a query string. The calling method returns a string containing name/value pairs in the format of a query string.

The encoder class has a method for adding a name/value pair to it and a method for generating a string that contains all the name/value pairs that were added to it. The string is formatted for the caller service method.

The decoder class parses the response from the caller service method into a map of name/value pairs.

To make a call to a PayPal service
1. Add name/value pairs to an encoder
2. Set the PayPal credentials
3. Create the request string from the encoder
4. Send the request string to the service
5. Decode the response

Table 8.2 SetExpressCheckout parameters

Name	Value
METHOD	SetExpressCheckout
VERSION	For now, the version is 51.0
RETURNURL	The return URL if the user confirms the transaction
CANCELURL	The return URL if the user cancels the transaction
PAYMENTACTION	For this example, it will be set to *Sale*, but other options are available
CURRENCYCODE	For this example, it will be set to *USD*, but other options are available
AMT	The dollar amount. The amount must have exactly two decimal places

There are three different calls to be made to PayPal. Each call has its own set of parameters. An encoder class will be created for each call and populated with the correct parameters. The encoder will be sent to this method for each service.

```
Map paypalService(NVPEncoder encoder) {
    NVPDecoder decoder = new NVPDecoder();
    NVPCallerServices caller = new NVPCallerServices();

    try {
        caller.setAPIProfile(getAPIProfile());
        String NVPRequest = encoder.encode();
        String NVPResponse = caller.call(NVPRequest);
        decoder.decode(NVPResponse);
        return decoder.getMap();
    } catch (PayPalException ex) {
        Logger.getLogger(ControllerHelper.class.getName()).
            log(Level.SEVERE, null, ex);
    }
    return null;
}
```

PayPal: SetExpressCheckout

When the user clicks the PayPal button, the transaction to PayPal must be initiated. The service request to PayPal must include the type of service. The service is contained in the method parameter. The name of the method that starts the transaction is SetExpressCheckout. The service call has the following parameters (Table 8.2).

A helper method has been added to the controller helper that creates an encoder and adds the properties required by the service. The helper then passes the encoder to the service method. The helper returns the map of properties that is returned by the service method.

The helper method uses the getRequestURL to get the complete URL that made the current request. Additional query string parameters are added to the URL to indicate which page in the application should handle the return from PayPal.

Table 8.3 GetExpressCheckoutDetails parameters

Name	Value
METHOD	SetExpressCheckout
VERSION	For now, the version is 51.0
TOKEN	The token is in the request parameters returned from PayPal

To guarantee that the total amount has two decimal places, the `String.format` method is used. The format string `%.2f` means that the floating point number will have exactly two decimal places. Numbers with more than two decimal places will be rounded to two decimal places. Numbers with fewer than two decimal places will be padded with additional zeros.

```
Map SetExpressCheckout(double total) {
    NVPEncoder encoder = new NVPEncoder();
    encoder.add("METHOD", "SetExpressCheckout");
    encoder.add("VERSION", "51.0");
    encoder.add("RETURNURL",
        request.getRequestURL().toString()
        + "?buttonPayPalReturn=Return");
    encoder.add("CANCELURL",
        request.getRequestURL().toString()
        + "?buttonPayPalCancel=Cancel");
    encoder.add("PAYMENTACTION", "Sale");
    encoder.add("CURRENCYCODE", "USD");
    encoder.add("AMT", String.format("%.2f", total));
    return paypalService(encoder);
}
```

GetExpressCheckoutDetails

When control is returned to the application, additional details can be requested from PayPal, like the user's address. The method that requests this information is `GetExpressCheckoutDetails` and has the parameters listed in Table 8.3.

A helper method has been added to the controller helper that creates an encoder and adds the properties required by the service. The helper then passes the encoder to the service method. The helper returns the map of properties that is returned by the service method.

```
Map GetExpressCheckoutDetails() {
    NVPEncoder encoder = new NVPEncoder();
    encoder.add("METHOD", "GetExpressCheckoutDetails");
    encoder.add("VERSION", "51.0");
    encoder.add("TOKEN", request.getParameter("token"));
    return paypalService(encoder);
}
```

DoExpressCheckoutPayment: PayPal

When control is returned to the application, the transaction has been approved by the user, so the transaction must be finalised. The method that finalises the transaction and charges the user's PayPal account is `DoExpressCheckoutPayment` and has the parameters listed in Table 8.4.

Table 8.4 DoExpressCheckoutPayment parameters

Name	Value
METHOD	SetExpressCheckout
VERSION	For now, the version is 51.0
TOKEN	The *token* parameter is in the request parameters returned from PayPal
PAYERID	The *PayerID* parameter is in the request parameters returned from PayPal
PAYMENTACTION	For this example, it will be set to *Sale*, but other options are available
CURRENCYCODE	For this example, it will be set to *USD*, but other options are available
AMT	The dollar amount. The amount must have exactly two decimal places

A helper method has been added to the controller helper that creates an encoder and adds the properties required by the service. The helper then passes the encoder to the service method. The helper returns the map of properties that is returned by the service method.

```
Map DoExpressCheckoutPayment(double total) {
    NVPEncoder encoder = new NVPEncoder();
    encoder.add("METHOD", "DoExpressCheckoutPayment");
    encoder.add("VERSION", "51.0");
    encoder.add("TOKEN", request.getParameter("token"));
    encoder.add("PAYERID", request.getParameter("PayerID"));
    encoder.add("PAYMENTACTION", "Sale");
    encoder.add("CURRENCYCODE", "USD");
    encoder.add("AMT", String.format("%.2f", total));
    return paypalService(encoder);
}
```

PayPal Button

This is the method that handles the click of the PayPal button. The method must initiate the transaction to PayPal with a call to the `SetExpressCheckout` service. If the call to the service is successful, then the request must be redirected to the PayPal site.

If the service call returns with success, then the response method `sendRedirect` is used to redirect the response to the PayPal site. Once there, the user will have the chance to confirm or cancel the transaction. The parameters to the `SetExpressCheckout` service include the URL for a confirmed transaction and a URL for a cancelled transaction. The method returns a null address to indicate that the servlet should not forward the request and response to a JSP.

The URL for the redirect can be obtained from the PayPal developers' site. The `SetExpressCheckout` service returns a token that identifies the transaction. This token must be sent as a parameter in the redirect. At this time, the address is `https://www.sandbox.paypal.com/webscr?cmd=_express-checkout&token=XXXXXX`. Replace the *XXXXXX* with the token returned from the request.

If the service returns an error, then an error page is displayed. The information from the failed service request is placed in the request so the error page can display the reason for the failure.

The name in the `ButtonMethod` annotation has a `.x` appended to it. The button that initiated the request is the PayPal button. It is not a typical submit button, but an image button. Image buttons always send the x and y coordinates of where the mouse was clicked in the image. This application does not need to know the coordinates; it is only testing the name to check if it is in the query string.

```
@ButtonMethod(buttonName = "buttonPaypal.x")
public String methodClickedPayPalButton() {
    Map map = SetExpressCheckout(cart.getTotal());
    String result = (String) map.get("ACK");
    if ((result.trim().toLowerCase().equals("success"))) {
        try {
            response.sendRedirect(String.format("%s%s%s",
                "https://www.sandbox.paypal.com/webscr",
                "?cmd=_express-checkout&token=",
                map.get("TOKEN")));
            return null;
        } catch (IOException ex) {
            Logger.getLogger(ControllerHelper.class.getName()).
                log(Level.SEVERE, null, ex);
        }
    } else {
        request.setAttribute("paypalErrors", map);
    }
    return jspLocation("paypal/PayPalError.jsp");
}
```

Transaction Confirmed: PayPal

After the user confirms the transaction at PayPal, control is returned to the application via the return URL that was passed in the service request. The URL can include a query string to help process the page. In this example, the query string of the return URL included a button name, so the request will be directed to the corresponding button method.

There are two service requests in this method. The first request retrieves information about the user, including the user's address and name. Table 8.5 lists the properties that are returned from the first service request.

The second request finalises the transaction. The user's PayPal account is not charged until this method is called. Table 8.6 lists the properties that are returned from the first service request.

If either of the service requests fails, then an error page is displayed. The information returned from the failed service request is placed in the request so the error page can display the reason for the failure.

This method uses new pages that were created for this application. They are accessed by adding path information to the string in `jspLocation`. Since this

Table 8.5 Parameters returned from GetExpressCheckoutDetails

TRANSACTIONID	BUILD	AMT
CORRELATIONID	TAXAMT	ORDERTIME
PAYMENTSTATUS	PENDINGREASON	PAYMENTTYPE
REASONCODE	VERSION	FEEAMT
ACK	TIMESTAMP	TRANSACTIONTYPE
CURRENCYCODE	TOKEN	

Table 8.6 Parameters returned from DoExpressCheckoutPayment

SHIPTOZIP	ADDRESSSTATUS	BUILD
CORRELATIONID	SHIPTOCOUNTRYNAME	SHIPTOCITY
SHIPTOCOUNTRYCODE	COUNTRYCODE	FIRSTNAME
PAYERID	SHIPTONAME	VERSION
ACK	EMAIL	SHIPTOSTREET
SHIPTOSTATE	PAYERSTATUS	TIMESTAMP
LASTNAME	TOKEN	

application uses a sub-package of the catalogue application from Chap. 7, the JSPs for this application can be found by using a sub-path.

```
@ButtonMethod(buttonName = "buttonPayPalReturn")
public String methodPaypalReturn() {
    Map mapDetails = null;
    Map mapFinal = null;
    String address = "paypal/PayPalError.jsp";

    mapDetails = GetExpressCheckoutDetails();

    String result = (String) mapDetails.get("ACK");
    if ((result.trim().toLowerCase().equals("success"))) {
        request.setAttribute("paypalDetails", mapDetails);
        mapFinal = DoExpressCheckoutPayment(cart.getTotal());

        result = (String) mapFinal.get("ACK");
        if ((result.trim().toLowerCase().equals("success"))) {
            request.setAttribute("paypalComplete", mapFinal);
            address = "paypal/PayPalReturn.jsp";
        }
    }
    if (address.equals("paypal/PayPalError.jsp")) {
        Map mapPayPalErrors = mapFinal;
        if (mapFinal == null) mapPayPalErrors = mapDetails;
        request.setAttribute("paypalErrors", mapPayPalErrors);
    }
    return jspLocation(address);
}
```

Transaction Cancelled: PayPal

If the user cancels the transaction at PayPal, control is returned to the application via the cancel URL that was passed in the service request. The URL can include a query string to help process the page. In this example, the query string of the cancel URL included a button name, so the request will be directed to the corresponding button method.

```
@ButtonMethod(buttonName = "buttonPayPalCancel")
public String methodPaypalCancel() {
    return jspLocation("paypal/PaypalCancel.jsp");
}
```

8.3.3   JSPs: PayPal

The current application is extended from the catalogue example with the shopping cart from Chap. 7. It will use the regular pages for that application, with a slight modification to the process cart page. It will also add other pages for handling the click of the PayPal button, the return page for the PayPal service and an error page in the event that something fails.

Process.jsp: PayPal

The process page will be modified with the addition of a PayPal button and a form for submitting it. PayPal requires that the button display one of the PayPal buttons. The URL for the image can be obtained from PayPal.

There is another type of input element that is for an image. When the image is clicked, two values are added to the query string: name-of-button.x and name-of-button.y. The button can be processed the same way as a normal submit button, except that the button method attribute must add .x to the name of the button.

The new input element has a type of *image* and has a *src* attribute that specifies the location of the image. The *src* attribute behaves the same way as the *src* attribute in the HTML *img* tag.

```
...
<form action="Controller">
  <input type="image"
         src="https://www.paypal.com/en_US/i/btn/btn_xpressCheckout.gif"
         name="buttonPaypal">
</form>
...
```

As part of the agreement to use the PayPal web service, it is required to use one of the buttons from the PayPal site.

PayPalReturn.jsp: PayPal

When the PayPal button is clicked, the controller helper will redirect the request to the PayPal service. The request to PayPal contains a URL for a return address. This address should be part of your application. The controller helper will request more information from PayPal and finalise the transaction.

The PayPal return page in your application should report the success of the transaction to the user. In this example, the return page displays the names of all the

properties that can be retrieved from the PayPal service. It then displays all the
properties that PayPal returns when the transaction is finalised. The properties will
be placed in the request by the controller helper.

```
...
<body>
    Paypal Return with Account Details
    <div class="container">
        <div class="clear">
            <hr>
            The details request returns a
            query string with these parameters:
        </div>
        <core:forEach var="detail" items="${paypalDetails}">
            <div class="detail">${detail.key}</div>
        </core:forEach>
    </div>
    <div class="container">
        <div class="clear">
            <hr>
            The payment request returns a
            query string with these parameters:
        </div>
        <core:forEach var="finalDetail" items="${paypalComplete}">
            <div class="detail">${finalDetail.key}</div>
        </core:forEach>
    </div>
</body>
...
```

The page uses a style sheet to layout the property names in columns of three. The
style sheet is similar to the one used for the original catalog. Note that the page
includes both style sheets. The sheet that is declared last will override any styles in
the other sheet that have the same name.

```
div.detail {
  position: relative;
  float: left;
  overflow: auto;
  padding: 3px;
  width: 31%;
}

div.container {
  position: relative;
  width: 600px;
}

div.clear {
  position: relative;
  float: left;
  width: 100%;
}
```

PayPalError.jsp: PayPal

When a request is made to a PayPal service, there is always the possibility of an error. The controller helper will detect errors and will place a map of information into the request that can be displayed in the error page. The map of values was returned by the PayPal service and contains hints as to why the request failed.

```
. . .
<body>
    Paypal Error
    <table>
    <core:forEach var="error" items="${paypalErrors}">
        <tr><td>${error.key}<td>${error.value}
    </core:forEach>
    </table>
</body>
. . .
```

PayPalCancel.jsp: PayPal

After the request is redirected to PayPal, it is possible that the user will cancel the transaction. An additional URL is passed to the PayPal service to handle this event. This address should be part of your application. The page only has to let the user know that the transaction has been cancelled.

```
. . .
<body>
    The Paypal transaction has been cancelled by the user.
</body>
. . .
```

8.4   Legacy Database

As has been seen in the previous chapters, it is a straightforward process to create an application that saves a bean to a database. The Hibernate package can create all the SQL statements that are needed to create the necessary database tables and to save data to those tables. Not all developers have the luxury of starting from scratch and creating the database tables. Many applications must interface with an existing database. Reverse-engineering the beans that could write to the database can be difficult.

The JBoss community has a set of tools for Hibernate. One of these tools is for reverse-engineering a bean from a database table. The created bean will use annotations to define the interaction with the table. Once there is a bean, all the techniques of this book can be used to interact with the legacy database.

This section is an introduction to reverse engineering. A simple example will be created that shows how a simple bean class could be created from a database.

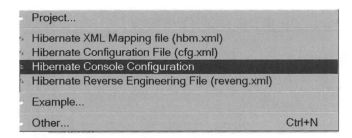

Fig. 8.8 Wizards in the Hibernate perspective

In order to develop a more robust example, it would be necessary to introduce many advanced database topics. The discussion is best left to a book on database design and on advanced Hibernate features.

8.4.1   Eclipse Tools

It is necessary to use Eclipse to reverse-engineer database files. It is not necessary to develop a web application for this example, so it is not necessary to configure Eclipse with Tomcat. A simple Java application will suffice to implement the example.

The current version of Eclipse is Indigo. The reference to the JBoss tools is for this version. If you are using a different version of Eclipse, then be sure to get the corresponding version of the Hibernate tools.

Eclipse has sites for downloading plugins. The link for the site to download JBoss plugins for Eclipse is http://download.jboss.org/jbosstools/ updates/indigo/RC2/. It is called the *JBoss Tools Requirements – Composite Indigo RC2 Mirror*. Add this site to your Eclipse installation by opening Help -> Install New Software. If this site is not already available, then add it.

Once the tools are installed, open the Hibernate perspective. This will limit the wizards to the Hibernate wizards (Fig. 8.8).

Access the Database
Create a simple Java project in Eclipse. The project will need to connect to a MySQL database. One way to do this is to create a Hibernate console that can connect to the database. Via the console, all of the tables can be viewed in a database without writing any code. The tool can connect to many types of databases, not just MySQL.

From the Hibernate perspective, open the console wizard with File -> New ->Hibernate Console Configuration. For the database connection, select New. On the next page, select MySQL as the connection profile. Next to the Drivers drop-down list, select the icon for New Driver Definition (Fig. 8.9).

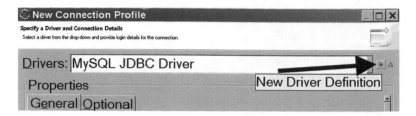

Fig. 8.9 Click the icon for a new driver

Fig. 8.10 Locate the correct JAR file for the driver

Select the driver for the version of MySQL being accessed. If there is an error locating the JAR file, click the JAR List tab and edit the current JAR file listed. Navigate to the JAR file for MySQL that was used in Chap. 5 (Fig. 8.10).

Once the driver and JAR file have been found, fill in the information for connecting to the database and test the connection (Fig. 8.11).

Code Generation

With the Hibernate tools installed, there is a new option in Run menu (Fig. 8.12). The new option is named Hibernate Code Generation Configurations, and it performs reverse engineering.

After following this run option, select Hibernate Code Generation Configurations to open the wizard for reverse engineering. In the wizard

Fig. 8.11 Enter credentials and test

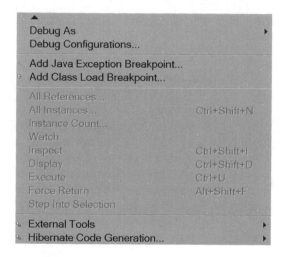

Fig. 8.12 The Hibernate run menu in eclipse

(Fig. 8.13), the Main tab is where the console configuration that connects to the database is set. Set the output directory to the src folder of the project. Click the Reverse Engineer from JDBC Connection check box. Select a package for the output and click the setup button for creating a new reveng.xml file. This will open a new wizard.

The wizard for creating a reverse engineering file has to have a console configuration specified. Select the one that you created earlier and click the refresh button. The databases from the console configuration should appear. Open the database and

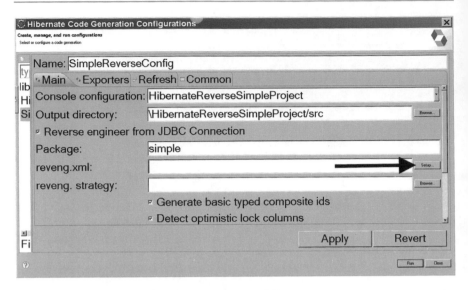

Fig. 8.13 Click the setup button to create a reveng.xml file

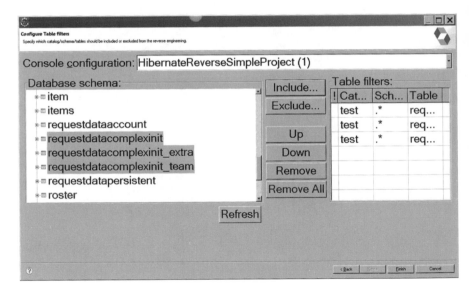

Fig. 8.14 Selecting the tables

select the tables that should be reverse-engineered. If there are related tables, be sure to select all of them. Click finish to close the wizard (Fig. 8.14).

After returning to the first wizard, click the Exporters tab (Fig. 8.15). Check both the Java 1.5 and Generate EJB3 Annotations check boxes. Select the Domain code (.java) check box. Click Run and the files for the beans will be created in the application.

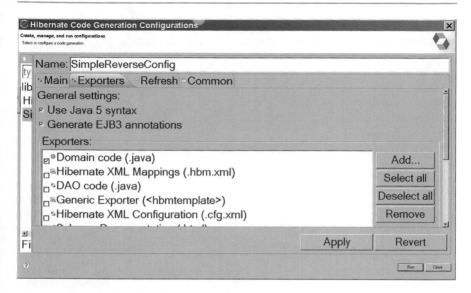

Fig. 8.15 Setting the exporters

The new bean classes will be created in the package that was specified in the wizard. Since this is only a simple Java application, it does not have all the packages that are referenced in the newly created files. Copy the bean files to the web application that will be using them. The web application that was used in Chap. 5 will have all the necessary libraries in it.

8.5   Summary

Accessing web services usually requires that the developer set up an account and obtain credentials. The credentials will be used each time a service is called. Many sites offer a development area where test accounts can be created and applications can be tested. Once the application is running, it can be moved to a production site. Sites provide many resources for developers, including libraries, code examples and tutorials. It can be a challenge to connect to a web service, but the resources from the web service site are essential to getting things to work.

RESTful web services are gaining popularity. A WADL file can be used to know how to communicate with the site. If there is a public WADL file, then it can be added to the NetBeans list of web services, which allow service calls to be drag and dropped into an application. The goal of RESTful services is to make it easier for an application to discover how to communicate with the service. Google Maps is an example of a RESTful service. An application for Google Maps was developed.

SOAP web services have been popular for many years. A WSDL file is used to describe the service. If there is a public WSDL file, then it can be added to the NetBeans list of web services. Each SOAP service has its own method for making a request.

The WSDL file gives details on how to make a request. The FedEx service is an example of a SOAP service. By examining the generated code for the service and reading the documentation on the FedEx site, it is possible to make connections to the FedEx service.

The PayPal services can be accessed either with SOAP or something like REST. REST services use the HTTP mechanism to deliver request instead of wrapping the data in a SOAP envelope. PayPal has an additional method to connect to services using name/value pairs sent in the HTTP request. PayPal supplies an SDK and online documentation to assist the developer in connecting to its services.

Web services allow the developer to extend an application without having to write a lot of code. While it can be tedious to set up the communication with a web service, the benefits far outweigh the configuration difficulties. It is always a challenge to set up a service for the first time. The developer must register with the site, read documentation and run examples.

When developing a user interface that interacts with an existing database, it is useful to be able to create annotated beans that correspond to the existing tables. With such beans, Hibernate can be used to manage the database. The JBoss community maintains a set of tools for Hibernate, including a tool to reverse-engineer annotated Java classes from database tables.

8.6   Chapter Review

Terms
1. Google Maps
   (a) RESTful
   (b) WADL
2. FedEx Rate
   (a) SOAP
   (b) WSDL
3. PayPal Express Checkout
   (a) Name/Value Pair (NVP)
   (b) Express Checkout
   (c) PayPal SDK
4. Reverse Engineering Database Tables
   (a) Eclipse Tools
   (b) Console Configuration
   (c) reveng.xml

New Java
1. Google Maps
   (a) getGoogleMap
   (b) getDataAsString
   (c) getDataAsObject
   (d) RestResponse

2. FedEx Rate
    (a) Address
    (b) Dimensions
    (c) streetLines
    (d) addressShipper
    (e) addressRecipient
    (f) RateService
        getRateServicePort
    (g) RatePortType
        getRates
    (h) RateReply
        getRateReplyDetails
3. PayPal Express Checkout
    (a) NVPEncoder
    (b) NVPDecoder
    (c) NVPCallerServices
    (d) SetExpressChckout
    (e) GetExpressChckoutDetails
    (f) DoExpressCheckoutPayment

Questions
1. How are credentials obtained for accessing the Google Maps service?
2. How are credentials obtained for accessing the FedEx rate service?
3. How are credentials obtained for accessing the PayPal ExpressCheckout service?
4. Which type of description file did the Google Maps service use?
5. Which type of description file did the FedEx rate service use?
6. Explain the steps that are followed to call the Google Maps service.
7. Explain the steps that are followed to call the FedEx rate service.
8. Explain the steps that are followed to call the PayPal Express Checkout service.
9. What does the Google Maps service return?
10. What does the FedEx service return?
11. How is control returned to your application after the user is redirected to PayPal?
12. Why was a console configuration created when accessing a legacy database?
13. Explain the steps that are followed to create a Java bean class from an existing database table.

Tasks
1. Create an application for a store locator.
    (a) Create a database of stores, including name and location.
    (b) Display the names of the stores in a drop-down list.
    (c) The user should select a store name and click a submit button.
    (d) The application should display the map for the store.

2. Modify the catalogue controller from Chap. 7 so that it calculates shipping information.
   (a) Modify the database of books so that it contains the dimensions and weight of each book.
   (b) When the user processes the cart, obtain the user's shipping address.
   (c) Calculate the weight and dimensions of the shipping container.
   (d) Contact the FedEx rate service to calculate the shipping cost.
   (e) Display the total cost of the books and the shipping to the user.
3. For the PayPal example in this chapter, obtain the address of the user and calculate the shipping cost.
   (a) Modify the database of books so that it contains the dimensions and weight of each book.
   (b) After the user returns from PayPal, obtain the shipping address from the PayPal service.
   (c) Calculate the weight and dimensions of the shipping container.
   (d) Contact the FedEx rate service to calculate the shipping cost.
   (e) Display the total cost of the books and the shipping to the user.
4. Reverse-engineer the database tables that were created for the persistent controller in Chap. 5. Compare the tables with the tables from the book.
5. Reverse-engineer the database tables that were created for the persistent controller in Chap. 6. Compare the tables with the tables from the book.
6. Reverse-engineer the database tables that were created for the persistent controller in Chap. 7. Compare the tables with the tables from the book.

Appendix

9

While simple Java applications can be created with a text editor, it is more difficult to create web applications because they run on a servlet engine. It is more efficient to use an IDE that can interact seamlessly with the servlet engine. A brief introduction will be given to two popular IDEs: NetBeans and Eclipse.

The relationship between the CLASSPATH and packages is explained. When complex applications are developed that require the use of many additional packages, it is necessary to understand how Java finds packages at runtime.

Hibernate can be used without any knowledge of SQL. For those that still want to see what Hibernate is doing on the database server, simple commands for the MySQL database server have been explained. Using these commands it will be possible to log onto the server and list the contents of the tables that have been created by Hibernate.

The remainder of the Appendix lists the contents of the auxiliary classes that were used in the book. The helper classes use many standard Java techniques to implement some of the features in the book. A detailed explanation of these techniques belongs in a book on Java. Hopefully, the contents of these files are easy to understand. The Javadoc statements have been removed from the listings in the book, but can be accessed at `http://bytesizebook.com/book/doc`.

9.1 Integrated Development Environments

NetBeans and Eclipse are two popular development environments for creating web applications. Each has advantages and disadvantages. Proponents of one extoll the advantages of one and deride the disadvantages of the other. Each environment can be used to edit web applications. Each has similar features: code completion, syntax highlighting, refactoring, fixing imports, debugging.

The biggest advantage that NetBeans has is that it is fully integrated with the Tomcat server. This is important for a novice. It is easy to download NetBeans and start running web applications without any configuration beyond the standard installation wizard.

T. Downey, *Guide to Web Development with Java: Understanding Website Creation*,
DOI 10.1007/978-1-4471-2443-6_9, © Springer-Verlag London Limited 2012

It is necessary to download Tomcat separately for Eclipse. Eclipse must be configured so that it will run with Tomcat. While the steps are straightforward, there is the possibility of doing something wrong, before writing one line of code. For this reason, I recommend that students start with NetBeans.

Eclipse has the tool for creating Hibernate files from an existing database. The tool is not supported for NetBeans.

Both IDEs have tools for implementing web services. NetBeans has a drag-and-drop interface for generating web services code. Eclipse has a wizard for creating a new web service that is easy to use.

Chapter 8 has examples for creating web services using the NetBeans drag-and-drop feature. Chapter 8 includes an example for creating Hibernate files from an existing database.

9.1.1   NetBeans

The installation of NetBeans and Tomcat are easy. A novice user can install NetBeans and run a web application in a few minutes. The web application will only write 'Hello World', but it will be a running web application. After that, it is up to the user to create a fully functioning web application, but the environment will not get in the way.

NetBeans uses a project to store all the files for a web application. The project is not the web application. A web application has a specific structure; a NetBeans project does not have that structure. Every time that the project is cleaned and built, a WAR file will be created that contains the structure and files for the complete web application. The WAR file can then be deployed to a remote server and run.

The NetBeans project has a project view and a files view. The project view does not show all of the files that are in the project, but the files view does. It is better to edit files from the project view.

NetBeans does not include the *.java* source files when it creates the WAR file. It is necessary to configure NetBeans so that it does.

NetBeans runs a local copy of Tomcat. It is possible to edit the configuration files so that it does not interfere with any other Tomcat installations on the computer.

NetBeans: Getting Started

Download the latest Java from http://www.oracle.com. Download the latest NetBeans from http://netbeans.org. NetBeans has many different packages, depending on a developer's needs. Download a version that contains Tomcat.

The first page of the installation wizard has check boxes for the servers that should be installed. Be sure to check the box for Tomcat. In older versions, the check box does not appear on the first screen; instead, click on the Customize button and then select Tomcat.

Create a web application by selecting File - > New Project. In the next window, select the Java Web folder in the left pane and Web Application in the right pane. Continue to click Next on each subsequent page. The defaults are

Table 9.1 NetBeans folders

Content	NetBeans	Web application
Visible	Web Pages	root folder
Hidden	Web Pages/WEB-INF	root folder/WEB-INF
Java classes	Source Packages	root folder/WEB-INF/classes
Java libraries	Libraries	root folder/WEB-INF/lib

Table 9.2 NetBeans wizards

Project folder	Wizard
Web Pages	Folder, JSP, HTML, Empty File
Web Pages/WEB-INF	Folder, JSP, HTML, Empty File
Source Packages	Java Package, Servlet, Empty File

good for now. The only changes that could be made are the name of the web application and its location. Click Finish on the last page.

Version 7.0 is the most recent version for NetBeans. It creates web applications that conform to the Java Servlet 3.0 specification. The *web.xml* file for the web application is not created by default. In order to create a *web.xml* file, select File – > New File – > Web. From the list of options, select *Standard Deployment Descriptor* (*web.xml*).

Once the application has been created, right-click on the name of the application in the Projects tab and select Run. A simple page will appear. It may not look like much, but it is a fully functional web application running on the local server.

NetBeans: Project Folders

There are four areas in a web application: visible content, hidden content, Java classes and Java libraries. Visible content files that can be accessed directly from the web, like HTML files, JSPs and images. Hidden content contains the same type of files as the visible content, but the files are only accessible from a servlet. All Java classes belong in the classes and JAR files belong in the libraries. Each of these areas corresponds to a folder in a web application. When the web application is cleaned and built, a WAR file will be created that contains the structure and files of the web application.

Table 9.1 shows the relationship between a folder in the NetBeans project and the corresponding folder in the web application.

Add content to each area by right-clicking the appropriate folder in the project and selecting a wizard from the New menu. The libraries use a different process and will be discussed next. Table 9.2 shows the wizards that can be used for each area. If the name of the wizard is not visible from the top level page, then select Other and choose the category Web, Java or Other: all the wizards can be found in these three categories. Do not enter an extension for the file name when using a wizard for a specific type. If there is no wizard for the type to be created, use the

Empty File wizard. An extension must be entered for the Empty File wizard
when naming the file.

To add JAR files to the libraries, first download the JAR files to your computer.
The entries in the project libraries are just links to the JAR files on the computer.
When the WAR file is created, the JAR files will be copied to the *lib* folder of the
web application.

JAR files can be added individually by right-clicking the Libraries folder in
the project and selecting Add JAR/folder. Browse to the location of the JAR
file and select it. More than one can be selected at once.

JAR files can be placed in a user library first; then it is an easy matter to add or
remove a group of JAR files at once. First, create the library by right-clicking the
Libraries folder in the project and selecting Add Library. From the next
page, select Create. Name the library; then on the next page add all the JAR files
to the library. Once a library has been created, all the JAR files in it can be added or
removed from the Add Library page.

NetBeans: Web Application Files
A NetBeans project is an abstraction of a web application. When the WAR file for
the project is built, the corresponding web application structure is created. However,
not all of the directories are visible from the project view, but they are visible from
the *Files* view.

The *web* sub-directory of *build* contains the actual web application directory for
your project.

The *dist* directory contains the WAR file.

The .class files for your servlets are located in the *build* directory. Open the
web sub-directory of *build*. In the WEB-INF is located the *classes* directory, which
contains the .class files for the servlets.

Do not edit files from this tab. Whenever the project is built, the WAR file is created, and these files are recreated. The files from the project folders are copied to the
files in the web application. Any changes that were made directly to files in the web
application folders will be lost when the Project is rebuilt. Always edit files in the
project folders.

Including Source Files in a WAR File
Developing locally and deploying on a remote server is a common practice for creating web applications. By default, Eclipse adds the .java files to the WAR file,
but NetBeans does not. In order to be able to modify servlets on the remote server,
the source files need to be added to the WAR in NetBeans. To have them added to
the WAR file, right-click on the name of the project in the project window and select
properties.

From the properties screen, select Build -> Packaging. Edit the Exclude
From WAR File box and remove **/*.java. This will allow the .java files
to be included in the WAR file.

When the WAR file is uploaded to the remote servlet engine, it can be deployed
without modification. This is the standard way that web applications are created:
develop locally, run remotely.

NetBeans: Managing Tomcat

NetBeans uses a local copy of the Tomcat configuration files. By setting the properties for Tomcat properly, it is possible to have many instances of Tomcat running on the same computer. The properties to change are the server port and server shutdown port.

Both ports can be set by editing the *server.xml* file. Find the file by opening `Tools -> Servers` and reading the value of the `Catalina Base` path. Copy the path and select `File -> Open File` from the main menu. Paste the base path into the file name and open. Navigate to the *conf* folder and open *server.xml*.

Search for the `server` tag with the port and shutdown parameters. Change the value of the port to some number between 1024 and 65535. Be sure this number is unique across all Tomcat server installations on the computer.

Search for the `service` tag for Catalina. This is a paired tag. Search for a connector with a protocol for HTTP. Change the port to some number between 1024 and 65535. Be sure this number is unique across all Tomcat server installations on the computer.

Restart Tomcat and you will see that it starts on the port that was set for HTTP.

9.1.2   Eclipse

The installation of Eclipse is straightforward. After installing Eclipse, it will be necessary to download Tomcat and configure Eclipse to use it. The Tomcat configuration is also straightforward. When configuring Tomcat for Eclipse, it is best to create a local copy of Tomcat.

Eclipse uses a project to store all the files for a web application. The project is not the web application. A web application has a specific structure; an Eclipse project does not have that structure. A WAR file can be created from the Eclipse project. The WAR file contains the structure and files for the complete web application. The WAR file can then be deployed to a remote server and run.

Eclipse has the ability to run a local copy of Tomcat. It is possible to edit the configuration files so that it does not interfere with any other Tomcat installations on the computer.

Eclipse Installation

Download the latest Java from `http://www.oracle.com`. Download the latest Eclipse from `http://www.eclipse.org`. Download the latest Tomcat from `http://tomcat.apache.org`. Eclipse does not need to be installed. Unpack the files from the download, find the Eclipse executable in the `eclipse` folder and execute it.

Once Eclipse is downloaded, Tomcat must be configured to run with it. Start Eclipse and select `Windows -> Properties -> Server -> Runtime Environments`. To add the Tomcat server, click the `Add` button and select the version of Tomcat that was downloaded. Be sure to check the box for `Create a new local server`; then the local server can be configured so it does not interfere with other Tomcat instances on the computer. Click `Next` and browse for the folder where the Tomcat files were unpacked. Click `Finish`.

Table 9.3 Eclipse folders

Content	Eclipse	Web application
Visible	Web Content	root folder
Hidden	Web Content/WEB-INF	root folder/WEB-INF
Java classes	Java Resources/src	root folder/WEB-INF/classes
Java libraries	Java Resources/Libraries	root folder/WEB-INF/lib

After the runtime has been created, click `File` `->New` `->Other` `->` `Dynamic Web Project`. Click `Next`. Choose a project name, select the target runtime as your Tomcat runtime and select the latest Dynamic web module version. Select the default values for the rest of the pages in the wizard, except the last page. On the last page, be sure to check the box for generating a *web.xml* file. Click `Finish`.

At this time, the web service tools only work up to version 2.5 of the Dynamic web module version, so select that version to use those tools. Soon, the web services tools will support version 3.0. This is only applicable in Chap. 8. For examples in all other chapters, select the default version of 3.0.

The web application is devoid of files. Before running the web application, create an `index.jsp` file by right-clicking the `Web Content` folder inside the project and clicking `New` `->JSP File`. Name the file `index.jsp`. Once the file has been created, open it in the editor and type some text between the opening and closing `body` tags.

To run the web application, right-click the project name in the `Project Explorer` and select `Run As` and then `Run On Server`. On the next page, select the Tomcat server. On the next page, be sure that the name of the web application appears in the right-hand pane and click `Finish`.

Eclipse Project Folders

There are four areas in a web application: visible content, hidden content, Java classes and Java libraries. Visible content contains files that can be accessed directly from the web, like HTML files, JSPs and images. Hidden content contains the same type of files as the visible content, but the files are only accessible from a servlet. All Java classes belong in the classes and JAR files belong in the libraries. Each of these areas corresponds to a folder in a web application. When the WAR file for the project is created, it will contain the structure and files of the web application.

In the Java perspective (instead of the Java EE perspective), the `src` file is within the project folder directly, not in a sub folder named `Java Resources`. This is also true for the libraries.

Table 9.3 shows the relationship between a folder in the Eclipse project and the corresponding folder in the web application.

Add content to each area by right-clicking the appropriate folder in the project and selecting a wizard from the `New` menu. The libraries use a different process and will be discussed next. Table 9.4 shows the wizards that can be used for each area. If the name of the wizard is not visible from the top level page, then select `Other` and choose the category `Web`, `Java` or `General`: all the wizards can be found in

Table 9.4 Eclipse wizards

Project folder	Wizard
Web Content	Folder, JSP File, HTML File, File
Web Content/WEB-INF	Folder, JSP File, HTML File, File
Java Resources/src	Package, Servlet, File, Class

these three categories. Do not enter an extension for the file name when using a wizard for a specific type. If there is no wizard for the type to be created, use the *File* wizard. An extension must be entered for the *File* wizard when naming the file.

In the Java perspective (instead of the Java EE perspective), the *src* file is within the project folder directly, not in a sub-folder named *Java Resources*.

To add JAR files to the libraries, first download the JAR files to your computer. The JAR files must be copied to the project *lib* folder in the Eclipse work space. In the file system (not Eclipse), navigate to the work space, then the name of the project, then the *Web Content* folder, then to the *WEB-INF* folder, then to the *lib* folder and place the JAR files there. It does not seem possible to add JAR folders to the library from within the IDE.

Back in Eclipse, right-click the project folder and select `Build  Path  - >` `Configure Build Path`. On the `Order  and  Export` page, be sure that `Web App Libraries` is checked. Click `OK` and then refresh the project.

This is a disadvantage for Eclipse. It is odd that the libraries cannot be added to the web application from within the IDE.

Eclipse: Managing Tomcat

When creating the runtime for Tomcat in Eclipse, be sure to check the box to `Create a new local server`. This will create a local copy of the Tomcat configuration files. By setting the properties for Tomcat properly, it is possible to have many instances of Tomcat running on the same computer. The properties to change are the server port and server shutdown port.

Both ports can be set by editing the *server.xml* file. Find the file by opening `Servers` folder in the project tab in Eclipse. Open the *server.xml* file.

Search for the `server` tag with the port and shutdown parameters. Change the value of the port to some number between 1024 and 65535. Be sure this number is unique across all Tomcat server installations on the computer.

Search for the `service` for Catalina. This is a paired tag. Search for a connector with a protocol for HTTP. Change the port to some number between 1024 and 65535. Be sure this number is unique across all Tomcat server installations on the computer.

Restart Tomcat and you will see that it starts on the port that was set for HTTP.

9.2   CLASSPATH and Packages

When using Java, it is important to understand the concepts of the CLASSPATH and packages. The two concepts are intertwined; one will not make any sense until the other is understood. When Java looks for packages, it searches the CLASSPATH.

9.2.1   Usual Suspects

There is a great scene at the end of the movie *Casablanca*. Humphrey Bogart has just killed the German Commander in front of the Chief of Police. The Chief then calls his office and informs them that the Commander has been murdered, and that they should round up the usual suspects.

For Java, the CLASSPATH variable is a list of the usual suspects. When Java wants to find a class file, it searches through all the directories that are listed in the CLASSPATH. In order to have Java look in new places, just add more paths to the CLASSPATH variable.

For example, suppose the CLASSPATH contains
1. /myData
2. /myFiles
3. /myStuff

Java will check the following paths to find a class file named `myFile.class`:
1. /myData/myFile.class
2. /myFiles/myFile.class
3. /myStuff/myFile.class

There are also system paths that are searched that are not listed in the CLASSPATH.

9.2.2   What Is a Package?

The simplest definition of a package is a folder that contains Java class files. However, packages do more than that. They also indicate where a Java class can be found. Essentially, packages allow for an extension to the CLASSPATH list without adding new paths to it.

If the class file `myFile.class` was in a package named `jbond007`, then Java will check the following paths to find the class file:
1. /myData/jbond007/myFile.class
2. /myFiles/jbond007/myFile.class
3. /myStuff/jbond007/myFile.class

If the class file `myFile.class` was in a package named `agents.jbond007`, then Java will check the following paths to find the class file:
1. /myData/agents/jbond007/myFile.class
2. /myFiles/agents/jbond007/myFile.class
3. /myStuff/agents/jbond007/myFile.class

Every section of the package name corresponds to a sub-directory in the file system. The first part of the package name corresponds to a directory on the file system that must be a sub-directory of a path in the CLASSPATH variable.

9.3   JAR File Problems

Java loads .class files when they are first accessed. At different times, Java uses different class loaders to create the class that is defined in the .class file. When a class is created, its information is stored in a separate part of memory that is never garbage-collected by the JVM. The memory can be released when the class loader is removed; however, if there is still a reference from a different class loader to any object that was created by the class loader be removed, then none of the class definitions that were loaded by the class loader will be released. This is known as a memory leak.

Each web application has its own class loader. This is what makes it possible to restart a web application without restarting the entire JVM. There are class loaders for running the JVM, and there is a class loader for the web application. When the web application is restarted, the class loader is reinitialised. As long as there are no active references to the objects created by the web application's class loader, all of the permanent memory that was allocated by the class loader will be released. If there is still an active reference, then none of the class information will be released and there will be a memory leak.

Other memory leaks can be caused by the programmer. Many packages have methods that should be called in order to release all the resources that are being used by the package. This is analogous to closing a file: there is a method to close the file, but the programmer must call it. If the file is not closed, then some data might not be written to the file. In the same way, the methods that exist for releasing resources must be called by the programmer, or the application will have a memory leak.

There are two types of memory leaks: catastrophic and one-timers. Catastrophic errors can cause the servlet engine to crash. The one-timers will usually not cause the servlet engine to crash; they will only force the engine to hold onto more resources than it needs.

If a web application with a catastrophic leak is reloaded enough times, then it will crash the servlet engine. Each time it is reloaded, it maintains a reference to the previous class loader. All the class data from the old class loader cannot be released, and then a new class loader is created. If it is reloaded ten times, then there will be ten copies of the class data. If it is reloaded enough times, all of the memory in the servlet engine will be used and the engine will crash.

The one-timers only hold onto extra memory during the first reload; they do not leak more memory on subsequent reloads. The one-timers are usually caused by a static reference to an object. When the static reference is loaded by one class loader and the object is loaded by a different class loader, then there is a memory leak. Often, these leaks can be removed by using a weak reference to the object.

As of the release of Tomcat 6 and Hibernate 3.2.4, these catastrophic leaks have been removed. However, it is still up to the programmer to call all the necessary methods to release resources; otherwise, there will be catastrophic memory leaks.

9.3.1 Hibernate

Hibernate can cause a catastrophic memory leak, if the programmer does not release Hibernate's resources. There is a method in the Hibernate package that must be called before the web application closes: closeFactory(). If this is not called, then every time the web application is reloaded, the previous class loader and all of its memory will not be released.

The call to this method has been encapsulated in the `closeHibernate` method of the `HibernateHelper` class.

9.3.2 MySQL Driver

The MySQL driver is used in this book, but this section applies to any SQL driver that is used. Once the driver has been registered with Java, then it must be deregistered before the web application is stopped; otherwise, there will be a catastrophic memory leak.

One technique is to deregister all of the drivers. An enumeration of all of the drivers can be obtained from the `DriverManager` class. Loop through each driver and deregister it.

```
try {
    Enumeration<Driver> enumer = DriverManager.getDrivers();
    while (enumer.hasMoreElements()) {
        DriverManager.deregisterDriver(enumer.nextElement());
    }
} catch (java.sql.SQLException se) {
    se.printStackTrace();
}
```

9.3.3 Hibernate Annotations

This section is not about a memory leak, but it is a warning to developers who have used earlier versions of Hibernate. In earlier versions, a multiple-valued bean property was annotated with @OneToMany to indicate that it will have a separate table created for it in the database. This table was created by Hibernate without having to be defined. In Hibernate 3.2, this annotation is only to be used for entities that have been defined by the programmer; an implicit table cannot be created by using this annotation. The @ElementCollection annotation should be used, instead, to indicate that Hibernate should create an implicit table, related table in the database.

9.4   MySQL

Although Hibernate eliminates the necessity of knowing SQL, sometimes curiosity gets the better of us and we want to see what Hibernate is doing. An example will be presented that demonstrates how to issue a few SQL commands in the MySQL database server to see the structure of the tables that Hibernate has created. A command will also be supplied that shows all the records in a table. These commands are very simple SQL commands. Only the bare minimum of statements will be introduced.

Additional commands will be supplied that are specific to the MySQL database. These additional commands are needed in order to log onto the server. The MySQL server is a free relational database. The source code can be obtained at `http://mysql.org`.

There are four essential pieces of information that are needed to log onto any server: host, port, username and password.

To access the MySQL database, issue the following command. This command will connect to the MySQL server at the specified host. If the host is the local machine and the port is 3306, then the host and port can be omitted from the command. Enter your password after MySQL prompts you for it.

```
mysql -u username -h http://server.com -P 3306 -p <Enter Key>
password
```

View all databases in the server with the following command. Don't forget the ; at the end.

```
show databases;
```

Select a database named *db_name* with the following command. This is the only command that does not need a ; at the end.

```
use db_name
```

Once a database has been chosen, the names of all the tables can be displayed.

```
show tables;
```

There won't be any tables until you create a servlet that saves data to a database. Once you have a table, you can view the structure of a table named *name-of-table* with the following command:

```
describe name-of-table;
```

Use the select statement to see all the records in the table.

```
select * from name-of-table;
```

Exit MySQL with the following command:

```
exit;
```

These are the only commands that are needed to see what Hibernate has done.

9.5   Auxiliary Classes

Many classes that were used in the book were not explained in complete detail. The parts that were relevant to the theme of the book were covered, but the remaining parts of these classes were not covered. Most of the uncovered details deal with annotations, enumerations, error handling and reflection. A complete explanation of the code from these files belongs in a Java programming text.

9.5.1   Annotations

In addition to the annotations that are used by Hibernate, two other annotations were used in the book. ButtonMethod was used to annotate a method that does the processing associated with a button on a form. SetByAttribute was used on bean property accessors to indicate if the property is initialised by including an extra attribute in the definition of the form element in the JSP.

ButtonMethod
Listing 9.1 is the ButtonMethod annotation. Place this annotation before a method that does the processing associated with a button in a form. The method that is annotated should have no parameters and should return a string.

```
package shared;

import java.lang.annotation.*;

@Retention(RetentionPolicy.RUNTIME)
@Target({ ElementType.METHOD} )
public @interface ButtonMethod {
      String buttonName() default "";
      boolean isDefault() default false;
}
```

Listing 9.1 The ButtonMethod Annotation

SetByAttribute
Listing 9.2 is the `SetByAttribute` annotation. Place the annotation before the accessor of a bean property that is associated with a form element that is a button group or a select list. These types of form elements are initialised by including an extra attribute in the element. This type of the additional attribute is defined in the `AttributeType` parameter of the annotation.

```
package shared;

import java.lang.annotation.*;

@Retention(RetentionPolicy.RUNTIME)
@Target({ ElementType.METHOD} )
public @interface SetByAttribute {
    AttributeType type();
}
```

Listing 9.2 The `SetByAttribute` Annotation

9.5.2 Cookie Utility

The cookies that are retrieved in a servlet cannot be accessed randomly; it is necessary to do a linear search each time a cookie is needed. To facilitate this task, a utility class of static methods was created that will perform such linear searches. A cookie can be retrieved by name; either the cookie or the cookie's value can be returned (Listing 9.3).

```
package shared;
import javax.servlet.http.Cookie;
import javax.servlet.http.HttpServletRequest;

public class CookieUtil {

  static
  public Cookie findCookie(HttpServletRequest request,
                           String name)
  {
    if (request.getCookies() == null) return null;
    for(Cookie cookie : request.getCookies()) {
      if (cookie.getName().equals(name)) return cookie;
    }
    return null;
  }

  static
  public String findCookieValue(HttpServletRequest request,
                                String name)
```

```
  {
    Cookie cookie = findCookie(request, name);
    if (cookie != null) {
      return cookie.getValue();
    }
    return null;
  }

}
```

Listing 9.3 The CookieUtil class

9.5.3 Enumerations

Enumerations are new in Java 1.5. They are an excellent way to create self-documenting code. The SessionData enumeration is used to indicate if the data that is already in the session should be read or ignored. The AttributeType enumeration is used by the SetByAttribute annotation to indicate the type of the attribute that is used to initialise a form element.

Session Data

Listing 9.4 is the SessionData enumeration, which is defined in the HelperBaseCh4 class. It is used as a parameter to the addHelperToSession method. While this parameter could have been implemented with a Boolean variable, it is clearer to understand what SessionData.READ means than to remember what true means in this context.

```
protected enum SessionData {

    READ, IGNORE
```

Listing 9.4 The SessionData enumeration from HelperBaseCh4

Attribute Type

Listing 9.5 is the AttributeType enumeration. This is used in the SetByAttribute annotation. Certain form elements are initialised by adding an attribute to the form element. This form element attribute is either named checked or selected. This enumeration encapsulates these values.

```
package shared;

public enum AttributeType {  CHECKED, SELECTED }
```

Listing 9.5 The AttributeType enumeration

9.5.4 Helper Base

The helper base classes have been used since Chap. 4. The subsequent helper base classes from each chapter extend the helper base from the previous chapter. Most of the details of the classes were covered in the book, but not every version of an overloaded method was covered. Reflection was also used in several places to simplify the work of the controller helper; the details of using reflection should be covered in a Java programming text.

Helper Base Chapter Four

This base class has member variables for the request, response and logger. These are initialised when the base class is constructed. There are also default implementations of the doGet and doPost methods that only display an error. The session is used to store data, the population of a bean is automated and reflection is used to execute a method that is associated with a button. Listing 9.6 is the helper base class from Chap. 4.

```java
package shared;

import java.io.IOException;
import java.lang.reflect.InvocationTargetException;
import java.lang.reflect.Method;
import javax.servlet.ServletException;
import javax.servlet.http.HttpServlet;
import javax.servlet.http.HttpServletRequest;
import javax.servlet.http.HttpServletResponse;
import org.apache.log4j.Level;
import org.apache.log4j.Logger;

public abstract class HelperBaseCh4 {

    protected enum SessionData {

        READ, IGNORE
    } ;
    private Method methodDefault = null;
    protected HttpServlet servlet;
    protected HttpServletRequest request;
    protected HttpServletResponse response;
    protected Logger logger;

    public HelperBaseCh4(
            HttpServlet servlet,
            HttpServletRequest request,
            HttpServletResponse response) {
        this.servlet = servlet;
```

```java
    this.request = request;
    this.response = response;
    initLogger();
}

protected void initLogger() {
    String logName = "bytesizebook.webdev";
    String initName = servlet.getInitParameter("logName");
    if (initName != null) logName = initName;

    Level logLevel = Level.DEBUG;
    String strLevel = servlet.getInitParameter("logLevel");
    if (strLevel != null) {
        logLevel = Level.toLevel(strLevel);
    }

    logger = Logger.getLogger(logName);
    logger.setLevel(logLevel);
}

protected void doGet()
        throws ServletException, IOException {
    response.getWriter().print("The doGet method must be overridden"
            + " in the class that extends HelperBase.");
}

protected void doPost()
        throws ServletException, IOException {
    response.getWriter().print("The doPost method must be overridden"
            + " in the class that extends HelperBase.");
}

protected abstract void copyFromSession(Object helper);

public void addHelperToSession(String name,
        SessionData state) {
    if (SessionData.READ == state) {
        Object sessionObj =
                request.getSession().getAttribute(name);
        if (sessionObj != null) {
            copyFromSession(sessionObj);
        }
    }
    request.getSession().setAttribute(name, this);
}

public void addHelperToSession(String name,
        boolean checkSession) {
    if (checkSession) {
        Object sessionObj =
                request.getSession().getAttribute(name);
        if (sessionObj != null) {
            copyFromSession(sessionObj);
        }
```

```
    }
    request.getSession().setAttribute(name, this);
}

protected String executeButtonMethod()
        throws ServletException, IOException {
    String result = "";
    methodDefault = null;
    Class clazz = this.getClass();
    Class enclosingClass = clazz.getEnclosingClass();
    while (enclosingClass != null) {
        clazz = this.getClass();
        enclosingClass = clazz.getEnclosingClass();
    }

    try {
        result = executeButtonMethod(clazz, true);
    } catch (Exception ex) {
        writeError(request, response,
                "Button Method Error", ex);
        return "";
    }

    return result;
}

protected String executeButtonMethod(Class clazz,
        boolean searchForDefault)
        throws IllegalAccessException, InvocationTargetException {
    String result = "";
    Method[] methods = clazz.getDeclaredMethods();
    for (Method method : methods) {
        ButtonMethod annotation =
                method.getAnnotation(ButtonMethod.class);
        if (annotation != null) {
            if (searchForDefault && annotation.isDefault()) {
                methodDefault = method;
            }
            if (request.getParameter(annotation.buttonName())
                    != null) {
                result = invokeButtonMethod(method);
                break;
            }
        }
    }
    if (result.equals("")) {
        Class superClass = clazz.getSuperclass();
        if (superClass != null) {
            result =
                    executeButtonMethod(superClass,
                    methodDefault == null);
        }
        if (result.equals("")) {
            if (methodDefault != null) {
```

```
                    result = invokeButtonMethod(methodDefault);
              } else {
                logger.error(
                        "(executeButtonMethod) No default method "
                        + "was specified, but one was needed.");
                result = "No default method was specified,.";
              }
          }
      }
      return result;
}


protected String invokeButtonMethod(Method buttonMethod)
        throws IllegalAccessException, InvocationTargetException {
    String resultInvoke = "Could not invoke method";
    try {
        resultInvoke =
                (String) buttonMethod.invoke(this,
                (Object[]) null);
    } catch (IllegalAccessException iae) {
        logger.error("(invoke) Button method is not public.",
                iae);
        throw iae;
    } catch (InvocationTargetException ite) {
        logger.error("(invoke) Button method exception",
                ite);
        throw ite;
    }
    return resultInvoke;
}


public void fillBeanFromRequest(Object data) {
    try {
        org.apache.commons.beanutils.BeanUtils.
                populate(data, request.getParameterMap());
    } catch (IllegalAccessException iae) {
        logger.error("Populate - Illegal Access.", iae);
    } catch (InvocationTargetException ite) {
        logger.error("Populate - Invocation Target.", ite);
    }
}


public void populateThrow(Object data)
        throws IOException, ServletException {
    try {
        org.apache.commons.beanutils.BeanUtils.
                populate(data, request.getParameterMap());
    } catch (IllegalAccessException iae) {
        logger.error("Populate - Illegal Access.", iae);
        writeError(request, response,
                "Populate - Illegal Access.", iae);
    } catch (InvocationTargetException ite) {
        logger.error("Populate - Invocation Target.", ite);
        writeError(request, response,
```

```
                              "Populate - Invocation Target.", ite);
        }
    }

    static public void writeError(
            javax.servlet.http.HttpServletRequest request,
            javax.servlet.http.HttpServletResponse response,
            String title,
            Exception ex)
            throws IOException, ServletException {
        java.io.PrintWriter out = response.getWriter();
        response.setContentType("text/html");
        out.println("<html>");
        out.println("  <head>");
        out.println("    <title>" + title + "</title>");
        out.println("  </head>");
        out.println("  <body>");
        out.println("<h2>" + title + "</h2>");
        if (ex.getMessage() != null) {
            out.println("    <h3>" + ex.getMessage() + "</h3>");
        }
        if (ex.getCause() != null) {
            out.println("    <h4>" + ex.getCause() + "</h4>");
        }
        StackTraceElement[] trace = ex.getStackTrace();
        if (trace != null && trace.length > 0) {
            out.print("<pre>");
        }
        ex.printStackTrace(out);
        out.println("</pre>");
        out.println("  </body>");
        out.println("</html>");
        out.close();
    }
}
```

Listing 9.6 The helper base class from Chap. 4

Helper Base Chapter Five
The Chap. 5 helper base class adds the enhanced interface for accessing the Hibernate validation messages (Listing 9.7).

```
package shared;

import java.util.Set;
import javax.servlet.http.HttpServlet;
import javax.servlet.http.HttpServletRequest;
import javax.servlet.http.HttpServletResponse;
import javax.validation.ConstraintViolation;
```

```java
import javax.validation.Validation;
import javax.validation.Validator;
import javax.validation.ValidatorFactory;
import org.hibernate.validator.engine.PathImpl;

public abstract class HelperBaseCh5 extends HelperBaseCh4 {

    public HelperBaseCh5(
            HttpServlet servlet,
            HttpServletRequest request,
            HttpServletResponse response) {
        super(servlet, request, response);
    }

    protected static final ValidatorFactory validatorFactory
            = Validation.buildDefaultValidatorFactory();
    protected static final Validator validator
            = validatorFactory.getValidator();

    java.util.Map<String, String> errorMap =
            new java.util.HashMap<String, String>();

    public void setErrors(Object data) {

        Set<ConstraintViolation<Object>> violations =
                validator.validate(data);

        errorMap.clear();
        if (! violations.isEmpty()) {
            for (ConstraintViolation<Object> msg : violations) {
                PathImpl value = (PathImpl) msg.getPropertyPath();
                errorMap.put((String) value.getLeafNode().getName(),
                                msg.getMessage());
            }
        }
    }

    public void clearErrors() {
        if (errorMap != null) {
            errorMap.clear();
        }
    }

    public boolean isValid(Object data) {
        setErrors(data);
        return errorMap.isEmpty();
    }

    public java.util.Map getErrors() {
        return errorMap;
    }

    public boolean isValidProperty(String name) {
        String msg = errorMap.get(name);
```

```
        return msg == null || msg.equals("");
    }

}
```

Listing 9.7 The helper base class from Chap. 5

Helper Base Chapter Six

The Chap. 6 helper base class adds the maps for initialising complex form elements (Listing 9.8).

```java
package shared;

import java.lang.reflect.InvocationTargetException;
import java.lang.reflect.Method;
import java.util.HashMap;
import java.util.Map;
import javax.servlet.http.HttpServlet;
import javax.servlet.http.HttpServletRequest;
import javax.servlet.http.HttpServletResponse;

public abstract class HelperBaseCh6 extends HelperBaseCh5 {

    protected Map<String, Map<String, String>> checked =
            new HashMap<String, Map<String, String>>();
    protected Map<String, Map<String, String>> selected =
            new HashMap<String, Map<String, String>>();

    public HelperBaseCh6(
            HttpServlet servlet,
            HttpServletRequest request,
            HttpServletResponse response) {
        super(servlet, request, response);
    }

    protected void setCheckedAndSelected(Object data) {
        setCheckedAndSelected(data, data.getClass());
    }

    protected void setCheckedAndSelected(Object data,
            Class clazz) {
        Method[] allMethods = clazz.getDeclaredMethods();
        Method methodDefault = null;
        for (Method method : allMethods) {
            SetByAttribute propAnnotation =
                    method.getAnnotation(SetByAttribute.class);
            if (propAnnotation != null) {
                String property = method.getName();
                java.util.regex.Pattern pattern =
```

```
                       java.util.regex.Pattern.compile("get(.+)");
               java.util.regex.Matcher matcher =
                       pattern.matcher(property);
           if (!matcher.matches()) {
               logger.error(property + " must be an accessor.");
           } else {
               property = matcher.group(1);
               property = property.substring(0, 1).toLowerCase()
                       + property.substring(1);
               clearProperty(property,
                       propAnnotation.type());
               if (method.getReturnType().isArray()) {
                   Object[] result =
                           (Object[]) invokeGetter(data, method);
                   if (result != null) {
                       for (Object obj : result) {
                           addChoice(property, obj.toString(),
                               (AttributeType) propAnnotation.type());
                       }
                   }
               } else {
                   Object result = invokeGetter(data, method);
                   if (result != null) {
                       addChoice(property, result.toString(),
                               (AttributeType) propAnnotation.type());
                   }
               }
           }
       }
   }
   Class parentClass = clazz.getSuperclass();
   if (parentClass != null) {
       setCheckedAndSelected(data, parentClass);
   }
}

protected Object invokeGetter(Object obj, Method method) {
   Object result = null;
   try {
       result = method.invoke(obj, (Object[]) null);
   } catch (IllegalAccessException iae) {
       logger.error("(invoke) Accessor needs public access",
               iae);
   } catch (InvocationTargetException ite) {
       logger.error("(invoke) Accessor threw an exception",
               ite);
   }
   return result;
}

public Map getChecked() {
   return checked;
}

public Map getSelected() {
   return selected;
}
```

```
public void addChecked(String group, String item) {
    if (checked.get(group) == null) {
        checked.put(group,
                new HashMap<String, String>());
    }
    checked.get(group).put(item, "checked");
}

public void addSelected(String list, String item) {
    if (selected.get(list) == null) {
        selected.put(list,
                new HashMap<String, String>());
    }
    selected.get(list).put(item, "selected");
}

public void addChoice(String list,
        String item,
        AttributeType type) {
    if (type == null) {
        return;
    }
    if (AttributeType.CHECKED == type) {
        addChecked(list, item);
    }
    if (AttributeType.SELECTED == type) {
        addSelected(list, item);
    }
}

public void clearProperty(String property,
        AttributeType type) {
    Map<String, String> propMap;
    if (AttributeType.CHECKED == type) {
        propMap = checked.get(property);
        if (propMap != null) {
            propMap.clear();
        }
    } else if (AttributeType.SELECTED == type) {
        propMap = selected.get(property);
        if (propMap != null) {
            propMap.clear();
        }
    }
}

public void clearMaps() {
    checked.clear();
    selected.clear();
}
}
```

Listing 9.8 The helper base class from Chap. 6

9.5.5 Hibernate Helper

The Hibernate helper class encapsulates access to the Hibernate methods. Hibernate uses transactions and session to access the database. The details of using these are placed in the Hibernate helper methods.

Saving Data

The saveOrUpdate method is used to add new objects in, or update existing objects to, the database. Hibernate uses sessions and transactions to interact with the database. The details of sessions and transactions are outside the scope of this text.

```java
static public void updateDB(Object obj) {
    Session session = null;
    try {
        session = sessionFactory.openSession();
        Transaction tx = session.beginTransaction();

        session.saveOrUpdate(obj);

        tx.commit();
    } finally {
        if (session != null) {
            session.close();
        }
    }
}

static public void updateDB(java.util.List list) {

    Session session = null;
    try {
        session = sessionFactory.openSession();
        Transaction tx = session.beginTransaction();

        for (Object obj : list) {
            session.saveOrUpdate(obj);
        }

        tx.commit();
    } finally {
        if (session != null) {
            session.close();
        }
    }
}
```

Retrieving Data

Retrieving data is accomplished by using a `Criteria` object. This method returns all the records from the database. If a key and value are sent to the method, then only the records that match the value for that key will be returned. This method could be extended to include additional criteria, so that a more complicated search could be performed.

```java
static public java.util.List getListData(
        Class classBean, String strKey, Object value) {
    java.util.List result = new java.util.ArrayList();

    Session session = null;
    try {
        session = sessionFactory.openSession();
        Transaction tx = session.beginTransaction();

        Criteria criteria =
                session.createCriteria(classBean);
        if (strKey != null) {
            criteria.add(Restrictions.like(strKey, value));
        }
        result = criteria.list();

        tx.commit();

    } finally {
        if (session != null) {
            session.close();
        }
    }
    return result;
}
```

Removing Data

Once a record has been found, Hibernate will remember that it was retrieved from the database. By sending the same object to the remove method, it will be deleted from the database.

```java
static public void removeDB(Object obj) {
    Session session = null;
    try {
        session = sessionFactory.openSession();
        Transaction tx = session.beginTransaction();

        session.delete(obj);

        tx.commit();
```

```
    }   finally {
        if (session != null) {
            session.close();
        }
    }
}
```

Hibernate Helper Class

Listing 9.9 is the complete Hibernate helper class.

```java
package shared;

import java.util.ArrayList;
import java.util.List;
import java.util.Properties;
import org.apache.log4j.Logger;
import org.hibernate.Criteria;
import org.hibernate.HibernateException;
import org.hibernate.Session;
import org.hibernate.SessionFactory;
import org.hibernate.Transaction;
import org.hibernate.cfg.Configuration;
import org.hibernate.cfg.Environment;
import org.hibernate.criterion.Restrictions;

public class HibernateHelper {

    static protected Logger log =
            Logger.getLogger("bytesizebook.webdev.hibernate");
    static protected List<Class> listClasses = new ArrayList<Class>();
    static protected SessionFactory sessionFactory;

    static public void initSessionFactory(Properties props,
            Class... mappings) {
        if (addMappings(listClasses, mappings)) {
            closeSessionFactory(sessionFactory);
            sessionFactory = createFactory(props, listClasses);
        }
    }

    static public void initSessionFactory(Class... mappings) {
        initSessionFactory(null, mappings);
    }

    static public void createTable(Properties props, Class... mappings) {
        List<Class> tempList = new ArrayList<Class>();
        SessionFactory tempFactory = null;

        addMappings(tempList, mappings);
        if (props == null) {
            props = new Properties();
```

```
        }
        props.setProperty(Environment.HBM2DDL_AUTO, "create");
        tempFactory = createFactory(props, tempList);
        closeSessionFactory(tempFactory);
    }

    static public void createTable(Class... mappings) {
        createTable(null, mappings);
    }

    static protected boolean addMappings(List<Class> list, Class... mappings) {
        boolean bNewClass = false;
        for (Class mapping : mappings) {
            if (!list.contains(mapping)) {
                list.add(mapping);
                bNewClass = true;
            }
        }
        return bNewClass;
    }

    static protected SessionFactory createFactory(
            Properties props,
            List<Class> list) {
        SessionFactory factory = null;
        Configuration cfg =
                new Configuration();
        try {
            if (props != null) {
                cfg.addProperties(props);
            }
            configureFromFile(cfg);
            for (Class mapping : list) {
                cfg.addAnnotatedClass(mapping);
            }
            factory = buildFactory(cfg);
        } catch (Exception ex) {
            log.error("SessionFactory creation failed.", ex);
            closeSessionFactory(factory);
            factory = null;
            throw new HibernateException(ex);
        }
        return factory;
    }

    static protected void configureFromFile(Configuration cfg) {
        try {
            cfg.configure();
        } catch (HibernateException ex) {
            if (ex.getMessage().equals(
                    "/hibernate.cfg.xml not found")) {
                log.warn(ex.getMessage());
            } else {
                log.error("Error in hibernate "
```

```
                        + "configuration file.", ex);
            throw ex;
        }
    }
}

static protected SessionFactory buildFactory(Configuration cfg)
        throws Exception {
    SessionFactory factory = null;
    try {
        factory = cfg.buildSessionFactory();
    } catch (Exception ex) {
        closeSessionFactory(factory);
        factory = null;
        throw ex;
    }
    return factory;
}

static public void closeSessionFactory(SessionFactory factory) {
    if (factory != null) {
        factory.close();
    }
}

static public void closeFactory() {
    closeSessionFactory(sessionFactory);
}

static public void updateDB(Object obj) {
    Session session = null;
    try {
        session = sessionFactory.openSession();
        Transaction tx = session.beginTransaction();

        session.saveOrUpdate(obj);

        tx.commit();
    } finally {
        if (session != null) {
            session.close();
        }
    }
}

static public void updateDB(java.util.List list) {

    Session session = null;
    try {
        session = sessionFactory.openSession();
        Transaction tx = session.beginTransaction();

        for (Object obj : list) {
            session.saveOrUpdate(obj);
```

```
          }
          tx.commit();
      }  finally {
          if (session != null) {
              session.close();
          }
      }
}

static public void saveDB(Object obj) {
    Session session = null;
    try {
        session = sessionFactory.openSession();
        Transaction tx = session.beginTransaction();

        session.save(obj);

        tx.commit();
    }  finally {
        if (session != null) {
            session.close();
        }
    }
}

static public void removeDB(Object obj) {
    Session session = null;
    try {
        session = sessionFactory.openSession();
        Transaction tx = session.beginTransaction();

        session.delete(obj);

        tx.commit();
    }  finally {
        if (session != null) {
            session.close();
        }
    }
}

static public java.util.List getListData(
        Class classBean, String strKey, Object value) {
    java.util.List result = new java.util.ArrayList();

    Session session = null;
    try {
        session = sessionFactory.openSession();
        Transaction tx = session.beginTransaction();

        Criteria criteria =
                session.createCriteria(classBean);
        if (strKey != null) {
```

```
            criteria.add(Restrictions.like(strKey, value));
        }
        result = criteria.list();

        tx.commit();

    } finally {
        if (session != null) {
            session.close();
        }
    }
    return result;
}

static public java.util.List getListData(
        Class classBean,
        String strKey1, Object value1,
        String strKey2, Object value2) {
    java.util.List result = new java.util.ArrayList();
    boolean withParent = false;
    int age = 0;
    Session session = null;
    try {
        session = sessionFactory.openSession();
        Transaction tx = session.beginTransaction();

        Criteria criteria =
                session.createCriteria(classBean);
        if (strKey1 != null) {
            criteria.add(Restrictions.like(strKey1, value1));
        }
        if (strKey2 != null) {
            criteria.add(Restrictions.like(strKey2, value2));
        }

        criteria.add(
          Restrictions.or(
            Restrictions.and(
              Restrictions.gt("age", 13),
              Restrictions.lt("age", 18)),
            Restrictions.eq("withParent", true)
          )
        );

        result = criteria.list();

        tx.commit();

    } finally {
        if (session != null) {
            session.close();
        }
    }
    return result;
```

```
    }

    static public java.util.List getListData(
            Class classBean) {
        return getListData(classBean, null, null);
    }

    static public Object getFirstMatch(
            Class classBean, String strKey, Object value) {

        Object result = null;
        Session session = null;
        try {
            session = sessionFactory.openSession();
            Transaction tx = session.beginTransaction();

            Criteria criteria =
                    session.createCriteria(classBean);
            if (strKey != null) {
                criteria.add(Restrictions.like(strKey, value));
            }
            criteria.setMaxResults(1);
            result = criteria.uniqueResult();

            tx.commit();

        } finally {
            if (session != null) {
                session.close();
            }
        }
        return result;
    }

    static public Object getFirstMatch(
            Object data, String strKey, Object value) {
        return getFirstMatch(data.getClass(),
                strKey, value);
    }

    static public Object getKeyData(Class beanClass, long itemId) {
        Object data = null;
        Session session = sessionFactory.openSession();

        data = session.get(beanClass, itemId);

        session.close();

        return data;
    }

    static public boolean isSessionOpen() {
        return sessionFactory != null;
    }
}
```

Listing 9.9 The Hibernate helper class

9.5.6   InitLog4j Servlet

A servlet is used to configure log4j. Listing 9.10 is the complete InitLog4j servlet.

```java
package shared;

import java.io.IOException;
import javax.servlet.http.HttpServlet;
import org.apache.log4j.FileAppender;
import org.apache.log4j.Level;
import org.apache.log4j.Logger;
import org.apache.log4j.PatternLayout;
import org.apache.log4j.RollingFileAppender;

public class InitLog4j extends HttpServlet {

  public void init() {
    String initPath = getInitParameter("logPath");
    String logPath = "/WEB-INF/logs/error.log";
    if (initPath != null) logPath = initPath;
    FileAppender appender = getAppender(logPath);
    if (appender == null) return;
    initLogger(null, appender, Level.ERROR);
    initLogger("org.apache.commmons.beanutils",
               appender, Level.DEBUG);
  }

  private FileAppender getAppender(String fileName) {
    RollingFileAppender appender = null;
    try {
      appender = new RollingFileAppender(
          new PatternLayout("%-5p %c %t%n%29d - %m%n"),
          getServletContext().getRealPath(fileName),
          true);
      appender.setMaxBackupIndex(5);
      appender.setMaxFileSize("1MB");
    } catch (IOException ex) {
      System.out.println(
          "Could not create appender for "
          + fileName + ":"
          + ex.getMessage());
    }
    return appender;
  }

  private void initLogger(String name,
```

```
                                  FileAppender appender,
                                  Level level)
  {
    Logger logger;
    if (name == null) {
      logger = Logger.getRootLogger();
    } else {
      logger = Logger.getLogger(name);
    }
    logger.setLevel(level);
    logger.addAppender(appender);
    logger.info("Starting " + logger.getName());
  }
}
```

Listing 9.10 The InitLog4j servlet

9.5.7 PersistentBase Class

It is a repetitive task to make a bean into a persistent bean. To facilitate this task, a
base class was created that contains the definition of a primary key (Listing 9.11). y
extending this class, a primary key will be added to the bean.

```
package shared;

import javax.persistence.GeneratedValue;
import javax.persistence.Id;
import javax.persistence.MappedSuperclass;

@MappedSuperclass
public class PersistentBase {

    protected Long id;

    @Id
    @GeneratedValue
    public Long getId() {  return id;  }

    private void setId(Long id) {  this.id = id;  }


    public PersistentBase() {
    }

}
```

Listing 9.11 The PersistentBase Class

It is recommended that such a primary key is used, even if there is a natural primary key in the data. This is because the primary key plays a fundamental role in how Hibernate maintains state.

9.5.8   Webapp Listener

In order to be sure that Hibernate is closed before the web application is stopped, a reference to a context listener was added to the *web.xml* file. Listing 9.12 contains the source code for this listener.

```java
package shared;

import java.sql.Driver;
import java.sql.DriverManager;
import java.util.Enumeration;
import javax.servlet.ServletContextEvent;
import javax.servlet.ServletContextListener;
import javax.servlet.annotation.WebListener;

@WebListener
public class WebappListener implements ServletContextListener {
    public void contextInitialized(ServletContextEvent sce)
  { }

  public void contextDestroyed(ServletContextEvent sce)
  {
    try {
      Enumeration<Driver> enumer = DriverManager.getDrivers();
      while (enumer.hasMoreElements()) {
        DriverManager.deregisterDriver(enumer.nextElement());
      }
    } catch (java.sql.SQLException se) {
      se.printStackTrace();
    }
    shared.HibernateHelper.closeFactory();
  }
}
```

Listing 9.12 The WebappListener class that is used to close Hibernate

Glossary

CSS	Cascading Style Sheets
EL	Expression Language
HTML	Hypertext Markup Language
HTML5	Hypertext Markup Language Five
HTTP	Hypertext Transfer Protocol
IDE	Integrated Development Environment
JAR	Java Archive
JSP	Java Server Page
JSTL	Java Standard Template Library
JVM	Java Virtual Machine
MIME	Multipurpose Internet Mail Extensions
MVC	Model, View, Controller
NVP	Name/Value Pairs
SDK	Software Development Kit
SQL	Structured Query Language
URL	Uniform Resource Locator
W3C	WWW Consortium
WAR	Web Archive

T. Downey, *Guide to Web Development with Java: Understanding Website Creation*,
DOI 10.1007/978-1-4471-2443-6, © Springer-Verlag London Limited 2012

Bibliography

Additional Resources

Books

Bauer C, King G (2005) Hibernate in action. Manning, Greenwich
Burke B (2010) RESTful Java with JAX-RS. O'Reilly, Sebastapol
Chopra V et al (2002) Professional Apache Tomcat. Wrox, Birmingham
Hall M (2002) More Servlets and Java Server Pages. Sun, Palo Alto
Hall M, Brown L (2004) Core Servlets and Java Server Pages, 2nd edn. Sun, Santa Clara
Ragget D et al (1998) Raggett on HTML 4, 2nd edn. Addison-Wesley, Harlow
Stein L (1997) How to set up and maintain a Web site, 2nd edn. Addison-Wesley, Reading

Web Sites

Apache Commons Beanutils, http://commons.apache.org/beanutils
FedEx Developer Site, http://www.fedex.com/us/developer/
Google Developer Site, http://code.google.com/apis/maps/documentation/webservices/
Hibernate, http://www.hibernate.org/
Hibernate Annotations, http://docs.jboss.org/hibernate/annotations/3.5/reference/en/html/
Hibernate Tools, http://www.hibernate.org/subprojects/tools.html
Hibernate Validator, http://www.hibernate.org/subprojects/validator.html
HTML 5, http://dev.w3.org/html5/spec/Overview.html
Java, http://java.com/
Log4j, http://logging.apache.org/log4j/1.2/
Memory Leaks and Class Loaders, Frank Kieviet Blog, http://blogs.oracle.com/fkieviet/entry/
    how_to_fix_the_dreaded
NetBeans, http://netbeans.org
PayPal Developer Site, https://developer.paypal.com/
Regular Expressions, http://download.oracle.com/javase/tutorial/essential/regex/
Tomcat, http://tomcat.apache.org/
Validator for CSS, http://jigsaw.w3.org/css-validator/
Validator for HTML, http://validator.w3.org/

Index

T. Downey, *Guide to Web Development with Java: Understanding Website Creation*,   375
DOI 10.1007/978-1-4471-2443-6, © Springer-Verlag London Limited 2012

Printed by Printforce, the Netherlands